Vilgot Sjöman

L136
DIARY WITH
INGMAR BERGMAN

Translated from the Swedish
by
ALAN BLAIR

*I am reluctant to make my own personal
affairs the object of attention, partly because they are of little import to know,
partly also because I, as a foster child of
the present age, cannot free myself entirely from its prejudices, of which shame of
poverty is one. But as I have no regard to
others in the exposure of weak and sensitive sides, I should have none to myself
either. This presentment can, moreover,
for many people, comprise a "Behold the
man!" as well as in general spread light
over the way of life and conditions in
these parts, this being one of the main objects of these lines.*

Petrus   Læstadius:
*Journal of Missionary Travels in Lap-
land.* 1831, 1833.

1978
KAROMA PUBLISHERS, ANN ARBOR

© Vilgot Sjöman 1978
Cover: photo by Lennart Nilsson
Typography: Patti Eldridge
Karoma Publishers, Inc.
Ann Arbor 1978

ISBN 0-89720-015-2 (Cloth)
ISBN 0-89720-016-0 (Paper)

CONTENTS

PREFACE

L-136 is a book that achieves two great, seemingly contradictory goals: it tells you more than you ever expected to know, and leaves you hungering for still more. The first accomplishment is obviously satisfying; but so too, though less obviously, is the second. You do not feel overwhelmed by the information; rather, your imagination is allowed, even obliged, to busy itself with certain questions about artistic creation— just as WINTER LIGHT, the film whose birth is chronicled, ends with certain unanswered, or only partly answered, questions about religion and love.

Vilgot Sjöman's monograph strikes me as a very rare, perhaps unique, and surely invaluable achievement. How often is a writer or a journalist allowed or able to follow the various phases of the making of a film? And even if he is, how often is he taken into the creator's intimate confidence, enjoying the privileges of an old friendship? And how often, then, is he himself a filmmaker, critic, observer, and writer of Sjöman's stature? And even supposing that all these conditions were met, how often does the film turn out to be a masterpiece such as WINTER LIGHT? Had Sjöman undertaken his project in conjunction with THROUGH A GLASS DARKLY or THE SILENCE, the film that preceded or the film that followed this one, he would have recorded the making of a considerably lesser work. So much devotion and evocative ability, then, were further rewarded by luck. It is safe to say that there is absolutely no such record of the making of a masterwork in the history of the cinema; indeed, very few comparable documents exist for the making of any *other* kind of masterpiece.

The book, short as it is, functions on many levels. Of course, no book can tell us how a genius *creates*, but this one tells us more about how that strange genius Ingmar Bergman *thinks* and *works* than any previous one was able to do, including all the critical studies and book-length interviews. But L-136 does not stop there: tactfully— by a snatch of conversation here, an inference there— it tells us something about the private life and daily existence of Bergman; and that, moreover, during the period when he was happily married to a fellow artist, the pianist Käbi Laretei. That the marriage, mutually stimulating as it evidently was, did not last, adds peripheral drama to this account.

On another level, L-136 should be of prime interest to actors and directors, both in film and in theater, for its eye-opening insights about how a great director works with two such remarkable performers as Ingrid Thulin and Gunnar Björnstrand. This relationship is not without its ups and downs— any more than that between the director and the brilliant cinematographer Sven Nykvist and other members of his technical staff. It is to Sjöman's credit that he allows even the minor characters in the drama— or comedy, and sometimes downright farce— of the making of WINTER LIGHT voices and personalities of their own. And beyond them, there are other people, including famous men and women like Igor Stravinsky and Greta Garbo, who have cameo roles, or are glimpsed through Bergman's gaze. There are also flashbacks to Bergman's childhood, and occasional flashforwards, in which Sjöman tells a-head of time about something that was to happen later. Like any good book of fiction or non-fiction, L-136 has a density, complexity, and internal structure (even if some of it was the result of pure chance) that require us to view it globally— as a world in which relationships and fields of force can be perceived and pursued in various directions. It is to Sjöman's credit that he tries, with footnotes and cross references, to facilitate the reader's task.

The uninitiated reader— though he will not remain so for very long— may wonder even about the meaning of the book's title. L-136 is simply the serial number by which the script of WINTER LIGHT was identified, Svensk Filmindustri (SF) assigning such identification marks to all its films. By his very title (which must have pleased Bergman, who always insists that he is not concerned with making art, only objects that people can use, like a chair or a table), Sjöman indicates that his project too is workmanlike reportage, a no-nonsense relation of relevant happenings and conversations, with merely such commentaries and speculations added as address themselves to questions the reader himself might have raised.

And yet, as is inevitable with any book that was not written entirely by some automaton, whether tape-recorder or computer, a point of view has to be present, a tone has to make itself felt. Sjöman's attitude is both appropriate and interesting. Though the age difference between him and Bergman is not very great, he nevertheless shows him the respect, indeed reverence, due a much older master. Yet, as with any truly intelligent disciple, this reverence never excludes critical scrutiny of what the master is up to, and, when unavoidable, honest disagreement, which Bergman scrupulously demanded from Sjöman.

About the reverence, you will permit me, I hope, an illustrative episode. On my first visit to Stockholm, Sjöman took me and my then girl friend to the dress rehearsal of a production of Pirandello's ENRICO IV at the small auditorium of the Royal Dramatic Theater. This was in 1964, a couple of years after the events described in L-136. Who should arrive at the theater simultaneously with us but a small group that included Ingmar Bergman, Erland Josephson and (if memory serves me) Anita Björk. Vilgot rushed up to talk to Ingmar, while my friend and I were left standing a couple of feet away, like a pair of gaping idiots. And agape we certainly were, amazed that the always considerate and gentlemanly Sjöman did not introduce us to a man we both admired as much as he did. Later, Sjöman explained that it would have upset Bergman terribly to be introduced to total stangers. This struck me as absolute nonsense: Bergman was in a radiant mood, laughing and bantering, and could not have cared less one way or the other. But it does show in what awe Sjöman, who had by then had his own international success with I AM CURIOUS (YELLOW), held the hero of L-136, which had come out in Sweden the preceding year.

What L-136 does superlatively is to give a rounded picture of Bergman at work. Very sensibly and sensitively, this includes all sorts of details— from hotel accommodations on location, meals eaten, and books read at the time to conversations about Ingmar's wife and her way of working, landscapes traversed by the car taking Bergman to the day's shooting, even little differences of mood between the protagonist of the book and its writer. It would be sufficient to say, as the worthy cliché has it, that Sjöman gives you the sense of being there; he often gives you several "there"s, even a whole spectrum of "there"s, and lets you choose what you think may have been the reality or meaning of a particular scene or event. Another cliché springs to mind: you read L-136 like a thriller, unable to put the damned thing down. Yet unlike a thriller, you know how it comes out, because you know WINTER LIGHT. What you don't know is how it was done; what led to what; what was rejected, changed, or insisted on fanatically; what feelings were involved, suppressed, hurt. In a sense, it is a thriller told in flashback: the end was the austere, uncompromisingly stern, yet also at times very delicate, and ultimately shattering film we know; the story of the book reveals how arduously that end was attained.

The books sheds invaluable light on the vexed question of the director as auteur. As we all know, the formerly very powerful and still not entirely negligible auteurist school of criticism holds that the film director is, no matter how strong a corporate structure he has to buck, the sole author of the film; indeed, the more of a studio system he has to contend with, the more he is assumed to leave his defiant mark on every frame of the film. Hence the auteur critics tend to pick their auteurs mostly among American directors, because they are the ones who have had to fight the giant cookie mold of the System more than anyone.

Still, even though they tend not to write books about him, most auteurist critics would concede auteur status to Bergman. I, on the other hand, always considered Bergman one of the few unquestionable auteurs in the history of cinema— if that term means anything at all. For even Bergman, as this book sovereignly demonstrates, is dependent to a substantial extent on the brilliant actors and technicians who work *with*, rather than *for*, him. How touching are the sections on Sven Nykvist, P. A. Lundgren, Ulla Ryghe, and, most moving of all, on K. A. Bergman, the hunchbacked property man who becomes the inspiration for Algot Frövik, the "angelic" sexton, and thus also the coach and stand-in of Allan Edwall who plays the part.

These relationships are by no means unilateral; they are quite complex, and sometimes vehement. With Nykvist, his great cameraman, Bergman feels that he has something like an "old marriage," as he has repeatedly said in interviews. And the relationship with the actors, as we see so clearly in L-136, is even more demanding, exhausting for both parties. Bergman's attitude here is wonderfully mercurial. On the one hand he recognizes "the warm sympathy of mankind" to be the actors' deepest need, and he gives them as much of it as he can muster. But he also looks at the matter jocularly, as when he says that he must "influence the actors' feelings," which also means "talking nonsense— whenever you can — so that they don't get cramps from sheer concentration."

Here we already glimpse the dualism in Bergman, the man who sometimes seems to be more serious, even dour, than anyone, and then bursts forth with a wonderfully childlike, indeed impish, sense of humor. Altogether, the notion of Bergman as a chilly and humorless Norseman should be laid to rest once and for all by this book. Sjöman evokes a man who goes into an interview tense, but relaxes as soon as he utters the first swearword; who displays for the benefit— or discomfiture— of the TV audience a paperweight in the shape of a small Asiatic goddess with a large, obscene posterior. Here we meet a Bergman who says about WINTER LIGHT, his most uncompromisingly harsh, downright forbidding film, that it "needs all the laughter it can get," and who finds ways of sneaking humor in. His is often a sardonic humor, as when he explains to his actors that "Christ has suffered all of mankind's sufferings— except, perhaps, marriage"; but it can also be the sweet, almost serious, jollity of basically solemn children, as when he tells Nykvist about a shot, "Make a beautiful light, Sven. Frövik is an angel." Or he will appoint someone on his production team "a special 'shadow hunter', which he pronounces in English .... to give the title a dignified sound."

Repeatedly Bergman has stressed the childlikeness of genius— with what relish he has told Sjöman, Charles Thomas Samuels, or myself about the "big child" quality he has discovered in the face or personality of this or that great man— Picasso, Stravinsky, or some other— a child that is very evident in him too. I find it in a lovely vignette Sjöman evokes for us: Bergman and Nykvist looking at a somber Northern landscape together and Ingmar exclaiming, "Look at that! The entire scale of grey!" It takes a very sensitive man to perceive the entire scale of grey; but it takes a spontaneous child to exclaim about it with uninhibited joy.

Yet the child can be harsh and even cruel. So much so that Sjöman envies Bergman's ability to hit out and be spared that ideal of kindness that enmeshes his own feet. Even when Bergman is trying to be kind, the capacity to hurt sometimes infiltrates his own concern. I wonder how comforting Ingrid Thulin, who complained that she could never make sense of the written word, found Ingmar's reply: "Actors never do. They understand only the spoken word"? The fact that this may be true does not mitigate its tactlessness. And yet a number of times during the narrative we find Bergman being exquisitely, unambiguously solicitous. And then, again, quite brutal.

It is, as our own Walt Whitman first pointed out, the privilege of genius to be self-contradictory. The man who can so delightfully declare that he has taught himself to sleep with his head tilted downward during theater rehearsals because that way the actors on stage think that he is studying the script, can wax quite rabid on the subject of critics, and speak of an "awful aggressiveness [that] awakens in one" and advise not having anything to do with critics at all.

Yet Bergman can take criticism from Sjöman even under the most trying circumstances and be a true collaborator with his technicians rather than a mere dictator. Thus he takes the archaic-looking wooden figure of the crucified Christ figure that P. A. Lundgren has carved for him, and twists off a finger from one of the convulsed hands, to provide the final authenticating touch. Auteur that he is, Bergman inspires co-auteurship, so to speak, in his staff. Here it is illuminating to reflect on something Nykvist tells Sjöman: "One must never say: Oh, we won't bother with that, the audience won't notice it anyway. The only principle to go by is what we ourselves, Ingmar and I, think of what we have done. If it's not what we meant, then we go in and do it over again until we get it right."

And that is what the work on WINTER LIGHT is about: not so much a doing, as a doing over and over again. Seldom before have I been so reminded of Goethe's famous dictum about genius being a long patience. Particularly revealing are the accounts of how the film's three greatest scenes come to be: Märta's letter monologue, the fight in the schoolroom, and Märta's final prayer for Thomas, her symbolic assumption of his burden. In particular the first of these required fanatical attention to detail— down to such things as finding the right handwriting for Märta— and unending retakes. The reader becomes deeply aware, for instance, of the importance and difficulties of getting the correct sound, or of the actress's mood at a given moment, or (in the schoolroom scene) of the influence of non-participating onlookers. The drama of getting a shot right is second only in intensity and complexity to the drama in the shot. And the hell of it is that to the viewer it all looks so simple: "In this [letter] scene we have tried the resources of technique to the utmost," as Bergman puts it. "Though no one will believe it, of course. They think all you have to do is plunk down a camera head on, and that's it." Mike placement, camera hum, unwanted shadows, sudden changes in the natural light (where this figures) are so many plagues visited on the director. And if he is as fussy as Bergman, he will worry the sound department even about the bark of an invisible dog ("None of your dachshunds; it must be a Lapland spitz!") And then, again and again, the contemptuous rejection of dogs from the sound effects department ("Another recorded dog! .... You'll damn well have to get a real .... dog!"), culminating in an exasperated "We can't go on like this!"

The book tells us a good deal about the problems of film acting, which most of us tend to dismiss as much easier than stage acting, because here you can piece a performance together from several takes— buy perfection, as it were, on the installment plan. Whereas on stage you've got to come up with everything on the first and only try. But precisely because you can keep reshooting (within certain budgetary limits, to be sure), both the actors and the director can find themsleves in the position of Balaam's ass. Since there is no rehearsal period such as that in the theater, one comes to every scene with less preparation and more uncertainty, and the temptation to keep experimenting, like the difficulty of choosing from among all the experiments, is immense. And indeed we see film acting and the directing of film actors as a continuous traipsing between alternatives, or attempting to improve on what to lesser artists might seem perfectly good. It is too bad that Max von Sydow's part in the film is too small to afford us significant glimpses into his work; at least, however, we learn a great deal about Ingrid Thulin and Gunnar Björnstrand as actors and as persons, and how the two things blend into performance.

L-136 is rich in all kinds of information, and, of course, more so for the reader well acquainted with Bergman's work. Thus, it is fascinating, as we follow Bergman planning a scene, then rejecting it, to recognize with a shock that the scene was not wasted but incorporated into a later film. So on page 55 we have a rejected scene that was to end up, *mutatis mutandis*, in PERSONA; on page 60, one that was to crop up in THE PASSION OF ANNA (or A PASSION, as the English title, following the Swedish, ought to run). Consequently, we come to realize how closely related all these movies are: that Bergman's oeuvre is, in certain respects at any rate, a single work— a *film fleuve*. Another thing that, as we see, is continuous in Bergman is his cinematic sense. "Very good. But it's theater," he tells Sjöman concerning some concept the latter has about structure. With exquisite sensibility, Bergman defines film as "nothing but small curves leading imperceptibly one into the other .... so that when the film is finished, all those small curves have formed one long line, a single dramatic arch."

And just as there is foreshadowing of future films in these pages, there is also a proleptic view of Bergman's coming biography, as in the discussion of how afraid Swedes really are of the police. For "police" read "authority" or "officialdom," and you have a flash-forward to Bergman's troubles with the Internal Revenue people that caused him to leave the country— not, I trust, forever.

Still, the most interesting elements of the book are those that most lastingly encapsulate Bergman's personality— for example, his fear of intense sunlight. Or take his self-contradictory placing on the WINTER LIGHT script, after its completion, the initials S.D.G.: Soli Deo Gloria (To God alone the Glory) on a film that is supposed to settle Bergman's account with God by, as it were, settling God's hash. And we see Bergman making good at every step of the way his noble pronouncement at the WINTER LIGHT press conference that the salient artistic fact for him "in this strange age of non-art" is not to "lose man out of the center, but keep searching for an expression by which to portray human beings .... " Accordingly, we find Bergman practicing, and confessing to, his "mania for close-ups." As he tells Sjöman in a TV interview, he wants "to look [people] straight in the eye and .... get their mental movements to reflect in their faces." But this is no simplistic obsession with close-ups at the exclusion of all else such as often mars the work of, say, Carl Dreyer. Bergman, as we repeatedly see here, is always equally conscious of other possibilities and needs. Now we find him giving the actors "the right movement," whose execution will bring with it the appropriate "state of feeling"— a shrewd perception; now we find him, with regard to the scene in which the fisherman's corpse is discovered, realizing (as he also told Charles Samuels in the excellent interview in EN-COUNTERING DIRECTORS) that the scene is "more creepy" in a long shot "with the thing lying far away."

And so, again and again, we get the priceless insights into the Bergman workshop— even into that workshop within a workshop, Bergman's mind. But— and this, for me, lends the book a touch of tragic mystery— some ultimate secrets remain hidden. Because, on one occasion, Sjöman forgot his tape recorder, and, on another, studio noises drown out Bergman's instructions to Björnstrand, certain key elements remain forever lost. I confess that I rather like that: it is good to know a great deal, but it is also good to be

reminded that some things, even if the words had not been obliterated, could never be fully understood. There exists a realm of the
undefinable where, at best, our intuition may hope to meet up
with the intuition of the artist— a realm into which definitions
cannot penetrate.

Allow me to conclude by quoting a relevant passage from the
Bergman interview that serves as an introduction to my book
INGMAR BERGMAN DIRECTS: "I think I have made just one picture
that I really like, and that is WINTER LIGHT. That is my only picture about which I feel that I have started here and ended there
and that everything along the way has obeyed me. Everything is
exactly as I wanted to have it, in every second of this picture. I
couldn't make this picture today .... but I saw it a few weeks ago
together with a friend and I was very satisfied." Vilgot Sjöman's
book records, in full detail and for all time, how Ingmar Bergman's
greatest satisfaction came about.

JOHN SIMON
July, 1978

PART I

THE SCREENPLAY

BETWEEN CHRISTMAS AND NEW YEAR 1960

Dinner with Ulla Isaksson. Ingmar and Kābi come up for coffee. Artistic interpretation problems: Kābi talks about Hindemith; Ingmar about direction as interpretation— then he tells wild and funny stories about animals he has filmed: the snakes in THIRST, the squirrel in THE SEVENTH SEAL, and the cat in THE DEVIL'S EYE.

Suddenly the conversation switches to suffering. Ingmar tells of one of his co-workers out at the film studios who suffers from Bechterew's disease— his deformed back, his constant pains; the only thing that saves him is always being on the move. I have spoken to him out at the studios: a man of about forty; his name too is Bergman, Karl Arne, always called just K. A. He has been property man for IB for many years now; he procures all the thousand and one props that are needed in the films; he puts all his emotional energy into work.

"K. A. is *impassioned,* I love him for that."

Ingmar speaks of K. A. with warmth and fascination, with an understanding of his suffering that is mixed with horror.

That was the first time I heard anything that had to do with WINTER LIGHT; but I didn't know that then.

(I recall the whole of this Christmas conversation six months later when I read the screenplay and meet the churchwarden Algot Frövik, former (retired) railroad clerk, thirty-nine years old; a very sick man who compares his own physical suffering with that of Christ:

"Please excuse me, it sounds presumptuous of course, but physically I have, in all diffidence as it were, suffered just as much as Christ. His torment was fairly short, what is more. About four hours or so?")

MONDAY 27 FEBRUARY 1961
Next film a Sergel film

"Funny thing about women, they want to be tormented ....
don't they? Don't you think so?"

A subject of conversation while the shrimp shells pile up on the plate. Over the meat course Ingmar talks about THE SEA GULL (which he has just directed at the Royal Dramatic Theater) and about THE RAKE'S PROGRESS (which he is to direct in the spring

3

at the Opera). I have come down to Stockholm from my writer's existence at Strömsund to do a TV program about American film censorship ; and towards the end of dinner I ask him what film he's going to do next (the last was THROUGH A GLASS DARKLY, which he made last summer).

"A film about Sergel! And his 'marriage in the eyes of God'."

The streetcars screech going around the bend outside *Konstnärsbaren*; the air has a strange spring warmth in the middle of February. And as we go into his director's room at the Royal Dramatic Theater he paints four big pictures from the Swedish 18th century.

The first picture represents the sculptor Sergel at the height of his powers, just home from Italy. On his walks into Stockholm to his studio in the city it is his custom to stop at an inn and have breakfast. He is served by a young woman. After breakfast they usually go to bed together for a while. Strengthened and satisfied, Sergel continues on his way into town.

"A pastoral picture. Utterly bucolic. Everything is carnal between them. The girl delights him with her warmth, her lush femininity."

"Who is there for a part like that?"

"Ulla Jacobsson. Can *you* think of anyone else? She has all the roundness, all the femininity."

"And Sergel?"

"Ulf Palme."

The second picture: The whole of the poet set, with Bellman and Kellgren, somewhere outside Stockholm, in a rustic idyll. The girl, Anna Maria Hellström, called "Anna-Rella," walks about under the shady trees with a new little naked Sergel on her arm.

"Sergel has drawn all that. He did drawings of Anna-Rella in every possible situation, some of them so damned realistic that they have been hidden away in the secret archives of the National Museum. But I was allowed to look at them in connection with this idea of mine. They are wonderful drawings, quite fantastic."

The third picture: A fête with Gustav III out in Drottningholm. Darkening colors, flickering flares, moral decay, hollowness and stage scenery.

The fourth picture: Anna-Rella alone with Sergel, several years later. Bleak and bare all around them, in small rooms right in

4

Stockholm. Sergel has his severe fits of melancholy— but Anna-Rella is there the whole time, at his side. Then the line is deepened. What began as carnal lust matures into deep affinity.

"She was much younger than he was, you know. And she died awfully young."

Actually, the whole thing didn't start with Sergel at all. By mere chance he stumbled on the story of Sergel's unlegalized marriage in Ragnar Josephson's books when he was reading up about the 18th century for another idea altogether: a story about an ego-centric young nobleman at the time of Gustav III. His wife is deeply attached to him, but he casts her aside for all kinds of affairs.

"He's the man who cannot accept love, who rejects it. Who can't put up with it. Until at last he realizes how hopelessly dependent he is on his wife, and goes back to her."

Ingmar gives a laugh.

"But that story's far too easy for me to write, I've written it many times before. That's why it's much more exciting with Sergel, it demands something new of me. It must rest in itself, be enclosed in itself in some way. It will need an awful distance .... and objectivity."

UNDATED, APRIL 1961
"I'm writing something else now"
The week after the triumphal first night of THE RAKE'S PROGRESS, I see Hogarth etchings on the dining-room wall in the Djursholm villa.

"If you knew how much I looked at them when I was working on THE RAKE."

Everything is carefully harmonized in the villa: colors, wall-papers, textiles. They did argue about the floral cushions when they were furnishing their home: Ingmar stuck to his urge for purity, Kābi to her hopeless love of pretty-pretties; that argument is one of the stories they tell now.

There have been matriculation exams over at Djursholm High School today: processions of raucously singing students a while ago. Now the wide expanse lies silent in the sunset haze, and no one really wants to leave the view. Kābi is to play a piano concerto by Gösta Nyström at the Concert Society on Friday and ought to go inside and practice. "I'll go soon," she laughs, "soon now, I

5

promise .... "; and the conversation jumps from tussock to tussock: jealousy, relation persons (I point out which persons I would like most to have praise from). Craving revenge (Ingmar tells what a relief it is to be able to murder his persecutors in his imagination by lampooning them in some film). The practicing of one's art. Kābi says that "after all there are limits to what an artist can achieve," but Ingmar shakes his head:

"I don't agree. I think that man's capacity is fantastic. That mentally he can extend himself as much as he likes."

Late in the evening there is a ring at the door. Both of them give a start. The doorbell at this hour of day? Out here, in this quiet residential district? Ingmar disappears, mumbles in a friendly tone out by the front door and comes back with an old-fashioned suitcase, held together with string, in his hand. A stranger has given it to him: a schizophrenic or a manic-depressive?

"I bet you there's a dead baby in it. Or a bomb. A time bomb."

Both work themselves up: a game with fear. But when Ingmar has undone the string an entire human destiny spills out: bundles of manuscript, photographs, authentic letters—someone is giving away his life to him.

A raw mist hangs over the meadow when they see me off. Chill, damp night air and the delicate tracery of the early spring branches around the empty railroad station. I ask Ingmar how far he has got with the Sergel film.

"Which? Oh, that! No, I've put it aside."

Pause.

"I'm writing something else now .... "

UNDATED, MAY 1961

What is it about? He doesn't tell Ulla J. either. Only his anxiety: "Guess how it feels: I'm to do a new film in the fall and I haven't written a line of it yet. The whole thing exists only in my head."

The only thing he reveals to Ulla is that it is to form the final phase of a trilogy:* THE VIRGIN SPRING, THROUGH A GLASS

—

*He likes working with the idea of a trilogy; it is just that by degrees he moves the trilogy forward a step: the first part drops out when a new one appears. When we do the TV interview at Torō (8-12-61), THE VIRGIN SPRING has been omitted. Now THROUGH A GLASS DARKLY is the first part of a trilogy.

6

DARKLY—plus the new one.
In that case it should have a religious theme.

UNDATED
An old wish
In the fall of 1946 I began studying at the University of Stock-holm: from the military service I came straight to Agne Beijer's lectures on Queen Christina's court ballets and encountered the extraordinary methods and problems of theatrical history. How can one reconstruct something so fleeting as the stage moment? Even the theatrical life we ourselves move in is gone tomorrow morning. Then why not try to capture it just now, when it is top-ical? In my spare time I wrote dramatic criticism, time and again aware of how little I knew about the director's and the actor's share in the whole. *That* was a brilliant detail— but who conceived it: the director or the actors? When was it born? Was it there from the start of the rehearsals? And I had a wild idea: day by day to describe how four different directors prepared a particular theatri-cal production— if they could think of letting a recorder into the very workshop.

I never got as far as daring to ask Olof Molander, Alf Sjöberg, Torsten Hammarén; I did however ask Ingmar Bergman once at the beginning of the 1950's when I had gone down to Malmö to write an article on Bengt-Åke Benktsson for the magazine *Vi*. Oh, no, he wouldn't mind. It was after lunch; I went with IB into the vast innards of the Malmö City Theater; in this dark forsakenness he was rehearsing the last act of Strindberg's GHOST SONATA with Gaby Stenberg and Folke Sundquist (" .... I love the first two acts as much as I loathe the last; but it's my blasted duty as director to give shape to it with just the same objectivity .... "); I felt the mag-ic and the attraction, the desire to report what happened in the workshop, meticulously, factually, as vividly as possible.

THURSDAY 1 JUNE 1961
SF needs screenplays; Ingmar has commissioned one from me; when it is ready I am seized by the devil and ask to direct it my-self. "You're crazy! If you had the faintest notion of all the work it takes to direct .... " He fires off a fifteen-minute sermon in his office today: a graphic horror picture of what can happen to a be-ginner in the film studio; then the agreement is fixed. (He is to

7

check all my rushes; else he cannot accept responsibility to the board. Sensible condition.) I want to call the film THE MISTRESS.

IB suggests that I prepare myself by following the shooting of his next film: a kind of course in direction.

All the better: then I can make my old dream come true at the same time. Does he agree? Oh yes. Will he really be able to stand having me in the studio every day— recording, making a note of every detail? Yes, it will be okay, he thinks. As long as I don't let him down. It has happened to him before, he says. Such and such a person let him down at such and such a time.

"In what way?"

"A stab in the back. He went around telling others what I was like. Others— but never a word to me. And when I found *that* out .... "

UNDATED
My belief in authority, my ambivalence in the presence of IB
It began actually in the fall of 1942. I was seventeen and had just started at the Norra Latin High School; then came the chairman of the school literary society *Concordia:*

"We're going to do A MIDSUMMER NIGHT'S DREAM at the annual party in the fall. And guess who's going to direct it? Ingmar Bergman!"

Now, long afterwards, I think how typical: the very first time I hear of him, his entrance is signalled with a blast of trumpets.

He was twenty-four and had produced plays at the University and the Saga Theater: he demanded that we should work. This was no game *en passant*; we slaved at the rehearsals, the theater was more important than schoolwork: the only thing that *was* important. He had his fiancée beside him, Else Fisher, she did the dances. Erland Josephson played Oberon. I learned the boring declamatory lines of the Duke.

One day I anxiously brought along my first drama, written at one go during four summer nights of excitation. At the corner of Sveavägen and Kungsgatan in those days lay a Norma café; IB stood me a coffee: the twenty-four-year-old gave the seventeen-year-old his opinion. How did he come to have such authority that I immediately believed what he said? That hour over coffee at Norma branded me for years to come: it bolstered up my self-confidence and forged links of friendship that have lasted ever since.

8

I guess many of his co-workers have become attached to him in a similar way: he has helped them to gain self-confidence.

The roles were thereby assigned. I longed for an authority, and I got it; thus began the pupil's typical fluctuation between fierce admiration and timid criticism. In 1943 Ingmar produced Kaj Munk's NIELS EBBESEN for the Dramatists' Studio. I had a walk-on part and followed his work as director with fascinated school-boy's eyes. In the spring of 1944 he was appointed head of the Hälsingborg City Theater; he asked in fun: "Like to come down with me?" but the pull of his theatrical world felt dangerous. Safer to stick to my studies and take my matriculation; and there, inside this studious existence, his first film hit me like a violent conflict. I didn't dare to like such an openly aggressive film as FRENZY.* It offended me that he made no attempt to understand the mentally ill teacher ("Caligula"). I would soon show that one could portray a difficult and complex teacher *from inside*, and during my military service I wrote a play that had the same triangle pattern as FRENZY (schoolboy— slovenly girl— middle-aged teacher). Ingmar picked the play to pieces, but the material wouldn't leave me alone: out of the play came my first novel, THE SCHOOLTEACHER.

SF showed an interest in the novel when it was published, three years later— so our patterns interlocked again. In the fall of 1949 we were both on our way to Paris and IB undertook the task of guiding me in the writing of a screenplay based on a novel which was a protest against his own film; that was an amusing situation. Every morning for three weeks, I took the bus over to his hotel in the Rue St. Anne with a newly-written scene. He dictated too much in those days— that was his failing as a teacher. But time and again he was suddenly transformed into a genuine ped-agogue who coaxed me to size things up and to try them out: "Can't you feel how it sags here and gets dull? .... can't you *feel* it!"— thus arousing all my curiosity about how a film scene could be constructed, about cinematic crescendos, rhythms and cli-maxes. I shared his nervousness over the première of THIRST, and one evening we saw LE MISANTHROPE at the Comédie Française. He lit up like a torch on meeting, for the first time, the French Molière tradition. I remember his excitement at intermission when

---

*The Swedish title is *Hets*.

he described Alceste: " .... oh, this hot heart!" and my own astonishment, the astonishment of a studious person: is *that* how one could regard art and the classics! As nakedly and directly— not filtered through literary history, not with the dramatic critic's anxiety to put the performance "in its right context."

I saw the other plays together with an actor from the Royal Dramatic Theater who was the same age as I was, Kenne Fant; several times the three of us ran across each other and argued over our likes and dislikes. I was collecting theatrical impressions so as to write theatrical letters home to my magazine, *Vi*. But I was evasive when Ingmar insisted that I should tell him what I thought about the performances I had seen. I thought he had a special technique at such interrogations. First he drew me out about play, acting, direction; then he squashed me with the whole of his authority and with a loud, provoking laugh that mocked my amateurishness and theatrical ignorance.

Not long afterwards did I hear *his* version of our Paris quarrels. I never dreamed that I was something for Ingmar to strike at, but I was because I belonged to the enemy camp: I was someone who had "opinions," a dramatic critic and an academic. Moreover my first novel had been praised for "maturity," while IB's films and plays were still being slated as "adolescent." What a strange disparity: there I was lapping up praise for "maturity" (comfortable protection against all inward insecurity) while IB went on rebelling as one does in puberty and he was seven years older than I was. A comic interweaving of mutual feelings of inferiority and envy. We stood at the window in the Rue St. Anne;* Ingmar was aghast that I could turn out such sloppy language as that in the day's bit of manuscript. There was amazement, anger and envy in his reaction: hell, the liberties they take, those who call themselves authors! Suddenly he confessed how painstaking he was over the

---

*Thirteen years later, in 1962, IB's Paris memories float to the surface when he makes THE SILENCE and makes Ester (Ingrid Thulin) stare through the window of the hotel room down to the strange street in the town of Timoka, whose language she can't even speak: "That's how creepy I thought it was to stand looking down at the Rue St. Anne ...." For IB foreign travel has never meant "open horizons" and "new perspectives"; on the contrary, it has given him nightmare feelings of insecurity and terror, of being "an outcast in the world"— this alien reality that you can't get the better of: Timoka reality.

10

language in his own scripts. He trained his style, he said, consciously and deliberately," .... so that I have the tools ready in case the day comes when I want to write a book." Then he went to his room and went on writing JOACHIM NAKED, his new play.

After that encounter we ran across each other at long intervals, often only by chance. We would then demonstrate our mutual tensions by continuing the Paris arguments: in our liking for each other there was an ambivalence. This ambivalence had the hampering effect on me that I was neither really critical of his films nor really enthusiastic about them; I felt mean and thwarted; and suffered as a result. I had just come home after spending a year in the USA when THE SEVENTH SEAL had its première: after six months in Hollywood I found the violent attraction of IB's film a pleasant relief; and when the radio asked me to review it I decided to settle accounts with my meanness. This was the first time I was unreservedly complimentary about an IB film; when we met some time later he told me how glad he had been. Then he looked at me, gravely, almost as though ashamed of having suspected anything so pure-hearted as I: ".... but of course there was this goddam voice inside me which couldn't help wondering: what's Vilgot after now? What does he hope to gain by this?" There I stood. I had brought home a carefully thought-out screenplay that I had written in the USA,   GAME ON THE RAINBOW. In it I had put into practice what I had learned from IB in Paris in 1949; how could I show it to him *now*?! Ingmar's suspiciousness; my own determination "not to be mean"— how did it all hang together? In a tangle of muddled feelings I put off sending the script month after month.

What comprises ambivalance? What comprised the ambivalence in regard to Ingmar in particular? This is what occurs to me (just now):

1. Envy of the greater talent. (Especially of his intensity, his wealth of ideas.)

2. Unfamiliarity with a different kind of talent: his emotional world is not mine. (The schoolboy puritan in me was slightly disgusted when he used four-letter words in his little manuscript-attic room out at SF. I was alarmed at the uninhibited sensualism in his films. I still have no sympathy for his moralism: these venomous truths with which his characters try to convert each other!)

3. Fear that his critics will "be right": Supposing he does only

11

turn out claptrap after all? (For many years this was *my* group: the authors, the university students, "the intellectuals.")

4. Attachment to his professional authority. What he said about films and theater during our sporadic meetings burned itself into me: fiery drops from another professional world— they incited me in my pursuit of the theatrical. (I remembered distinctly that he said *that* in 1950 when he made TO PLEASE (*Till glädje*); he said *that* in 1953 when he was shooting SAWDUST AND TINSEL (*Gycklarnas afton*), etc. And the more he attacked me as dramatic critic, the more I believed in his authority. God's words, literally: "Ingmar says that .... Ingmar thinks that ....")

Several other motifs make up ambivalence, but I can't get at them. (Something about IB has often intimidated me, but I don't know how or why. The sense of power he radiates? His tendency to dominate?)

I had better record his "prelude" in the diary— it would be strange if it were not to influence what I see.

WEDNESDAY 14 JUNE 1961
The new idea for a film
Envy of Christ

Lunch guest at Ingmar's table: a girl in a light kerchief, Inger Stevens who has come to see him. "Nice kid," he says (since she has confided to him that she is trying to get away from Hollywood). We see a test film of a young ballerina from the Opera, Kari Sylwan; then he tells me of an idea he has for a film:

"A parson shuts himself up in his church. And says to God: I'm going to wait here until you reveal yourself. Take all the time you want. I still won't leave here until you have revealed yourself.

"So the parson waits, day after day, week after week."

That was the original idea for the film, he says.

"Then I woke up one morning .... well, you know the state when you wake up still grasping at a dream. I realized that the parson didn't have to wait as long as I had first thought. A lot can happen in an hour and a half— the time the film itself takes.

"So now I'm going to start, without beating around the bush, by showing a communion service. Only six communicants— one of them being the parson's wife. After the service the parson stays behind in the church. He is waiting for a man who has made an appointment with him. The man doesn't show up. The parson

12

grows tired and irritated. But the man doesn't come because he has hanged himself."

"This film, too," he says, "is a chamber play, with only a few parts: the parson, his wife, one or two others— the chamber play has been neglected in films."*

He will depict the whole of the empty, dead, hollow routine in the communion service.

"How will you do it?"

"Oh, I've only to go to a country church north of Stockholm and show everything just as it is. I've driven around now the last few Sundays and had a look."

"With Kābi?"

"No, with my father." (Ingmar's father, the Rev. Erik Bergman.)

"Do you tell him about the ideas for your films?"

"No, never. But he helps me with practical details."

I'm sorry that the Sergel film has been put aside. Ingmar smiles.

"Can't be helped. I couldn't get rid of this idea once I had got ten it, I had to follow it up. But it's awful being pressed for time: I must start shooting in September. And I don't want to rush a theme like this. It must take its time to be born, labor pains and all."

He tells me far too little for me to grasp what the film is really about. And I'm alarmed at the prospect of having to watch yet another film parson who succumbs under doubt and lack of faith —however many has one endured! Is Ingmar really capable of renewing that theme? Then he adds something that makes me prick up my ears:

"You see, this parson has a hatred of Christ that he won't admit to anyone. He is envious of Christ."

"*Envious?*"

"Yes, and jealous. He feels something akin to the elder son's

—

*I don't know when IB first began using the term "chamber play"; but having once discovered that films lend themselves so well to what Strindberg calls "the intimate procedure," "the strong important theme," he has been the most energetic follower of the Strindberg chamber play tradition. But it is not easy to define a "chamber play." Even Strindberg had difficulties— see "Open Letters to the Intimate Theater"— and IB maintains that two such structurally different films as WILD STRAWBERRIES and THROUGH A GLASS DARKLY are both "chamber plays."

hatred of the prodigal son, who gets all the attention when at last he comes home: fatted calf and all the rest. It simply occurred to me that I would make a clean breast of my own envy and jealousy of the Christ figure."

"Envious of Christ"— it calls to mind IB's childhood. What is it like being a small child in a clergyman's family, with father going off every Sunday to devote his time to someone else, an utter stranger called Jesus Christ?

A parson who is envious of Christ— what a fascinating theme! And how original— I imagine it has never been used in literature before.

"Hard to give shape to it, though. I'll just have to lift up what I have found in myself— as cleanly as I can."

He goes on to say how long it has taken him to interest himself in the Christ figure at all. And it can be seen from his films: whenever he touched on a religious theme, it has been about the God motif. So now, for the first time, he is going to penetrate in towards the Christ motif?

".... because when the parson is waiting there in the church for the man who doesn't come, he understands for the first time how it must have been for Christ when he felt himself forsaken on the cross. It wasn't only that Judas betrayed him and that the disciples fell asleep at Gethsemane. But God forsook him when he hung on the cross .... "

"Who is to play the parson?"

"Gunnar Björnstrand. The very right one for the part, just now."

Talk of THE FACE, Tennessee Williams, Jean Anouilh; and then:

"When I've finished the script you can read it. And criticize it. I *want* criticism."

Pause. Swift, sensitive postscript:

"But you're not to criticize it in such a way that I lose my belief in this film and get scared of making it."

The fear of all writers that the theme will wither up, evaporate like fairy gold. And in the midst of this the literary inferiority complex.

"What the critics say about me as a director leaves me cold. They can say this and that is bad and this and that is brilliant— but when they say anything about me as a writer, I'm vulnerable."

On the bus going home from SF I notice that I am out of humor. I feel dogged by bad luck. Now that at last I can follow a film pro-

14

duction— why did I have to strike one of his religious films, of all things! Now I shall be forced to try and record the innermost twists and turns of the religious themes— am I capable?

(A few years ago I wrote a religious settling of accounts with myself in the travel book FLYGBLAD; I'll give it to him straight away, so that he knows where I stand.)

FRIDAY 16 JUNE 1961
Kābi gives a concert at home
Björnstrand's heavy working schedule this summer
Concert at home.

Kābi is going to Germany to give piano recitals ("Four Romantic Temperaments: Brahms, Chopin, Schubert, Schumann") and has a sort of dress rehearsal for a small circle in the Djursholm villa: Gunnar Björnstrand; Gunnel Lindblom and Sture Helander, who is a doctor, an old friend of Ingmar's and Gunnel's husband; Erland Josephson; Lenn Hjortzberg, Ingmar's secretary.

Kābi's simple blue dress against the black of the grand piano. The beautiful color scheme of the room. I watch her fingerwork with the keys and think how difficult it would be to write about her hands without lapsing into insipid lyrical similes of this type: she plays Chopin's *Barcarolle*— her hands fly to the side, resting; it is like a drop from an oar, these cool rings on the water.

Kābi's life story: born and raised in Estonia, her father a minister. Childhood journeys to Moscow, life a fixed aristocratic form that could not be shaken. Then the sudden changes of fortune: the breaking up of the home at the eleventh hour before the Second World War, the family leave everything behind them and flee to Sweden. The whole of this upheaval: the anonymity and defenselessness of a refugee's existence, the economic quagmire— but her mother generously keeps open house for anyone who wants to come and go in the new home, a market garden; and Miss Kābi Laretei makes her debut as a pianist in 1946 in Stockholm, at the age of twenty-four. She was born on the same day as Ingmar: July 14th.

Her early successes. Her joy in playing and in making contact with the audience. Her sensibility and devastating charm. How beautiful she is in the white woolly shawl as she talks afterwards to Gunnar Björnstrand. Gunnar regrets that he is not musical— but

15

he is in scintillating party mood: repartee, gaiety, the glittering silver shoal of anecdotes. A blue manuscript figures somewhat mysteriously in the evening's conversation: THE GARDEN OF EDEN, a comedy that Ingmar and Erland Josephson have written together; and Gunnar is worried about the double burden of work that awaits him: first the lead in THE GARDEN OF EDEN, playing opposite to Sickan Carlsson; then the part of the parson in Ingmar's film. Ingmar comes up to him with a reassuring.

"Oh, Gunnar, we've agreed that your scenes in THE GARDEN OF EDEN will be shot as early as possible in the schedule, so that you can lie fallow for three weeks before starting my film."

Käbi doesn't seem in the least tired as she moves among her guests— she is more vital than ever after the evening's trial of strength.

SATURDAY 17 JUNE 1961
Religious seeking for contact
On religious flirting

" .... and let me tell you that she had been practicing for five hours during the day before giving her recital last night," Ingmar says when he phones next morning.

His pride in her. And in her enormous strength.

"No one has the faintest idea of the resources hidden in that girl."

He has only slept an hour last night ("I'm always worked up when I've had guests or been out"). He has also read the religious "creed" in FLYGBLAD that I gave him last night. The telephone conversation turns into a quiet tug-of-war between us; I find myself thinking. Ingmar is eager, groping for contact, anxious to find a religious bridge between us: "What you write about 'God's water' in FLYGBLAD is the very same thing I say about love in THROUGH A GLASS DARKLY." But I'm on the defensive and mumble that I'm on exactly the same standpoint as before: "Christianity .... the biggest dream that humanity has invented, but *only a dream*, wishful thinking."

"But haven't you found, you too, that this business of religion goes in waves, like ebb and flood? When I made THE SEVENTH SEAL I was terribly taken up with religion. But having made it, I got rid of two things: my fear of death— I just didn't feel it any-

16

more. And my brooding about God, that left me for a long, long time— until just the last few years, with THE VIRGIN SPRING and THROUGH A GLASS DARKLY, then it has possessed me again."

I reply that the religious material I have inside me is there because I have soaked up what other people have experienced. I have listened to them, read, argued, felt what it was like to be in their mental world, but not had anything of my own to contribute. By degrees I felt all that to be religious flirting and resolved to clear it all out; then he bridles up:

"There's nothing worse: religious flirting! And I know what I'm talking about, for I've achieved quite a lot in that line. Oh yes, one must clear out all that sort of thing: be objective, see clearly ...."

Those words ring in my ears for a long time after I've put down the phone: *Clear up. Be objective. See clearly.* How they recur in his mouth. "Am I plain now? Am I talking so that people can understand me?"

What a fear he must have of anything blurred and chaotic, of being overwhelmed by emotional chaos in himself.

MONDAY 3 JULY 1961

This evening he ran the rough cut (unmixed) of THROUGH A GLASS DARKLY out at SF for Kenne and Janine Fant. Listening silently in the background: Ulla Ryghe who edited the film.

None of IB's films has gripped me so directly— a host of reservations gone. The feeling afterwards: that it pays. There is some point in an artist's fighting with his themes. It pays to scrape and cut. This is the barest thing he has done yet.

Amusing detail when talking it over afterwards: The author David, Gunnar Björnstrand, is in such despair over his own uncleanness that he burns the manuscript of his own novel in the stove— heroic gesture, sacrificial act. Ingmar feels his way:

"Shall I cut out that book burning? Perhaps it would be better if he didn't burn his goddam trashy novel and published it instead? That would be punishment enough."

He tells us how the wallpaper theme in the film comes all the way back from PRISON. Then we discuss the acting. His voice takes on a sudden tenderness and warmth:

"However excellent Harriet and Max are, do you know what *I* think is the best performance in the whole film? Gunnar Björnstrand. It's just great what he does."

UNDATED
Ingmar's literary inferiority complex
The mystification Ernest Riffe
The fight with the "hateful words"

Supposing that an author publishes a self-portrait in which he exposes his egocentric failings. He gains three things: He finds a new and subtle outlet for his egocentricity. He gets new food for his self-esteem by realizing that of his own accord he can lay bare his worst traits. And to crown it all he is sure to be praised for his honesty.

In November 1960 the magazine *Chaplin* issued an "anti-Bergman number." Ingmar was just then rehearsing THE SEA GULL at the Royal Dramatic Theater. I went to see him in his office; *en passant* he asked me what I thought of the issue. Then he added:

"I thought one of the articles had a point. This Frenchman—I've been thinking over what he says about the differences between the creative artist and the interpretative one."

I suspected nothing.

Chaplin's anti-Bergman issue contained four executions: three Swedish and one French. When the next issue of the magazine came out, the editors disclosed that the French execution was a camouflage. The Frenchman Ernest Riffe was Bergman himself. (His own name in full is Ernst Riffe Bergman.)

Read the three Swedish executions first! There it says that IB is admittedly brilliant technically— a clever image-creator, a past master at giving direction to his actors— but: He works with "artificial puppets," "puzzle pieces," "rattling constructions," "the extrinsic effects of pessimism." He is "utterly void mentally," his compassion is "strangely lifeless," his religious perspective "one-sidedly negative" and unclear. He replaces emptiness with "as titillatingly sensuous sensations as possible"; he is lacking in substance and must constantly "sponge off others and take substance from their films." Etc.

Read Ernest Riffe after that.

IB reads everything that is written about him, thoroughly; he knows all these opinions. It was only natural, therefore, that he should write a sarcastic pamphlet, gaily ridiculing his critics in Ernest Riffe's name.

But this article is black. That he did write it is an act of self-defense; but its contents I cannot regard as anything else but a self-confession. IB spews up all the abuse he has received, but the strength in this spewing comes from his own self-doubt: the article oozes pessimism and melancholy, fear that the critics' judgments may turn out to be justified.

1. The critics say that his compassion is "lifeless"— and Ernest Riffe scourges IB's "deep contempt for humanity" and "defective contact with the world around him."

2. The critics say that he "sponges off others"— and Ernest Riffe declares that he's really only "an actor, a portrayer of roles."

3. The critics say that he is "manic" and "mechanically repeats himself"— Ernest Riffe replies that IB often "mistrusts his intentions," that the ideas seem "pallid and lacking in oxygen," etc.

4. He is arrogant, Ernest Riffe goes on. He is alone in his desolate self-assertion, a spectral figure, void of love, warmth, etc.

5. Films, says Ernest Riffe, are his big trick to conceal his unoriginality as a writer: films are the trick which hides all his loans and gives a false impression of independence.

6. Last and first: The torment of not being regarded as a writer. "Bergman," Ernest Riffe writes, "who has never been considered an author in his own country, has no doubt suffered from this disdain of his literary colleagues."

Has he suffered!

Nowadays he pooh-poohs the idea of ever having had ambitions as a writer— but he obviously always had them.

The turning point came at the beginning of the 1950s.

Critics had slated him for being "a mere scribbler," but he had at any rate had his plays performed and the publishing house of Bonniers had printed three of them in 1948 under the title MORALITIES. He arrived home from Paris with JOAKIM NAKED and other plays and handed them in for publication. Bonniers refused. This was the peripeteia in his literary life. A draught of humiliation. The official seal that he was no good as a writer.

Redress came from abroad. After his international breakthrough a number of offers flowed in: he had his screenplays published in English, French, Italian— in handsome, massive volumes.

Then the Swedish publishers came back.

And then it was *his* turn to say no.

At first he did so out of wounded pride, the desire to give tit for tat, the need to triumph— but having given vent to his vindictive feelings, he seemed to notice that actually nothing had changed at home in Sweden. The literary disdain appeared to be as strong as ever. The opposition of the cultural elite looked just the same. Why should he feed it with new material?

That is why he has postponed the Swedish publication year after year: the matter touches IB to the quick— the literary value of what he does. The enthusiasm abroad didn't really redress the wrong; it merely acted as a balm. So the odd situation remains that a number of his screenplays have been printed in the principal languages abroad but not in Swedish.

It is the old story of someone's dependence on persons whose opinions he values. *Here* the defeat took place; *here* the rehabilitation must be made— otherwise it has no effect.

Odd that IB's capacity to write has not entirely left him— when the walls of his room echo with so many declarations of ineptitude. But all along the need to express himself has been stronger than all feelings of defeat. The only visible sign is that writing is such an effort for him: he can sound almost querulous when he talks of how he dislikes writing.

But he is interested in problems of style, he really struggles with the language— how then does he regard these problems? *I* think one of his handicaps is his unlyrical disposition. The young IB could not get hold of a lyrical image without believing that he had a simile in his hand; and then he overdid the metaphor until it creaked at the joints. A pedantic need of clarity that dives him into dryness— he can express a lyrical mood better in pictures than in words. His other handicap lies in his bent for the over-strong, for the terrible words. His emotional experiences are evidently so violent that they seem meager and scraggy on paper if he doesn't use fierce phraseology. But a warning voice inside him keeps on telling him how dangerous that phraseology is. Then the need of expression and the warning voice begin this vehement sparring, which exhausts the author David in THROUGH A GLASS DARKLY, who can't get to sleep and lies fighting with the "twisting sentences, the hateful words, the insufferable banality of the situations and the poverty without dimension of the characters." He stares at the manuscript of his novel:

She came towards him panting with expectation, cheeks all aglow with the strong wind ....

David groans. Good God, has he really written that? Seizing the pen, he changes it to:

She came running towards him, her face flushed with the strong wind ....

Does that sound better? No. He tries this:

She came running towards him.

He sighs, crosses the whole lot out and writes resolutely:

They met on the beach.

That is a summary of IB's own stylistic development. Stubbornly grappling with language he has, with the passage of time, come a long way towards the ideal of clean-washed prose: "They met on the beach."

David's fight with the language is in the script but not in the finished film; all that is left is that Gunnar Björnstrand writes a "They met on the beach." I grumbled when I discovered the cut.

"Pity you cut that out."

"It's too special. That sort of thing may amuse the initiated; but it's caviar to the general."

THURSDAY 13 JULY 1961
The first Thursday: A hint of the film's structure

At Torö, some distance outside Nynäshamn, Käbi and Ingmar have rented a summer retreat which he says is fantastic: a long stretch of beach facing the open sea. There he is writing the new film. Once a week he drives into town and SF: every Thursday. He goes through the pile of letters on his desk and crowds work into the day: he has a lot of irons in the SF fire; they all must be seen to.

How is the script going? Not so badly, he laughs, he gets so much thrown in now that he has decided on a radical step: to include the whole of the communion service at the beginning of the film.

"You can imagine: twenty minutes of the film in nothing but pictures. I only have to copy down the whole service."

Like this, in other words:

"First I get the whole of the communion service free. Then Gunnar Björnstrand has a monologue of fifteen minutes. Then a few things happen at the end, very quickly."

The first hint of the building of the script, in a drastic contentment. But this difficulty worries him instead:

21

"In THROUGH A GLASS DARKLY I could split myself up into three male characters: I could put myself into the writer, the doctor and the boy. In this new film there's only one character in which I can bare myself, that of the parson."*

(P. S. In the meantime he has decided to cut out the part where David burns his book manuscript in THROUGH A GLASS DARKLY.)

THURSDAY 20 JULY 1961
The second Thursday: The wife dead
Three sources for the new film
He settles accounts with THROUGH A GLASS DARKLY
A mixture of religion and sexuality

Last Thursday the parson still had a wife. Now she's dead.

"I woke up one morning and killed her off. It was a lovely feeling. And right." He gives a loud laugh as he tells me about it.

"The wife was to have played a big part, actually. But somehow I found it hard to write about her. Whenever I tried, nothing came."

These typical sudden changes in his ideas! Aversion mounts up: sluggishness, unwillingness to write; a sharp blow and his imagination is flowing swiftly again, in new channels:

"Now the parson has a mistress instead. An hysterical, lonely, middle-aged, flat-chested schoolteacher in the country. So now things are moving."

"Who is to play that part?"

"Ingrid Thulin."

Pause: for my surprise. He laughs delightedly.

"So actually I'm writing a new FANCY IF I MARRIED THE PARSON."

He's writing the script for the third time now. He is trying to apply his usual industrious working schedule with fixed writing times and relaxation in the evening. I can't grasp it. How can one avoid working around the clock when one is right inside a work?!

"Can you really put the characters out of your mind when you've finished writing for the day?"

"No, they're with me day and night. There is only one time when they have vanished completely: eleven o'clock, when I sit down

---

*At this stage the parson was the only leading character in the film— active, supporting. Märta Lundberg, the teacher, wasn't invented.

22

to write. Then they're gone with the wind, like schoolchildren who don't want to go inside to lessons."

Then the working moralist inside Ingmar shakes his finger and says that it is *dangerous* to give in to one's disinclination.

"The remedy is to sit down pedantically every day at a definite time, irrespective of whether you're in the mood or not. And then you get up and prowl around the house, once an hour .... until you start functioning."

Sighs, laughs, groans— I have never heard Ingmar speak of writing other than as torment, resistance, a necessary evil. Never as enjoyment, tingling desire.

"You see, this matter of working discipline .... It was when I was directing down in Malmö. Paul Kletzki came and was to conduct a concert. He was ill and wretched and rheumatic—sciatica, fever, the shivers— in such a bad way that he had to keep one foot in a slipper while he was rehearsing. And the Malmö orchestra has never played better in its life! That's how little he allowed his body to stop him. For me it was a damn good lesson— I was terribly down just then, for various reasons. It looked as though I was not going to get Käbi, and I was rehearsing THE VÄRMLANDERS after FAUST and it was a bit boring to work on .... But Kletzki hadn't a *thought* of pampering himself as some artists do. I notice the same thing with Käbi: she can coddle herself and fuss over little things— but when it really comes to it, not a word out of her! She doesn't mind how hard she works."*

Today I find that the film didn't at all arise merely out of the theme that he first indicated, with the parson who waits for God to come. We talk for a long time; the literary historian in me begins looking for clues.

One thread-end is this:

"Käbi and I were married in Boda church in Dalarna on September 1st, 1959, nearly two years ago. The same fall we went to visit the parson who had married us; but we were still only in the village store when we met his wife and she was very grave; she was
—

*An old interest of Ingmar's, an old problem. Of the final episode in TILL GLÄDJE (1950): the young artist falters in the first big solo part in his life, but is forced to accommodate himself to humble, simple working discipline. Isn't there a thread leading from this to the parson in WINTER LIGHT, who holds the service *notwithstanding*? (The framework changes, that is all: artistic ambition in the first case; religious ambition in the new film.)

23

talking to a schoolgirl. When we got to the parsonage we were told that this girl's father had taken his life. The parson had had many talks with him, but it hadn't helped."

Another thread, joined to this one:

"This parson had the same difficulties as nearly all Swedish clergymen: he found it heavy going when he tried to reach his parishioners. Hardly anyone came to church, and so on."

A third thread-end of an idea:

"I don't as a rule give a damn about foreign politics, but last spring I read in the papers about the Russians and the Chinese, and then I discovered that it's not the Americans the Russians are afraid of, it's the Chinese. The Chinese who are drilled so hard that they might very well start an atomic war. And reading all this put me in an awful state of mind."

"How does it come into the story?"

"I have a fisherman and his pregnant wife come to see the parson; they've made an appointment for a talk with him after the service. The fisherman has become introspective and brooding because he has read that the Chinese are going to destroy the whole world."

"Who will play the fisherman?"

"Max von Sydow."

"And his wife?"

"Gunnel Lindblom, I think. If I can get her for the part. It would all fit in very well— she's expecting a baby herself."

The new film has been given a name now: NATTVARDSGÄSTERNA (WINTER LIGHT). I like it— it smacks of pure Swedish tradition, going right back to Tegnér's *The Communion Children* and Runeberg's *The Moose Hunters*. Apparently Ingmar has made good headway with writing, as he ventures to tell me a little about it:

"It's a counterpart to THROUGH A GLASS DARKLY. An answer to it. When I wrote THE GLASS I thought I had found a real proof of God's existence: God is love. God is all kinds of love, even perverted forms— and the proof of God's existence gave me a great feeling of security .... "

A great feeling of security, he says literally.

".... and I let the whole film work out into that proof, I let it form (he has recourse to a musical term) the actual *coda* in the last movement. But that lasted only until I started shooting the film."

(Then how is it he didn't alter the ending of the film? No, in his

24

view that is one of the fundamental principles of work in the studio: don't leave your script in the lurch in the middle of shooting. Be faithful to what you wrote, even if now, here in the studio, you think it represents a bygone phase. Don't meddle with the unity it had *then*. That sort of thing is dangerous, from both an artistic and a practical production point of view. If you want to record new results, then wait until the next film.)

"That's why I break up that proof of God's existence in this new film. It's a settling-of-accounts film, more or less. I settle accounts with Daddy God, the god of auto-suggestion, the god of security."

IB is evidently in the habit of cutting up a tent into pedagogically clear sections so as to get order and a general picture of the whole. He divides the new film up into three parts:

1. THE BREAKING UP OF THE CODA. Squaring accounts with the god of auto-suggestion.

"Hard to write that part?"

"Not so hard."

2. THE VOID AFTER THE BREAK-UP.

"Not so hard to write either."

3. A NEW FAITH SHOWS SIGNS OF LIFE.

"That's the hardest to write. I think I've found a solution. Have you ever heard of "duplication"? On certain Sundays the parson has to hold two services: one in the main parish and then one in the chapelry, the sub-parish in the next district. Now it is the custom in the Swedish church that if there are no more than three persons in the congregation, no service need be held. What I do is this: when Björnstrand comes to the district church, the churchwarden comes up to him and says: "There's only one churchgoer here." Yet the parson holds the service all the same. That's all that is needed to indicate the new faith that is stirring inside the parson."

The opening of the film gives Ingmar the parson's son and moralist a few qualms of conscience. He searches his heart to see whether it is "only a gimmick," "a trick of the trade," to begin the film with the whole of the communion service. In that case he should refrain from it!

"But however much I turn it over in my mind, I still arrive at the thought that I *don't* do it just as a gimmick."

At times IB looks quite Asiatic. Eyes and lips gleam and he looks down on his co-workers from a height, conscious of position and psychological power. A smile like that on an Indian god's image. The sharpe eye-teeth; the dark-green copper tints of the skin of his face.

At other times he is helplessly serious, as appealing as a child: with all his sensitivity laid bare. As now when he talks of religion, his face softens with seriousness. I catch a glimpse of both torment and the need of honesty.

On the few previous occasions when we have touched on religion, we have both been on our guard. Today too I am on the defensive, closed around my naturalism. Ingmar senses it and tries to bridge the gap between us by telling me his conception of the difference between "conviction" and "knowledge."

"I have the same conviction as you, if you know what I mean."

" 'Conviction' is naturalistic: don't count on anything other-worldly."*

"But I have a *knowledge* which says just the opposite. A knowledge which is at once distinct and evasive."

" 'Knowledge' says that God exists."

"You see, I believe that one can cut oneself off from God. Or one can say yes. I really think so."

(So many times he has returned to this theme. Now this parson who cuts himself off from God and love— in the shape of a woman, typically enough.)

"And intercession: I am convinced that it is a reality."

In THROUGH A GLASS DARKLY Karin goes to pieces in the conflict between two powers. The good voices are behind the wall-paper.** Karin calls them mysteriously "the others"; Ingmar himself actually calls them "the saints." Opposed to them are the black voices, those who give fiendish promptings: when *they* get God into their hands, he becomes a repulsive and nightmarish spider-God.

As a young man he lived with a woman who from time to time was subjected to commands. Voices gave her orders; voices told her what to do— he drew on those memories for material for the

—

*The naturalistic perspective can be found in Thomas's words to the fisherman in this finished film: "If it is so that God does not exist, what is the difference? Life becomes comprehensible. What a relief. Death becomes an extinguishing, a dissolution of body and soul. Etc."
** The original title of that film was THE WALLPAPER.

26

character of Karin. And on one of his own most basic conflicts:
"There, in THROUGH A GLASS DARKLY, there I really succeeded in expressing that mixture of religion and sexuality which I have always found so hard— so painfully hard— to sort out."

SATURDAY 22 JULY 1961
An idea for a TV series
By chance I began making TV interviews with actors and directors last fall— but what can you find out about their *work* during a 15-minute interview? Never a real inside view— only a clumsy fumbling at the door of their workshop. But a TV series about how one novel is created, one theatrical performance, one film— that should be able to show what takes place "in the artist's workshop." Would TV be willing to venture something like that?
Yes-answer from TV this week.
Supposing I am doubly ambitious and *both* write a diary and make a TV program about IB's film— then surely there should be a pretty good heap of material to show how films were made in the old days (way back at the beginning of the 1960s).

THURSDAY 27 JULY 1961
The third Thursday: Writing difficulty
"The goddam technical slovenliness of the New Wave"
Lenn opens the mail
Thursday again, IB has come in from Torö.
"How far have you gotten now?"
"The thematic part is ready. But not the shaping of it. Not all the details. For a while I got nowhere. Then Käbi said: 'If you're writing about Our Lord, then you'll have to trust him to give you the right inspiration, and stop worrying.' I obeyed her and stopped writing for three days; then it solved itself."
Anxious just the same:
"I've never been so late with a script as I am this time."
But when Harald Molander, the studio manager, asks him in the canteen when he will have the script ready, the answer comes like a shot:
"August 15th, as I said."
The clothes designer Mago, Max Goldstein, is at the same table— he will be doing the costumes for WINTER LIGHT. We start talking about the New Wave; Ingmar snaps out the same criticism as he re-

27

cently fired off in the magazine *Chaplin*. Once again he plays off THE LADY WITH THE LITTLE DOG ("which will last forever") against TILL THE LAST BREATH ("which is only a jazzed-up QUAI DES BRUMES"). He detests the New Wave for "its goddam technical slovenliness" and loves THE LADY WITH THE LITTLE DOG because it has been made "with such enormous love and care and passionate patience."

The technical slovenliness is perhaps not the only reason for his dislike of the French New Wave (which first lifted him up, then let him down; can one not sum up like that?) but it is the only one he mentions.

As usual he began the morning by opening the week's pile of mail with Lenn, his secretary. One of the letters is from a "very kind" Frenchman. Another from an unknown, dotty woman in South America who bombards him with incessant ideas. One from an unknown Spanish girl ("I am a Spanish girl of 21, small, thin .... am studying for the stage in Madrid; last year I tried to go to Sweden to meet you but my money gave out in Copenhagen ...."). A business letter from *The New York Times* which wants an article of 2,000 words ("how many pages is that?"). Etc.

Lenn bends over the pile of letters with the pencil and shorthand pad in his hand. He was a dancer at the Malmö City Theater and started his secretarial work for Ingmar during that time. Hard to guess his age: the boyish face with the melancholy eyes, a small figure who has the ex-dancer's concern for the way he carries himself. I never see him relax: he writes down, telephones, types out and puts the same energy into details as into big things; serious, sensitive, a keen observer. Lenn puts up with the film world but loves the theater: *there* he is at home, in his native element; there he is spared protective masks and disguises.

"He does everything he has to do for me with an enormous ambition," Ingmar says. "But it's nothing compared to what happens if Käbi calls up: then he just drops everything he is doing and rushes to help her! They can be missing for hours on a round of shopping, in a world all their own; they have terrific fun together."

TUESDAY 8 AUGUST 1961
Fetch the script
S.D.G.
What about the envy of Christ?

Lenn calls up: he's going to the barbershop in Valhallavägen this afternoon; can I drop in and fetch the script? Then I'd have time to read it before the TV shooting on Saturday.

The script is brand-new, dated: "Torö, 7 Aug. 1961. S.D.G."

I recall a slip of paper on which Ingmar had printed "S.D.G." and stuck to a lamp on his desk at the Malmö City Theater. It was at the time of THE SEVENTH SEAL and he was of two minds as to whether he would tell me about it or not. Perhaps I would think it was silly and pretentious of him to borrow Johan Sebastian Bach's habit of writing at the end of every composition "S.D.G." — *Soli Deo Gloria*, 'to God alone the Glory'.

I wonder what Ingmar has done about the envy of Christ. He has said very little about it during these last Thursdays. Has he been up to carrying the theme through?

Surely he hasn't gone and mislaid it?

WEDNESDAY 9 AUGUST 1961

Question marks in the margin

Yes, just as I feared: the envy of Christ is missing. At any rate the motif has not been worked out— it is merely mentioned now in two speeches: once by the parson himself, the second time by the schoolteacher.

Why has it shrunk so much?

When it could be such a good scene, if Thomas were to kneel down before Christ on the cross and start a declaration of love: "I love you, Christ." But in the middle of this declaration of love, to his own astonishment, he begins to mumble, thinly, quietly: "I hate you, Christ. I have always hated you and envied you .... " and then his childish, boyish envy would pour out. Then horror at what he has said. And the Christ image who merely keeps silent. And Thomas so frightened and desperate that he could run amok there inside the church, among all the symbols .... .

As regards the end: I think that the drive to Frostnäs church should imply a *choice* for Thomas— so that it is plain that something has really happened inside him. As it is now, one doesn't really notice "a new faith showing signs of life." There is a possibility of choice here, a dramatic twist that Ingmar has not brought out.

I read the script over and over, keeping accounts of the themes, dividing up what I like and don't like. At length I have found so many objections that I won't be content until I have thought out suggestions for a complete reconstruction.

P. S.

With what tenderness the figure of Algot Frōvik, the church-warden, has been created! Is it inspired by K. A.?

THURSDAY 10 AUGUST 1961, FORENOON
Look in the mirror

A host of worries rises up inside me when I am to hand the script back. On the subway into town I get out my notebook. (Better jot down the impulses *now*; afterwards they will drown in rationalizations.)

1. My dislike of the choice of religious theme is perhaps *distorting* my judgment. A sour taste in my mouth from all the conventional film parsons ....

2. It would be silly to say anything to IB that I would never hear the last of. *I* give kicks on the behind; so does he (and *what* kicks!). More comfortable just to hand the script back and say that everything's fine as it is. Then I'll rescue the diary and any film future I may have.

3. No, I mustn't be ingratiating and subservient. But I must think of what is best for his *film* when I offer my criticism. Be matter-of-fact. Not criticize so clumsily that I put him off accepting a well-suggested alteration.

4. There's professional cockiness for you! Here's my suggestion for reconstruction, take it or leave it! I too know how to build up a drama.

5. Might as well confess it: I am childishly flattered at being entrusted with reading the script so early, with orders to say what I "really think."

6. Proceed warily at any rate. (Not from cowardice but from consideration for him: ".... you mustn't criticize in such a way that I lose my belief in this film and get scared of doing it.")

I put down paper and pencil wearily.

What a tangle!

Is it always like this, the co-worker situation?

THURSDAY 10 AUGUST 1961, AFTERNOON
Four hours of rough treatment of the script

He settles down in his little office at SF with a searching smile:

"Well? Do you think we should do this film?"

"Sure."

I myself can hear what that "sure" sounds like. This hedging, non-definite, unenthusiastic thing which is I; and which is the very opposite of his abrupt choice between cold and hot (either he is seized with enthusiasm or else he snaps and snarls). I brace myself and start according to plan reeling off everything I like about the script; but he waves all this aside impatiently, anxious about what is to come: the objections, the criticism.

"Why have you fought shy of the envy of Christ?"

"I haven't fought shy of it! It's there!"

"It's *talked* about, yes. In passing. But it's never dramatically formed, in picture and acting."

Ingmar gives a little smile.

"It *was* there, before, from the start. I even wrote it .... "

"How did you form it?"

"Oh, that's very simple: just by letting Thomas talk to the Christ image in the church. But I took it out."

"Why?"

"Because it didn't belong here, to *this* film. It belongs to the next film. You see, every object has its specific gravity, hasn't it? All that about the envy of Christ is too big to sort out this time, I felt very strongly that I must keep it till next time. This film is much simpler than that. I've had to begin at the beginning again, in fact, with a scraping bare of the God image."

(I seem to remember he sometimes spells it with a small 'g' in the script = the old god image that is to be rejected?)

"You see, I feel that I can't run before I can walk. I've done it so many times before: tried to force myself to a result of faith. But you just can't *make* yourself believe. It must take its time: one year or two years or ten. Perhaps the whole problem disappears entirely, for all I know. I must also be prepared for that. At any rate for a time. That's how it was after THE SEVENTH SEAL."

Suddenly a timid and sensitive voice:

"What are you smiling at?"

Because I am touched, I want to answer; but I find it hard to explain myself. It has something to do at any rate with purity in an artistic striving. The will to listen carefully to a theme; and be loyal to it. Do one thing at a time. The insistence on work well done, the strict morality of the handicraftsman. All this ideal of patience in an explosively impatient man like Ingmar.

Lay building stone to building stone, so they form a life's work. This is Ingmar's twenty-fifth film. Not all of them belong to his life's work; some are merely exercises. But even restricting oneself to ten. Ten well-made building blocks which together form a whole.

This leads me to think of Ibsen, who sedulously formed each new work as a rejoinder to the one immediately preceding: a continuous dialogue between drama and drama. WINTER LIGHT tests and displaces THROUGH A GLASS DARKLY— and then? So he is thinking of a sequel?*

"Something more you don't approve of?"

"Algot Frōvik's thoughts about Christ's suffering come so late. Can't you bring them in at the beginning?"

"No, because then people would have forgotten them. They must come last .... You see, Algot Frōvik is an angel to me. Really, literally: an angel. There is fifty times more religion in that man than in the whole character of the parson."

"How are you going to do Mārta's letter?"

"I start with Thomas reading it. Ordinary conventional shot of Thomas as he opens and reads it. Then close-up of her: she looks straight into the camera as she talks over the reading. Then I cut in between Thomas and Mārta in different kinds of shots. But both look straight into the camera. Close; scraped bare; like this."

"When Thomas meets the fisherman for the first time and then

—

* Yes, several times during the shooting that followed, IB hinted that he was contemplating a sequel. It was not to be about Thomas Ericsson and Mārta Lundberg at all, but it would— if I understood him correctly— carry on where WINTER LIGHT left off and in some way develop the new God image. At some time during 1962 there was a violent outburst against *both* the atheists and the religious dogmatists who think you can "round up" God. Then it suddenly seemed as if he were talking like someone who has left the religious "problem" behind him and had an inkling of mysticism.

But it was not THE SILENCE he was referring to in the summer of 1961 when he spoke of a sequel. THE SILENCE came quite unexpectedly as a third part of the trilogy. And in THE SILENCE God is present only by his absence. The scraping bare has merely advanced another step. When THE SILENCE ends, the boy Johan (Ingmar points out) sits spelling out the "new words" in the "foreign language." The beginner in mysticism. Those who are to accustom themselves to the Second Reality must begin with very simple words: "hand," "music."

32

when he meets Mārta .... I don't know how, but I think there's a little too much of yourself in those speeches, as yet. In THROUGH A GLASS DARKLY you managed to objectify yourself much more."

A shake of the head.

"There's much less of myself in the character of Thomas than you think. In fact, I've only one thing in common with Thomas: the clearing out of an old image; and the glimpse of a new God image that is much more difficult to capture, to explain, to describe. Otherwise he is not *I*. Anything else?"

I think of Thomas's words by the railroad crossing:

One evening, when I was a child, I woke up in a terrible fright. The train whistled down at the bend we lived in the old vicarage by the bridge. It was an evening in early spring with a strangely wild light over the ice and the forest. I got out of bed and ran from room to room looking for father. But the house was empty. I called and shouted but no one answered. Then I got dressed as best I could and ran down to the edge of the lake. The whole time I screamed and cried for father. Then the train came from the direction of the station. The smoke was quite black against all the white and there was a roar from all the freight cars.

(Shot of the train which "thunders past with a majestic roar in a cloud of steam and whirling snow.")

I was left without father and mother together with a huge dragon of iron and fire in a completely dead world. I was ill with terror. Father sat up with me all that night.

MÅRTA (absent-mindedly): What a kind father!

THOMAS: Father and mother wanted me to be a clergyman. (Pause.) And I did as they wanted.

"That childhood memory .... don't you think that Pär Lagerkvist has already laid claim to the locomotive as a symbol of anguish?"

"Where?"

"In FATHER AND I. One of his short stories."

"I've never read it."

I wonder how often that kind of thing has happened to IB? That which appears to be a literary loan is not a loan at all— it goes back to experiences of his own. His maternal grandfather built and owned the Södra Dalarna railroad; he spent all his summers as a child with his grandparents, the whole of his childhood was criss-crossed with locomotives, railroad tracks, whistlings, the smell of smoke. (The association train— anguish— death is to be found in one of his very first screenplays: the childhood episode in EVA.)*

—

*We lived at Duvnäs and sometimes I was allowed to go with mother when

33

"Good. Then I'll cut out that bit that they lived by the railroad.* But the train that trundles past while Märta and Thomas are sitting in the car. I'm not cutting that out! (Devilish little grin at my officiousness:) You don't insist on *that*, do you?!"

An embarrassed "no" from me.

"Okay then. It isn't important anyway to specify *what* frightened the boy. Only to show that he did get frightened and was then consoled by his father .... "

The boy gets a fright and is consoled by his Father. God himself is a reassuring, fatherly god "who admittedly loved mankind but me most of all" (Thomas says to the fisherman). "Father spoke to me," says the boy at the end of THROUGH A GLASS DARKLY— with an undertone of "God spoke to me." One ought to look a little more closely at all associations of "father" and "god" in these films, for Ingmar has put them there deliberately.**

Why has IB never (before) been interested in Christ? Swiftly-made theory: because his religious, emotional world has been poisoned (sated) with the association "father"-"god."

"Any more objections?"

"The end. One never feels that 'a new faith shows signs of life' in Thomas. He just goes in and holds the service .... "

"Exactly. He's the pack donkey that keeps struggling on. Far too weak to be of any use in God's work. God cannot put any strength into him— but he can into Märta! It's Märta who takes over the struggle for faith in the end, do you see?"

I hesitate. I have been reading the script for two days, backwards and forwards, but everything I have jotted down shows that I have thought of Märta as a non-believer right through the film.

—

she was going to Borlänge to the market. In the afternoon we came home with a freight train that made long stops at Lännheden and Repbäcken. Oh, hot summer days with flies and rails— I'll never forget it!" (Note jotted down at Rättvik, 1.25.62.)

*Memory shortens and condenses everything: in the spring of 1962 he maintains that I made him realize that that episode "was only *bad Pär Lagerkvist*— that's why he cut out the story, although it had already been shot. All he kept was: *"Father and mother wanted me to be a clergyman."*

**In THE SILENCE the dying Ester, Ingrid Thulin, thinks of her old father's death. He weighed 440 pounds when he died. She would liked to have seen the faces of the pallbearers who had to stagger along with him; and on the way back from a trial screening in a cinema in Rättvik, 5.8.63, Ingmar laughs at this leave-taking of the symbol for the old security-father-god:

34

"Then what about her intercession?" Ingmar says. "Right at the last."

Curtain. My own religious phobias have always played such an intellectual trick on me that I haven't even noticed that it *is* an intercession! I was just painfully affected by her kneeling down and mumbling a prayer about "being able to believe."

"But supposing you faced Thomas with a choice before the last service, so that we are more clearly aware of his decision? Then we'd feel more of 'the new faith showing signs of life'. All you need to do is give a slightly more dramatic touch to it .... "

"I'll think about it. I've a feeling that very little is needed to alter the mood. A few lines. A detail or two."

He nods a little, as though I had touched something that concerns himself.

"Everything you've said up to now is so foreign to me .... *this* I feel to be right; it strikes a chord in me. Not the other .... "

"But before, I might inadvertently have touched on something that you resist developing— the envy of Christ, for instance?"

He thinks this over carefully.

"No, I don't think so."

I hesitate about going on.

"Come on, out with it! What is it?"

"Blom, the organist, doesn't tell Märta what Thomas's marriage was like until the final scenes .... isn't that putting the yeast into the dough after it's in the oven? Why do you want it so late?"

"So as not to say too much at the beginning, of course. His relationship to his wife must be revealed bit by bit, don't you see? When Märta finally hears what a sham Thomas's married life was, the last obstacle is removed for her. Then she is seized with a great tenderness for Thomas. In fact, like this: what Blom tells her makes Märta capable of praying for Thomas."

"But if you put Blom's gossip at the beginning instead, one would understand better that Thomas formerly lived in a romantically religious world with his wife. Show him in a conventional cozy world where religion is romantically simple: "God is love"— *before* you cast him out into anguish .... the film now has hardly begun before you show his distress."

He ponders on the alternative.

—

" .... all that's left of it, a dead old man weighing 440 pounds."

"So you think I should start with the service?"

Picking up his yellow pad, he starts noting down my suggestion:

1. THE SERVICE

2. THE CHURCHWARDEN

3. ....

With pencil in hand:

"What then?"

At last I have my chance. Ambitiously I reel off *my* structure, the gist of which is that everything should be lumped together. I don't want two talks with the fisherman, but one; I don't want Thomas to have it out twice with Märta, but once. Let them quarrel in the vestry, then there's no need for the excursion to the classroom— and the whole drama can be acted out in the church, etc. Ingmar listens thoughtfully but after a while puts down the pencil. His eyes begin to smile. For a while I'm so taken up with my own plan of construction that I don't suspect anything; I think the smile is an acquiescence in the excellent solutions I have found. At last I come to the end of my suggested alterations. Then he smiles benevolently.

"Very good. But it's *theater*."

The shaft hit home.

"Had I written this thing for the theater, I'd have set it all out in big scenes as you suggest. And if I were to do it on TV, only two scenes would be needed for the whole play: the altar and the vestry."

The shaft hit home because it reminded me of his criticism of my first independent screenplay GAME ON THE RAINBOW. The fault of that script was that right through the film I had written rounded-off scenes, with beginning, middle and end— just as in the theater. "But a film, you see, a film is nothing but *small* curves leading imperceptibly one into the other .... so that when the film is finished all those small curves have formed one long line, a single dramatic arch."

So my neat little construction went up in smoke. Not much to be done about it. But if Ingmar sinks me with Principles of Building Technology, then I'll take out the equivalent from my own arsenal. Haven't I discovered by myself the principles by which A and B must change their attitude toward each other, if long, dull patches are to be avoided?

"What were you going to say?"

"I just want to ask whether you're not afraid of all the repetitions you make in WINTER LIGHT. I think it might be a bit boring when people have such a static relationship to one another."

For if character A and character B treat each other in exactly the same way in two similar scenes ....

"Repetitions? They're my device for making things stick. *First I give people a hint, then I ram it into them.* You have an overclear example in WILD STRAWBERRIES: the clocks with no hands."

"But when you let Märta say *twice* that she's so 'bossy'! Let her say it *once*— then we get the feeling that she has come to realize it. Though of course .... in real life one is always perceiving something with one's reason— and being just as helpless for all that .... "

Ingmar:

"Exactly."

Then I try to show him how much ammunition he wastes the first time Märta appears. Why must she *abruptly* pour out her religious scorn? Why not save it until later? In any case she confesses everything in the letter.

"You should have seen what her first scene was like at the start! Kābi helped me there. She got me to tone down Märta's outburst, to save it .... This is how it was."

Suddenly he helps me to get at the most important thing of all: how the ideas move about with an author. This is how the scenes between Märta and Thomas were at the outset:

"I wrote a scene in which Märta showed Thomas her eczema. I wrote that first.* Then I went still farther back. I wondered how it was they met. I wrote a scene showing how Märta went up to the parson and thanked him for the sermon when she was a newcomer to the district."

—

*This scene is not in the final script. But fragments of it are in the finished film. What happened was this: when IB decided to let Ingrid Thulin read *the whole of* the letter straight into the camera, it was an experiment that *might* fail. In order to safeguard himself he took long cut-in shots of Gunnar Björnstrand, and he also wrote out the entire scene anew, from memory: a) Märta asks Thomas to pray for her hands, b) Thomas hesitates, which makes Märta so exasperated that she kneels down at the altar rail and prays for herself. Everything was shot. At the cutting table he experimented by putting both (a) and (b) into the middle of Ingrid Thulin's letter reading. The result was jerky. Finally, he decided on the most radical procedure of all: to cut in only (b) into the letter reading.

(Theory: if the eczema scene was written first, then *it* was emotionally the most important for IB. It contained a fruitful kernel, something that released the imaginative impulses in him. For it's a common experience: for certain scenes a writer draws on that which emotionally concerns him most; other scenes he kneads deliberately in order to join together what has to be joined.)

"How did you go about it to put those scenes into the story?"

"In flashbacks, during their talks. Then followed the whole of their long settling up."

"Where did that take place?"

"In the church."

"In the church?!"

"Mmm."

"All in one go?"

He smiles.

"Sure. But it became a terrible cannonade. So I broke it up into several scenes .... "

I am suddenly aware of the comic situation that has arisen: unwittingly I have been suggesting to IB that he should revert to a structure which he has already rejected.

Ingmar:

"It was like this: at first I wanted *the whole thing* to be played in the church. It was to be played in front of the altar."

"A kind of morality play?"

"Yes. But I kept getting farther away from it as I wrote. I saw more and more clearly what I really wanted. I wanted everything to be simpler and more everyday, as it is "in real life." No heroic strains as between Jöns and the Knight in the THE SEVENTH SEAL — peel that all off! You object because the parson says trite things when he talks to the fisherman and his wife at the beginning...."

"Yes, when I think of all the film parsons I've seen in a spiritual crisis ...."

"I don't follow you. What parsons? By all means think they're platitudes," he says. "I've gone to a lot of trouble to find the worst clichés a parson can trot out when someone comes to him for comfort .... I can tell you this: it wasn't until I gave up the thought of shooting the whole thing in the church that this film started to work out for me. Not until I saw the whole film as a journey between two churches— two terminuses— two god images. The old god image and the new. Then everything arranged itself naturally for me. *This goddam car trip in the November snow* .... Everything became stations on the road for the parson. The first station: when he watches over the body in the snow although he himself is in a bad way, ill and feverish. Next station: the classroom. Next station: when he has to go to the fisherman's wife and tell her that her husband has shot himself. At that point I had a goddam long dialogue between Thomas and Mrs. Persson which I cut down to almost nothing."

"Stations" on a road. The word is charged with Strindberg associations: it belongs to Strindberg's dream plays, penitent dramas. And beyond that: stations on Christ's road of suffering to the cross, the object of meditation in catholic churches.

" .... saw that I must get away from the church play. Out into reality instead. As realistic and true to life as possible .... "

"In that case are you going to take out the oddities of the fisherman's second visit to Thomas? As you've written it now, we don't know whether Jonas is really there or not."

"He is a vision. Has never been there."

I frown, not understanding.

"But you've experienced that yourself, haven't you? One sits there and experiences something so intensely that it's just as if the person in question were there. Thomas sits there thinking so hard of what he is to say to the fisherman that he imagines Jonas *is* there. He goes and asks Mārta afterwards if she has seen Jonas."*

"That seems like a mystification to me. Especially if you're striving for everyday reality .... "

—

*The scene is still in the shooting script: Thomas goes out into the church and discovers Mārta. She is standing just behind the pulpit, screened from the sunlight. Exhausted, he sinks down in a pew. Long pause.
THOMAS: Did you see anyone go out here?
MĀRTA: No.
THOMAS: Did you just come or have you been here long?
MĀRTA: When I left you, I thought I'd go home, but I changed my mind and came back here. When I came into the vestry, I saw you sitting at the table asleep. (N.B.!) I didn't want to disturb you, so I decided to wait out here.
THOMAS: Then you didn't see Jonas Persson.
MĀRTA: (shakes her head).
THOMAS: Then he's not coming.
MĀRTA: Are you expecting him?
IB cut the whole of this dialogue during shooting.

His smile.

"So you think we should cut out the mystification?"*

My monosyllabic:

"Yes."

Ingmar ponders.

"If I make it so that it's not a dream talk, I'll be faced with a time problem of course: Jonas goes off; within two minutes he has shot himself. But good Lord! when have *I* ever bothered about realistic time. I can make a minute seem as long as an hour."

Pause.

"Anything more?"

I launch myself resolutely into the course of events after Jonas's suicide. First Thomas stands by the fisherman's body (the whole theodicy problem); *then* he chats with a schoolboy (who is going to be a "spaceman" when he grows up!); *then* he pours all his hatred over Mārta ....

"I think it feels funny rhythmically."

He looks at me questioningly.

"Funny rhythmically? *Rhythmically*, you mean? I'm usually pretty sure of the rhythm. What do you mean exactly?"

I rationalize swiftly and come up with this counter-question:

"Let me put it like this: which theme is the more important? The Jonas theme or the Mārta theme?"

"The Mārta theme."

"What! Surely the Jonas theme is the main theme, from a *religious* point of view? So shouldn't the Mārta theme be subordinated to it, so that the outburst of hatred against Mārta comes *before* Jonas's suicide .... "

"But the relationship to Mārta is the main theme. It too is a religious theme, isn't it? It's in relation to her that Thomas's final religious failure is evidenced: his inability to accept her love."

Always this theme with Ingmar: the woman wants to give a love which the man cannot accept. Just how inflamed by guilt is he?!

"What is it?" he asks.

"I'm beginning to realize what I meant by 'funny rhythm'. I think it looks awful for Thomas to stand naked in the presence of death and suffering and God— and then disgrace himself with a

—

*At the first read-through (10.2.61) it turns out that several have puzzled over the mystification. Cf. IB's reply why he considered it necessary.

40

stream of hatred against Märta. I want a nice neat curve to the story."

Ingmar laughs.

"I was thinking .... "

We began talking at one o'clock. At two thirty Ingmar went off to look at the rushes of THE GARDEN OF EDEN, the Alf Kjellin film that Ingmar is producing. I sat there annotating our discussion; at three thirty he came back and we went on.

Naturally it was rather a blow that he was so obstinate and strong in defense: there was not one objection that he didn't shoot to bits. I consoled myself by thinking it was because of twenty-five years of professional experience: a director is always being forced to find reasons when there's a hitch with actors and co-workers, and Ingmar discovered early on that reasons *tell* on people. As long as you can invent a reason for them, they give in— provided you rivet them with your eyes and speak with vehemence or gentle gravity when you give your reason. Every profession has its occupational diseases.

Besides: IB finds it frightfully hard to yield the point. Somewhere he has an old general inside him. A passing remark, and he immediately sees a chance of battle formation. Bring up the batteries, load the arguments! If anyone is to come off the victor, it is not the opponent.

Neither explanation really helped me. The position was simply that he had lived with Thomas Ericsson and Märta Lundberg for a whole summer. He had worked at the material thoroughly from several directions. Written large quantities, condensed, cut out. Tried out a solution and rejected it. No wonder his structure was better. My own objections were made in two days.

But the actual discussion is more free of tension than I thought it would be. He never squashes me. I feel relieved. So I am all the more astonished when IB says, suddenly, very quietly:

"I was a bit depressed when I went in to look at the rushes of THE GARDEN OF EDEN. I thought: Have I not managed to express myself in the script so that Vilgot grasps it? What's wrong with it all now? Is it *he* who can't understand me? Or is it I who can't express myself?"

Two egocentricities speaking to each other. I sit there with my private tangle of motives, satisfied that at least I have not been ingratiating towards IB. Yet I know from experience how sensitive

41

one is when showing something that one has just written. What don't I myself expect in the way of discretion and consideration for the newborn thing. And IB's script is only a couple of days old.

"This has been a cold shower. Very good for me."

He says it without smiling.

I am rather ashamed and remind him how hard it is to read a film script. It calls for an enormous amount of practice to read *pictures* out of those meager paper words. IB nods, with a hint of self-mockery.

"Something that I have pointed out in my writings."*

An exchange of tired smiles. IB raises his hand and bends down a finger for each point where my criticism has found a response in him. Total: two bent fingers. I mumble, coaxingly:

"And you'll bring out the envy of Christ a little more?"

He smiles.

"Perhaps."

The time is getting on toward four thirty, and we are both rather tired. I say that I myself could hardly stand fifteen minutes of a discussion like this. He replies that it all feels different now. His depression is gone.

"Whatever the reason may be. Perhaps because we've reached a result .... "

His worried look:

"I'm wondering now if you've gone and given in and backed out just for the sake of peace and quiet, or whether you've *really* understood me?"

"I haven't backed out. Your structure is *yours*, and it's the only right one in this case."

He is still not sure that I mean what I say. He looks hard at me, and says with an undertone of uneasiness:

—

* For instance in the essay "Every Film Is My Last Film."   Six months later I am given splendid proof of this difficulty on glancing through my notes from those days. In my opinion, one of the strongest scenes in the finished film is that in which Thomas, in spiritual vexation, sinks down at the altar and is patted and consoled by Märta. What did I get out of that scene when I read the script? This: *"Märta is there. Short, expressionless conversation between them to fill in the time of waiting until the woman is to come and say that Jonas has been found dead."*
The everlasting lesson.

42

"Promise me one thing: you mustn't change your mind just in order to please me; you're *not* to tell me anything you *don't mean.*"

FRIDAY 11 AUGUST 1961
After-thoughts
So:
While working on the idea, Ingmar lifted the whole material *out of* a literary tradition (type: morality play, altar play) *into* another literary tradition (type: "Strindbergian penitent drama"). The movement went from the stylization of the church to everyday realism. From theater to film. (Check later to see if the finished film bears traces of this transition.)

It was lucky all the same that I brought out my suggestions for reconstruction; otherwise I would never have found out about this course of events, since Ingmar always throws away drafts and rough copies.

Why does he?

Is he ashamed of them? Does he think his problems of literary style will be exposed just there?

As it is now, one must trust his sudden explanation afterwards.* Explanations that come by chance, *en passant*; like this one, for instance:

Once last summer he called THROUGH A GLASS DARKLY a "romantic" film, particularly if one compared it with the bleakness of WINTER LIGHT. "Romance" as against all chill penury. Yesterday afternoon, tired after our discussion, he told me something of himself and Käbi, how they gradually discovered that they were "two badly injured people. I most, perhaps. She had her time as a refugee behind her. And I, I felt myself to be dying." With great tenderness:

"It all began very romantically between us, awfully romantically. Then we changed together. The romance passed; now it's something else that binds us together. Something else, something much more real."

And suddenly, the psychological key, tossed out in passing:

"That romantic first time corresponds to Thomas's marriage in the film."

—

*Cf. Tuesday, January 23rd, 1962.

43

THROUGH A GLASS DARKLY was conceived during this first romantic phase— and was the only one of his films with a dedication: "To Käbi, my wife." Therefore this mysticism in the final coda: love exists. Love is real. Love is God. A mysticism which (so I guess) in a far too simple way soaked up the difficulties, the cruelties, the conflicts in life— therefore it must be contradicted and exploded, in expectation of a greater God image. The beautiful Karin mysticism in THE GLASS had to be succeeded by the harsh Märta Lundberg demand in WINTER LIGHT.

That must have been why Ingmar got nowhere as long as he tried to write about the parson and his wife.

Not until he broke the female image* into two halves did the situation become fruitful for his imagination: on the one hand the dead wife, pallid, dreamy, marked by death, standing for the romantic "God is love" declaration. On the other hand the schoolteacher— strong, demanding, real.

SATURDAY 12 AUGUST 1961
The first TV shooting out at Torö

"Today I cremated and buried an adder."

He shifts down to second and turns off on a twisting road.

"I killed the snake the other day and put it out for the gulls, but none of them wanted it. And no buzzard came and no eagle, so this morning I poured gasoline on it. Then I buried it properly on the beach, with stones and all. You'll see."

A glance in the rearview mirror to make sure that the four cars from TV are keeping up: suddenly he is somewhat embarrassed, feeling the demands grinning at him. This entire caravan— cameramen, sound truck, sound engineers, producer, interviewer— all just to record what he has to say about his film. The whole area down to the water is covered with small pine trees; IB jogs eagerly around the trees showing the cars where to park— anxious to make everything enjoyable for the TV guys: " .... nice to get rid of my nervousness," he says. Only then do I realize how he tenses himself at the thought of what he has to do.

The sea murmurs, a wide expanse, no horizon. The only mark: the lighthouse at Landsort.

—

*Cf. Thursday, July 20th.

44

The place is too rugged, lonely and vast for Kābi; but Ingmar loves it.

The interview takes a couple of hours to shoot; Ingmar is stiff at first. Not until the third reel (each reel uses up ten minutes of film) do I sense that he is relaxing— it's when the first swear-word comes, unintentionally, spontaneously, in the same tone of voice as he uses in his everyday speech. I embroider my questions onto the material that emerged in our long script discussion; and when we get to the question of the father-feeling-of-security-god, I try out the theory from last Thursday in a question about the development of the God image in his films. He shies rather at discussing the problem. (His emotional tension concerning the subject is noticeable from the way he ends so many sentences with a semi-question: "haven't I?" "didn't it?" "doesn't it?" "wasn't it?" etc., etc.)

IB: Let me put it this way: in the earlier films I've always left the question open— of a God's existence or not   haven't I? In the VIRGIN SPRING the folk song gave the answer, didn't it? The spring wells up, doesn't it? But *at that time* it was a way for me to make a shy approach to the subject and document my own conviction— my own conception — of a God's reality, wasn't it? In THROUGH A GLASS DARKLY you have it manifested very definitely. The gist of it and the credo is that "God is Love and Love is God" and that therefore the proof of God's existence is the reality of love: "Love's existence as something real in the world of mankind."

    Then, you see— and this is what is so awful and difficult— I've had to embrace the whole problem in WINTER LIGHT and shatter that entire god image, which is a kind of seeking for security. I've tried now to find my way to an even broader and distinct and clear god-conception.

INT: Why is it so essential to shatter the god image that is in THROUGH A GLASS DARKLY?

IB: Well, you can imagine that yourself. I mean: the fisherman comes with his terror of the Chinese and their latent threat of war, doesn't he? If you have a man like that sitting opposite you, it's awfully hard to say to him: "You don't have to worry about the Chinese, for God is Love. Feel safe, for after all love is the essential thing and it exists on earth as something real."

INT: Can you say that it was .... how shall I put it .... too narrow a god image that was based merely on security?

IB: Yes, that's what I think. At any rate, it felt so, more and more as time went on.

INT: Security in what sense? Like the child?

45

IB: Yes, exactly. And there I've had to put my own house in order— a very painful process incidentally. Make a clean sweep of an old god conception. The father-god. A father-and-son relationship in some way — an auto-suggestion god, a security god, eh? I've had to make a very searching inquiry into the whole of the concept. And deep down that's really what this film is about.

INT: If I were to classify your films, I'd say that in the first period there was all that rebellion against authority— against *fathers* of various kinds and in religious contexts. Then we have a long sequence of films with reconciliation: WILD STRAWBERRIES and all films in which you, as it were, accept the paternal secure god image.

IB: Yes, that's right. That had to be done first. That's the way it went of course: first one revolted— opposed the father image. Then one accepted it. And then it was a matter of quietly putting it aside— of not modelling the father image and the god image (on each other).

INT: I gather that you're extremely careful as regards the theme too in this new film: you don't supply any new god image?

IB: No, you couldn't say that. But the *drama*— the actual passion— is not enacted in the main character, Thomas, but in Märta, the non-believer. She who bears within herself the seed of a new god image; who has the possibilities of life within her and in time hands these over to Thomas.

With an hour's worth of interview answers in the bag, the TV caravan calls it a day. The twilight deepens under the pines, the dampness rising from the water's edge darkens the stones of the terrace, and over dinner Käbi tells me that she had never taken communion until she married Ingmar— it was part of the wedding ceremony.

She was only so disappointed in the wafer in the Swedish church.

"Bread," she says. "*Bread*, to me that was black Estonian bread .... not that little bit of white paper that the parson popped into my mouth."

Her eyes twinkle as she talks. Ingmar often speaks of her wonderful black humor; and he himself chimes in with:

"Bread! It shouldn't be bread at communion, it should be meat. Real meat. Tournedos."

Turning to me, the puritan:

"Shouldn't I say that? Oh come now. You see, in *my* childhood home religion was sturdy reality. Something to get hold of. Something substantial."

Then I remember this joy when he composed an opening shot for the TV series. He took the first handwritten page of the script of WINTER LIGHT. On it he placed a desk decoration that he generally uses as a paperweight: a small Asiatic goddess with a huge, obscene behind. Up to a point he did it to shock TV viewers, but very largely to depict himself.

Moreover: while the cameramen were busy around us today, he said that he often worked on some other script at the same time as he was writing the main script.

"This time I wrote a long story about a guy that found himself in a brothel."

He laughed.

"I got quite a long way before I tired of it."

Found himself in a brothel .... so did the hero in THE RAKE'S PROGRESS.

On the interview table lay a few yellow writing pads, full of handwritten jottings: the only rough drafts I've seen of WINTER LIGHT(he always writes by hand). On one of the pages I read: *"From my window I can see the cemetery, my wife's grave ...."*

I, Thomas Ericsson.

"At first I wrote the whole second act of WINTER LIGHT in the first person."

WEDNESDAY 30 AUGUST 1961
The technical preparations get started

Mixing of THROUGH A GLASS DARKLY: trouble with the fog horn. The newly-made sounds supposed to represent the fog horn sound awful; nothing left but to have K. A. go down with a man and record the real sound.

But over the afternoon tea IB is a pretty satisfied man. He has escaped from the monk's cell of writing, out into the open air. This pleasant phase when the whole production collective begins to gather around the script, which is finished at last!

"The other day we all went to church."

Lennart Unnerstad, chief sound engineer; P. A. Lundgren, the art director who is to build up Mittsunda church in the studio; Mago, Lenn .... After the service they all walked around in the country church, looking, trying out the sound and measuring the resonance.

The result was a thorough discussion about the *floor* in the studio church. As a rule the scene painters get to work with their brushes and paint a floor that looks like a stone floor. Is that what is to be done now too? Wouldn't it be wise to lay a real stone floor in the studio church— slab by slab? Think of the acoustics then! The footsteps through the church, the atmosphere around the speeches— think of the gain in sound, whatever the expense.

So be it.

Lars-Owe Carlberg, production manager, comes up to the canteen with Eddie Axberg, eleven years old. Eddie is going to play the boy in the classroom. An old stagehand already: he played the lead in the boy's film THE BRIG THREE LILIES.

"Are you going to be an actor when you grow up?"

Eddies looks at Ingmar with a pitying smile and shakes his head gravely.

"Unfortunately," Eddie says.

He says it with the expression of one who is genuinely sorry to have to say no. But he has more important things for the future.

"What are you going to be instead, then?"

"Farmer."

Ingmar eyes him delightedly.

The day after tomorrow he's going up to his usual recuperation spot (Hotel Siljansborg, Rättvik). The bonds linking him to the landscape of his childhood and summer school vacations are so strong that he feels an "utterly ambivalence-free happiness" every time he goes back to Dalarna.

UNDATED, 1962
Sacrificing the coast

In fact, the bonds are so strong that during his time up there he decided to take all the location shots in Dalarna.

But the script of WINTER LIGHT describes a typical Swedish coastal landscape— "and actually I should have shot it there." Didn't he give in to his own need of well-being when he moved Thomas and Märta inland? Did he not sacrifice something of the environmental atmosphere so as to be in a part of the country where he always felt secure?

I had no idea that this had been anything of a problem for him until he told me today, long afterwards, that his conscience pricked him when he made that change.

Hc smiled as he said it.

MONDAY 11 SEPTEMBER 1961
Gunnar Björnstrand's first reaction to the part

48

Lunch with Gunnar Björnstrand (in the little pink extra room that SF has gone to the expense of building in the old restaurant). Gunnar has nearly finished his part in THE GARDEN OF EDEN, but doesn't seem particularly tired. Previously we have met only in more nerve-racking contexts (a TV interview); now he is at ease, relaxed. I notice more clearly than before the care with which he likes to express himself: distinctly and with brilliance— he often gives the sentences a sharp literary edge before delivering them. And the actual delivery is performed with a rare verbal agility and cerebral rapidity.

He is frank and goes straight to what he is most skeptical of in WINTER LIGHT: how is one to interpret the end? He has discussed the final scene with Lillie, his wife— "her religious sensitivity is much greater than mine." (Both are converts to catholicism.) *She* took a brighter view of the end than he did.

"I think that the parson in the last scene is exactly where he was before."

But he makes an immediate reservation: he has read the script only once, so far. "When I get into it more, and Ingmar explains his intentions to me, I may feel differently." (Some time later, however, he returns to the same view, displaying a kind of weariness at the type of religious struggle that Ingmar represents. "He pulls at the religious problem but doesn't really get anywhere. At any rate very slowly, the movements towards something positive are so small." Such a slow advance towards Grace arouses a kind of opposition in Gunnar.)

Ingmar Bergman with his corroding protestant heritage, Gunnar Björnstrand who in middle age became a catholic convert— do they discuss religion at all? Evidently seldom. The point on which he feels the difference between himself and Ingmar most strongly is the perspective of eternity. He imagines that it plays a very small part in Ingmar's religious beliefs.

"For me as a catholic— and generally speaking for me as a believer— it goes without saying that what happens here on earth is part of a far greater context: the little that takes place here is important only in relation to what happens afterwards. It is, in fact, merely a preparation. A short preparation— for something else. But I've no feeling that Ingmar sees it like that. For him, everything is restricted to *here* and *now*."

When I interviewed Gunnar for TV last spring, he differentiated between various Bergman parts. He liked playing the squire, Jöns, with his doubts and love of his fellow men, in THE SEVENTH SEAL, just as much as he disliked playing the medical officer Vergérus in THE FACE— a man with no redeeming features: rationalistic, promiscuous, repulsive.

What does Gunnar think of the Rev. Thomas Ericsson? Is he fascinated by him?

My impression is: not really.

Not spontaneously fascinated, at any rate.

On the contrary: he is disappointed that the hero in the film is a man with such *small* proportions.

"A *small* man, an extremely *small* soul. Cold, lonely. A man who is utterly inadequate. Incapable of loving, of making the best of what is given him."

Bit by bit he draws a portrait of the Rev. Thomas Ericsson. The portrait has sharp outlines, an edge of disappointment to it.

"A frightfully *difficult* part. How is one to make the audience interested in him?"

In SF's program FILM NEWS, No. 4, 1961, I later find an interview with GB in which he speaks of the actor's need of "being a hero."

He pokes fun at this heroic need in himself and his colleagues. He speaks playfully and ironically of their desire to "attract the warm sympathy of mankind." All the same, he describes it as the actor's deepest need.

Is that why the parson's role feels extra difficult?

"There's nothing likeable about this parson. A role without a *particle* of glamour in it."

He makes a reservation— once more. He has been playing a comedy part in THE GARDEN OF EDEN for three months now; and the new part piles up so many problems in front of him:

"Maybe it's merely a reaction of fatigue, just at present."

WEDNESDAY 13 SEPTEMBER 1961
Final script version of "Feature Film No. 136"

The stenciling machine moves its jaws; the young people at the production office bind the sheets— today sees the making of the script copies to be used in shooting.

It's almost the same script read on August 9th. A little polishing here and there. But there are two fair-sized cuts.

1. The fisherman's wife tells of Jonas's fear of the Chinese. The

parson tries with a "We must rely on God." But the following attempt at consolation is cut:

> THOMAS: Love exists in the world. We know that, we have proof of it every day. Love is a reality, something palpable, a consolation. Lovelessness, on the other hand, is spiritual death. One can say that love is the great proof of God's existence.

This is an ironic repetition of the final words in THROUGH A GLASS DARKLY. With its removal, we have to wait until the organist Blom's sarcastic last scene before IB explicitly shatters "the final coda" in THE GLASS (Cf. July 20th, 1961).

2. Thomas confesses to Märta in the vestry window that he is tormented by "God's silence." How was it before? He said much more about it in the former version:

> THOMAS: I have always lived with god. He has existed as a security, immovable, ever-present. It has been like a blood vessel between me and him. I was an important detail in god's creation, he could not do without me.
> MÄRTA (smiles).
> THOMAS: And suddenly he's gone. During the communion service today I felt a strange portent. The words of the prayers seemed meaningless. Every gesture was empty and peculiar. The communion became a cult for cannibals. I was terribly frightened.
> MÄRTA: I see.
> THOMAS: Then Jonas Persson and his wife came. They demanded my faith. And it was no small matter either. It was a matter of life and death.

WINTER LIGHT has now been given a production number: feature film No. 136; in the production office they refer to is as "L-136."

FRIDAY 15 SEPTEMBER 1961
Sven Nykvist and the light

The entire technical crew have been up with IB at Rättvik: Sven Nykvist, P. A. Lundgren, Lars-Owe Carlberg, K. A.

They have ridden a trolley along Ingmar's childhood railroad, looking for a level crossing for the Rev. Thomas Ericsson.

They have driven around Lake Siljan inspecting about thirty churches, and Sven Nykvist has come home with a harvest of photographs which he pastes into his copy of the script. The photos are taken in Torsång church— the one finally chosen, the one that is to be copied in the SF studio by P. A. Lundgren.

51

They spent an ordinary, cloudy weekday afternoon in the church. Walked about, but mostly sat quietly in the pews. Sven had a Leica camera with him and caught the changes in light with it.

"Necessary?"

"Absolutely. In this way I am forced to be 100% realistic in my lighting."

In THROUGH A GLASS DARKLY the problem was to capture the hours of the Swedish summer night: "We wanted to keep a kind of leaden shade, without any big contrasts." Is he satisfied with the result?

"Yes, but it's disconcerting that one thought *then* that one could not get any farther. Now double-X has come, the new kind of film. Now it's a *real* challenge!"

The light problem in WINTER LIGHT is this: the action of the film takes place between midday and three in the afternoon of a typical cold, bleak, cloudy Swedish November Sunday with sleet in the air. What is expected of Sven: that he shall photograph with as few shadows as possible— a cloudy day is shadowless. For that reason they are thinking of constructing some very simple screens to use in the studio— wooden frames covered with greaseproof paper— and photograph throughout with indirect light.

In order partly that Sven will not be tempted to work with so-called illogical light— light that has no equivalent in reality (e.g., light from lamps in the studio roof)— P. A. is going to build a roof on the studio church. SF's studio hands are going to be church vault carpenters on top of everything else. They will copy Torsång church almost exactly. The only difference: the studio church will be a little longer than the real one— so that it will give a narrower impression.

I glance through Sven's working copy. *Perhaps mist*, he has noted about the first shots in the film. *Desolate and dreary. Heavy Sunday atmosphere.* Jotted down in accordance with Ingmar's instructions up at Siljansborg.

The first shot in the church is a close shot of Thomas. The camera follows Thomas right until "Our Lord Jesus Christ in the night when he was betrayed." Perhaps camera crane.

Find out whether there is zoom lens for blimped Arriflex. Ask Skaar whether there's zoom lens for De Brie.

Perhaps the whole of the communion service in a single focusing.

52

Sven Nykvist shot his first feature film, THE CHILDREN FROM FROST MOFJÄLLET, when he was only twenty.

Since then he has shot more than forty films. The first time he worked for Ingmar was in SAWDUST AND TINSEL. Kurt Hoffman, after having seen that photography, took him down to Germany; since then Sven moved regularly between Swedish and German studios and does at least one German film a year. The regular cooperation with Ingmar was not begun, however, until THE VIRGIN SPRING in 1959.

"Afterwards, when I think of all the tricks I've learned over the years .... it's enough to make me shudder. Impressive spotlighting and a welter of double shadows over the studio walls. A lot of uncalled-for direct light in a pretty girl's hair. And great, exaggerated foregrounds which you arrange merely to get an awfully dramatic perspective in the picture. A lot of overworked features, in fact."

All that is finished with now. Reality is the supreme teacher: everywhere it is ready to offer silent instructions in the technique of lighting, if only one takes the time and has the patience to listen.

"I have a much greater desire to study the real light now than I had before. Now that at last there are kinds of film available which can capture such subtle nuances."

"That simplicity is in some ways more unrewarding than the old 'pretty' lighting. People have no idea of the work behind it. But one mustn't think like that. One must never say: Oh, we won't bother with that, the audience won't notice it anyway. The only principle to go by is what we ourselves, Ingmar and I, think of what we have done. If it's not what we meant, then we go in and do it over again until we get it right."

Sven is forty, and bears the imprint of the environment in which he grew up: his father was a missionary. Right at the start of his career as a cameraman he went off down to Africa, seeking out his father's places and making a couple of shorts, UNDER THE SOUTHERN CROSS and ON THE TRACK OF THE FETISH MAN. He still has a love of Africa and a deep attachment to his father's African environment.

He was puritanically brought up: to be good and kind— the aggression inhibitions are so strong and the Christian upbringing so deep that, for example, a swearword can never possibly sound natural in Sven's mouth. Ingmar's and others' standing joke about Sven:

"When Sven really loses his temper good and proper, he comes out with a ————."

In a working environment like this, a ———— is far more noticeable than a ———— .

But when his rage does come, *then* .... say those who have borne the brunt of it.

Sven Nykvist has reddish-fair hair. When he smiles his eyes narrow to mere slits embedded in his face.

His eyebrows are so fair that they are barely visible against the light complexion.

SATURDAY 16 SEPTEMBER 1961
P. A. Lundgren, churchbuilder

A better churchbuilder it would be impossible to find: P. A. Lundgren has all the wiry strength of the countryman. He is fifty now. He has been a film art director for twenty years. He laughs when I ask him about his background:

"Actually I'm an old soldier."

By which P. A. means that he got his training in the traditional Swedish way of the ordinary people: he enlisted and rose to be a non-commissioned officer, before going to Stockholm and becoming a painter. Painter by trade.

He painted sets and scenery in the film studios of the 30s. But he was an unusual kind of painter, a colleague relates: in his spare time he would sit in a plaster room doing sculptures. He made reliefs, he painted pictures. His talent was noticed. An untrained talent that had run wild— a talent with all the inventive peasant strength in it. Sure enough, he got fed up with only painting scenery. He considered applying for a job as assistant to film art director Bibi Lindström. This step in his education he never had time to take; one day he was simply given an offer:

"Hasse Ekman is going to make a film based on Bertil Malmberg's HIS EXCELLENCY. Like to take it?"

He "took" it.

He has lost count of the number of films he has designed. But he knows that WINTER LIGHT is the thirteenth film he has done for Ingmar.

The art director must have the same semi-chameleonic gift as so

54

many other members of the film collective: a sense of all styles. P. A. can design fashionable interiors, of course; and does so when necessary. But he doesn't care for them. He simply detests having to produce a wealthy businessman's apartment.

That's one of the reasons why he and Ingmar get on so well together.

For Ingmar, P. A. means perseverence, reliability, stubbornness.

"There's a church painter in P. A., have you noticed?"

P. A. did the church paintings in THE SEVENTH SEAL— a game in the spirit of Albertus Pictor: "one of the nicest things I've been given to do in films."

For the same film P. A. also carved the huge wooden crucifix that is dragged along in the flagellants' procession. For six years this P. A. work has lain hidden away in SF's property storeroom; now it is brought out. Ingmar wants it in Thomas Ericsson's vestry.

P. A. is not phlegmatic by nature. He smiles when the subject is brought up.

" .... though one should be able to admit it about oneself by this time: that one is rather hot-tempered."

For a long time I made a mistake about the force of the wind when a storm is brewing in P. A. (just as I did with Sven). All I saw was the calm, even, secure surface. Now I would paint a lake and a Swedish forest glade if I were to portray P. A. First a thunderstorm bending the reeds at the lake's edge on a sultry summer day. Then the freshness afterwards, between the trunks of the pines.

UNDATED, SEPTEMBER 1961
Ingmar and DIARY OF A COUNTRY PRIEST

Yesterday evening Ingmar ran DIARY OF A COUNTRY PRIEST out at SF— Robert Bresson's film based on Bernanos's novel. Ulla I. was there. First, she said, Ingmar asked those present what they thought of it; then he said:

"It's the third time I've seen it."

Ingmar boggled at Bresson's film at first; *now* he is evidently beginning to accept it. But why did he see it again just now? Perhaps it was part of the preparations for WINTER LIGHT— there's always some detail to take up; or to reject and make different?

It's one of his working methods at any rate: see a lot of films, the whole time; soak up, reject— while going his own way, his

55

memory is loaded with newly captured, useful references.

SUNDAY 24 SEPTEMBER 1961
Special event at the Concert Hall: Stravinsky conducts his own works.

MONDAY 25 SEPTEMBER 1961
And today IB ought to know what Stravinsky really thinks of his production of THE RAKE'S PROGRESS: they are to meet for a while this afternoon, before Stravinsky leaves Stockholm this evening.

UNDATED, SEPTEMBER 1961
Make-up being tried out
How far has Börje Lundh come along with his make-up tests? He lends me one of his lists; I copied it down:

GUNNAR BJÖRNSTRAND: Hair cut short at sides. Dyed faintly. Parting. Thin skin-color. VC 2 PS. Powder and water. (?) Eyebrows plucked out. Brown pencil (to color eyebrows). Red-rimmed eyes and red at nostrils. Try out collodion near nose.
INGRID THULIN: Two tests taken with different hair-dos. If the curly one is approved, we'll make a half-wig. Hair toned with color spray. Complexion seemed a bit too dark, owing to her own sun tan.
"Medium blond."
Skin color PS CTV 3. No lashes. No lips. Eczema on hands done with Duo, sawdust, blood, gelatine, rice paper, perhaps collodion. (Ditto perhaps for face.) Red and white. Castor-oil make-up. Zinc ointment. Swollen eyes.

"What's castor-oil make-up?"

"Something you have to have in conjunction with Duo, because Duo is a latex, and you can't have ordinary make-up with a latex."

As a rule Börje writes down *all* ideas he gets for make-up. Nowadays he feels he has come so far in his cooperation with Ingmar that his thoughts are much the same as Ingmar's in regard to the characters' make-up.

"Or put it this way: I have my own train of thought and one à la Ingmar— when those two clash, we have to talk it over."

(The above list is a mixture of "already done and planned." The test with Ingrid Thulin, for instance, was not at all good. Three more tests were made on Ingrid— before her Märta Lundberg make-up was passed.)

56

WEDNESDAY 27 SEPTEMBER 1961
Actors' opposition to parts
"I've started a new film now"

Time to turn out with the TV team if we want to capture anything of the preparation mood: trying out costumes, make-up
tests, the half-finished sets. TV interview with Gunnar Björnstrand
tomorrow! Shall also ask K. A. Bergman for an interview.

During the two weeks that have passed since I last pumped
Ingmar about the position, I have had my own first taste of actors'
opposition to a part. (Bibi Andersson is doubtful about the lead in
my script; she thinks the girl in THE MISTRESS is "shabby.") Ingmar replies by telling me that Gunnar Björnstrand was really un-
easy about the part in WINTER LIGHT. Gunnar turned it over in his
mind for a whole day; at last he put his doubts before Ingmar, his
reason for wanting to give up the part.

I tell him of Bibi's reasons against THE MISTRESS.

"But it's *always* the way with good actors: they always have a
lot of objections to a part. Bad actors leap at anything."

Is he right? It would be reassuring, certainly. I soon have a
working hypothesis ready: opposition is part of an actor's working
process. It's *his* way of getting inside the skin of a character's
personality: during a suspicious search for cracks and holes and
hollows in the character. Until he has investigated them, he can't
assume the character.

"Though there are different kinds of opposition. Max von Sydow
always goes around terribly indolent about a part: the Great
Indolent Calm itself. He seems rather indifferent, rather sleepy—
that's how *he* gets into the part. While the others kick and fuss and
carry on .... I know myself," Ingmar says, "how I'd like to sneak
away from the job."

I don't believe him. I've never seen him anything else but appal-
lingly industrious.

"When did *you* ever want to sneak away?"

"Often. When I did THE RAKE'S PROGRESS for instance! Three
or four times I told them at the Opera that I didn't want to do it.
And every time Svanholm talked me into it .... Have I never told
you when the Stockholm Opera was on fire last winter while I was
rehearsing THE RAKE'S PROGRESS?"

"No."

(Someone persuades Svanholm. Svanholm persuades Ingmar. Ingmar persuades Gunnar .... is the whole profession full of persuasions?)

"Well, one day there was suddenly a goddam great alarm out here at SF and the SF newsreel got ready to turn out— it has been abandoned, you know, but it turns out on big occasions so as to have them in the archives. They drove up outside here and stood ready to turn out *in case* it was going to be a really big blaze .... And I was delighted. Because if the Opera burned down, I wouldn't have to do THE RAKE."

Suddenly he said, rather absent-mindedly:

"I've started a new film now."

His eyes twinkled at my blank surprise. Begin writing a new film right in the middle of preparing this one!

"It's to be called THE BIG PICTUREBOOK, and   goddam big at that .... "

"What about the sequel to WINTER LIGHT?"

"No, no, that doesn't come now; that's not the way I do it. This is something quite different....   You see, during those periods I was in the hospital, at Sophiahemmet— well, they have a fascinating park there. And one day I came out and along came a couple of big, hefty, strapping, flourishing nurses pushing a tiny, tiny old woman in a wheelchair. I could see Naima Wifstrand in the part .... The film was to begin there: with an old man-woman who doesn't have very long to live."*

After all the ideas he has had for a chamber play, he unrolls an enormous three-hour fresco.

"I've established my form so firmly now that I know it backwards: it's time now to break it up."

Then he tells me about it. The theme is the ages of Man. AGE comes first in the series. The little old man-woman in the wheelchair dies and lies in the coffin at the mortuary, belching ("corpses

---

*For a long time I regarded THE SILENCE as a preparatory exercise for THE BIG PICTUREBOOK. In May 1963 he says that "the old man in the wheelchair" is all that is left of THE BIG PICTUREBOOK. "The old man in the wheelchair" is in the *script* of THE SILENCE— the boy Johan sees an enormous old man being pushed along the hotel corridor. The scene was even shot, with Olof Widgren as the old man— but was cut out because it was "far too symbolic."

So what became of THE BIG PICTUREBOOK? Did it merge into THE SILENCE forever or will it crop up again, somewhere else, in an entirely new guise?

belch, you know" "they belch?" "yes, bubbles and air come out of them")— and from the dead person in the coffin, he'd dissolve into CHILDHOOD. A boy has a doll's house: when the boy opens the doll's house, this little old man-woman falls out in the shape of a doll. Then MANHOOD: the grown man who looks back on his childhood and *last*: YOUTH. The whole film would end with puberty's angry rebellion against the world. But it won't be a film with dramatic composition throughout, like his others.

"But only pictures, *pictures, pictures* .... long chunks of pictures. As in a dream. Not an ordinary passage of time, but dream time." P. S.

This evening he's going to run THROUGH A GLASS DARKLY for the special group who are usually there for the pre-viewing out at SF: co-workers and friends of Ingmar's. A small cluster collects out at the Film City's only good screening room (and which therefore is called "the Opera"). The first time *that* film encounters an audience.

THURSDAY 28 SEPTEMBER 1961
What kind of haircut is the Rev. Ericsson to have?
TV interview with Gunnar Björnstrand
GB's visit to the doctor

Gunnar Björnstrand is sitting in front of the mirror in one of SF's make-up rooms. Börje Lundh, the make-up man, stands brandishing the scissors— but how much of Gunnar's hair does he dare cut? In fact, what kind of haircut is the Rev. Ericsson to have?

Better go down to Ingmar. They take Mago with them. Ingmar picks up a paper-knife.

Gunnar takes it for granted that a "clerically charming" haircut must be avoided. He has therefore put a part in his thin hair.

"I'm all for the part."

Ingmar smiles behind his desk; the jargon is already in full swing:

"Do I have to see you with a part on the side right through this whole film, Gunnar?"

"A Kennedy tousle then?" Börje Lundh laughs. "If you'd rather see that?"

Then Ingmar looks at Börje Lundh and says:

"Thomas Ericsson should, of course, look like you, Börje, as regards his hair. Though then I suppose you'd look like Sven Milliander instead, Gunnar?"

Gunnar narrows his eyes and answers with his most amiable asperity:

"You mean, old make-ups that are left over?"

"What about a kind of peasant cut then?" Börje asks.

The whole office grows heavy with reflection. The Director Himself concentrates on giving us an outline of character. We listen.

"If you come to think of it, Thomas is a man who has a woman who never says anything to him. She doesn't say: 'You must wash your feet. You should have such and such a haircut.' On the contrary. She's the girl who's grateful for what she can get. Nor has Thomas a housekeeper who's always after him. And when he gets a haircut, he goes down to the barber's at Frostnäs .... "

We all imagine Thomas at the village barber's at Frostnäs and the laughter of a little male collective echoes around the room.

Suddenly Ingmar breaks off and says that he had a long talk with his father the day before.

"The old man," he says with affection in his voice. "The old man has read the script *three* times, can you imagine? And he has understood the end quite correctly," he adds (looking at Gunnar, as though the remark were addressed to him). "Father doesn't see Thomas as a static person with a strong sense of duty. He saw the end as something constructive: that Thomas shouldered the task at last. Father is not intellectual, he accepts things in an emotional way. Imagine, said Father, your parson even *writes* his sermon!— that impressed Father. And one scene in particular Father spoke about: when Thomas tries to comfort Mrs. Persson and asks if they shall pray together. And she merely shakes her head and says: No. Father felt that scene very much. Do you know what he said? — 'He was awfully ambitious, your Thomas, but he won't make a good parson.' "

Ingmar conveys to us the degree to which he was affected, and we get sidetracked from the discussion about the hair. (Ingmar's mother, too, has read the script— she on the other hand wanted Ingmar to make it a little more edifying at the end. "Mother is awfully intelligent and gifted. It's just that her artistic taste and mine are so different. Hers is at the Selma Lagerlöf stage.")

"Well, to get back to the haircut. This parson hasn't of course had his hair cut for a long time. And he still wears it the same way as he did in school."

"In college," Gunnar corrects him automatically.

60

Ingmar looks resignedly out the window. A sigh at the necessary retreat.

"I didn't want to think about this, *but* .... it leads inevitably up to the part on the side."

Presumably Thomas Ericsson is an open-air type. Presumably he has his best moments together with this woman when they are out walking. The four men who are to furnish Thomas Ericsson with body and soul toy for a moment with the thought. They egg each other on with lies and pretence; then they agree unanimously that Thomas Ericsson is a schoolboy.

He has not developed since he went to school.

This must be noticcable from his haircut as well.

"His hair must not look plastered down," Ingmar says, passing his hand across Gunnar's forehead. Gunnar's hair is dark at present: grey on top, yellowish lower down (the yellow is the stain left by the wig he has had in the color film THE GARDEN OF EDEN). At the moment it looks pretty lifeless. Ingmar:

"It mustn't look like this, of course. And it mustn't seem fly-away either. As it is now, it seems unorganic."

"Shall we decide on Old Schoolboy haircut then?" Gunnar says.

"Internally too!" Ingmar adds. "He never grows up."

The long training that Gunnar and Ingmar have had together! They know each other inside out, the weaknesses as well as the strengths: it is like a fencing match, with feint, thrust and parry. New jargon-attack: "It's essential that this baboon Gunnar Björnstrand gives the impression of having a *refined* face," Ingmar declares. Gunnar ripostes instantly:

"Then I should have played this part when I was twenty-three."

Ingmar's loud, contented laugh.

"Let's try and find someone whom Thomas might remind us of?"

Ingmar racks his brains.

"What about Kaj Munk. *Without* the touch of genius. Or The Svedberg. There we have it exactly! A combination of Kaj Munk and The Svedberg."

Up in the make-up room Börje Lundh decides to cut Gunnar Björnstrand's hair so that the old haircut is left under the newly grown hair. In that way one will get the impression that it's been a long time since the Rev. Thomas Ericsson went to the barber-shop down in Frostnäs village.

61

The discussion in Ingmar's office took half an hour. Out of it all— the play on words, the jargon— emerged an analysis of the part, and it all started because Ingmar, Mago and Börje Lundh together examined Gunnar Björnstrand's face, wondering how long the parson's hair might be.

In the meantime, the TV team has been getting ready for an interview with Gunnar and me. I count on our talking about the matter that cropped up in our lunch conversation three weeks ago (September 11th); but I have not taken into account the mechanism in actors which makes them reluctant to speak unfavorably of a part. Gunnar brings out all the good sides he can find in the Rev. Thomas Ericsson: "I think he's tough in the sense that he does his job with all the doubts he has. He has a strong will. He has an active will to do something constructive. And that, I think, is something to be admired. He keeps going, in spite of everything." During the interview I have a feeling that Gunnar will not of his own accord describe Thomas as a "small," "cold and lonely" man, "incapable of loving." So I incite him to do it, and the interview ends up as a description of the part's difficulties from the public's point of view. "It's hard to know what it is the audience will like about him. There's nothing appealing or attractive about him from the outside. There is nothing dramatic about the external course of action, but everything takes place on an inner plane."

The TV interview in itself involved a certain tension. Not until later do I find that Gunnar has other reasons as well for being anxious and keyed-up. Yesterday he had an important medical examination. Some doctors wrap up the truth in their reports; apparently that was not the case yesterday. Blood pressure too high; and a series of injunctions: so and so many cigarettes a day! Ease up on the work tempo (five days before shooting starts). Careful weight check, etc. If he obeys a number of doctor's orders it's possible he will survive.

"If I look after myself *properly*, I'll be spared a coronary. I'll be let off with a stroke in five years. So I was told. And you don't necessarily die of a stroke— you just lie there, incapable of any life worth speaking of."

Ingmar smiles, at the lunch table:

"I suppose I could trot out a lot of sympathy. But I know that is just what you don't want."

Gunnar's smile in reply:

"No, of course Gunnar does not want sympathy."

I look at them, remembering Mārta Lundberg's words to Thomas ("Do you want sympathy?") and bring out my interview technique intended to sting people into a reply:

"You look so goddam smug when you speak of Gunnar's illness."

Ingmar laughs in reply.

"Well, of course it's just great that Gunnar is so off-color and unwell when he's to play *this sort* of part. Imagine if I'd gotten a sun-tanned, hale-and-hearty guy to play someone worn out and ailing!"

He nudges Gunnar:

"Who knows if that isn't how things work?!"

I'm given what amounts to a sentence of death by a doctor. I absorb the shock and keep it to myself, because I know it's good for me just now— I'm to play a sick and wretched parson.

The thought may be self-evident for Ingmar. Is it for Gunnar himself? I can't figure this out: they play on each other's habits and behavior in such an initiated way that an outsider understands only half.

No more is said about illness. Period. After a few moments there is a roar of laughter in the lunchroom, wave after wave. Ingmar is telling a grossly obscene story about John Ekman and Nisse Lundell. Gunnar caps it with another story. He tells it with terrible verve and spirit— his experience of shock incapsulated.

These are all matter-of-fact happenings behind the scenes, inside "the artist's workshop"— but to open it up to the public view? I get an inkling of how foreign that thought is to an actor when Gunnar and I take the bus into town and I tell him that I'm going to interview K. A. tomorrow for the TV series. I have picked K. A. not only because he is such a representative figure in the working collective around Ingmar. I have also picked him because of the unique chance of being able, right "inside the artist's workshop," to interview the model for one of the parts— and for the most tenderly written part in the whole film.

"Sure. But people don't understand that sort of thing."

Then I remember:

One morning during the shooting of THE FACE Gunnar had a frightfully bad migraine. Instead of postponing the take, Ingmar and Gunnar agreed to take the scene just then, while the migraine was at its worst. The extra tension in the face, the pain in the eyes— it would all be very effective in a close-up.

Gunnar told me the story last spring, while we were preparing the TV interview. But when I wanted to include it in the actual interview I couldn't get him to agree by hook or by crook. Don't give away trade secrets.

" .... people don't understand that sort of thing. They haven't a clue as to how artists work. They'd only think it seemed cruel."

He's right, of course.

But if one could only break down the wall so that people did understand ....

Oh, this goddam inability of people to accept a complex picture of a man!

FRIDAY 29 SEPTEMBER 1961

K. A.'s treble contribution to WINTER LIGHT

The studio is taking shape; I do the TV interview with K. A. Bergman inside it; there is the best working atmosphere.

I try to bring out the passionate work that K. A. always puts into procuring all the props for whatever film he is busy on— and the fact that he always seems to feel physically better, the more he has to do. He describes his disease to the TV viewers: cartilage formation between the vertebrae; how knees, ankles, shoulders are attacked— "I've got a stiff neck. But the hands I can manage." Bechterew's disease is comparatively rare, most common in men between the ages of 18 and 25; K. A. came down with it in 1952, when he was out on a film production with Rune Lindström. He started working for Ingmar in WILD STRAWBERRIES. Ingmar's feeling for K. A. is certainly reciprocated: no doubt whatsoever that IB's exacting demands for detail spur K. A. on; he even goes so far as to say that the demanding work for Ingmar is the reason for the improvement in his condition the last few years.*

Toward the end of the interview I asked K. A. whether he had gotten together at all with Allan Edwall, who is to play the part of Algot Frövik. Oh yes, they were to meet that same evening. Edwall was going to study K. A.'s walk; K. A. smiled ironically in

—

*After the first TV program was run through, IB was violently self-critical: he thought he acted badly. "In fact there's only one good actor in this program— but he's *brilliant*: K. A.! When *he* says that it's wrong to go to bed when one is sick .... thousands of old men and women all over Sweden will leap out of their beds when they hear it and realize how pampered they are!"

64

front of the TV camera: "I dance along like a young ballet god." But he was looking forward very much to working with "such a swell guy" as Edwall.

Allan Edwall is heavily engaged at the Royal Dramatic Theater, and for a long time it looked as if it would not be possible to get him free for Frövik's part. But it's worth any changes backwards and forwards in the production schedule of WINTER LIGHT to get just him— no one could play the part better. The same arrangements will have to be made for Gunnel Lindblom: get a stand-in who can be used for all the long shots. As regards Allan Edwall, K. A. himself offers to be his stand-in.

K. A. therefore takes part in the creative process in more ways than one: as a model for the character, as instructor of and stand-in for Allan Edwall.

To say nothing of the painstaking work by which he procures all the props for the churches, vestries and the classroom!

SATURDAY 30 SEPTEMBER 1961
The author's disappointment
Ingrid and the part

Meeting with Ingmar and Ulla I. about quite different things. But before we can start, Ingmar must give vent to his disappointment over the screening on Wednesday evening: not a single goddam bastard seems to grasp how vulnerable it is to run one's film for the first time. Everybody just shut themselves up in their stiffness when the lights went on after THROUGH A GLASS DARKLY. No one except Ulla made any attempt to break the silence barrier.

".... one is thin-skinned and anxious and *wants to hear*. And nobody says anything. Oh, this ghastly lack of generosity. Of ordinary simple decency to the one who lays himself bare. And everyone who was there works in this game, they ought to know how it *feels* on such an evening!"

He tells how he used to preach theatrical culture to his pupils at the Malmö City Theater: you must learn to abuse what you don't understand! You must learn to show enthusiasm when you like something! *Both* .... "

To me with a piercing glance:

"And you, you bastard, of course you didn't dare say anything!"

I, no?

Had I in *that* circle repeated what I told him privately last sum-

65

mer: that none of his films has affected me so much— how ingratiating it would have seemed. That's why *I* kept quiet.

And the others? They kept quiet because ....

Doesn't he see that on an evening like this he too is a victim of his position as leader? With these evening run-throughs the parts have been cast once and for all: *he* must start the discussion, *he* must utter the first opinion— as it's his film being shown, no one knows how to break the pattern ....   That explains everything, doesn't it?

"*Oh Christ*. Let's talk about something else ...."

He tries to laugh it off. But he can't "talk about something else" until he has cleared his system of the whole lot:

"Oh, this goddam *meanness* in the Swedish artistic world ...."

Then he tells Ulla in passing what kind of hair Ingrid Thulin is to have in WINTER LIGHT.

"You see, it's the same fuss with Ingrid and her hair this time too, just as in CLOSE TO LIFE. Well, *that* time I had to show who was boss. This time .... well, suddenly the other day when we'd been arguing for a long time, I gave up and thought: it's all the same how long her hair is."

"How is she tackling the part otherwise?"

He laughs gaily.

"Hard at it making herself ugly, of course. We'll have to adjust the first make-up tests a bit so that she doesn't make herself *too* ugly."

MONDAY 2 OCTOBER 1961
The first read-through

"I thought we wouldn't read right through the script," Ingmar B. says. "Just one or two key scenes."

Gunnar Björnstrand asks his director in a gay but biting tone:

"Is there any special page you like?"

Ingrid Thulin murmurs harshly:

"All pages."

The read-through has started, with good-humored professional bandying.

They bandy themselves, colleagues and theatrical memories. They recall read-throughs that have lasted for several days, in fact someone took part in a read-through that went on for six weeks ("Was it because the director wanted to see if the actors would come out with something *themselves* first?" Ingrid Thulin asks, gravely.) Anecdotes, chat, laughter— all bounce to and fro across the green baize cloth.

The table is rickety, put there just for today. We are gathered in the foyer outside the Small Studio. The wall decorations are rather silly and vulgar, one sits there caught up in a quasi-modernistic maze of lines. There is no special room for this purpose— these are film studios and read-through is a theatrical term that seems all astray in this alien air. Afterwards I get a lift into town with Olof Thunberg, who is to play the church organist in the film. He had never before come across a film director who bothered to have a read-through; this all felt unusually well-prepared and reassuring, he says, "almost like in the theater."

In the theater it goes without saying that work starts with everyone getting together and reading through the play. The director gives the actors his interpretation of the text: "*This* is what I feel about the play, *this* is how we're going to do it ...." Sometimes he resembles a foreman who shows the building plans to his co-workers. Sometimes he resembles the schoolteacher who tells the class to open their textbooks to page fifteen.

Now and then I wonder how often the feeling of school is present in actors. They're always being given homework, small lessons or big lessons, but always a new lesson for each new part. (Not always can they hit on the same exit line as Max von Sydow one day during the shooting of WINTER LIGHT. Seizing the fisherman Jonas's typed but silent part, he gave a winning smile and said: "Now I'll go home and learn my pauses.") And they are always having to ask the teacher to "explain." Of course they themselves can explain what needs to be explained— but maybe their interpretation doesn't tally with that of the others? That's why they subordinate themselves to the pattern of teacher-and-pupil, just like those grownups who visit their old school and squeeze themselves down into seats at desks which are far too small and cramped: it's the best way to become part of the unity that is to be created. Actor Y. thinks that the fourth line on page 145 is uncalled-for; but there it is and obviously it has to be said. At home in his armchair he has puzzled out a reason for it; now he tries it out to see whether it agrees with the director's interpretation. The director is impatient: two explanations jostle each other. Next time Y., rather tired, contents himself with merely "asking teacher"; it's quicker. The school desk is too small and chafes a grown-up's joints— but in six weeks' time the whole thing complete must be down there on the stage, with no loose ends sticking out; so teacher had better have his way.

Three hours reading aloud today while the October light deepens outside the windows. The reading lamps are switched on. Pencils bounce in company against the green baize of the table. No one acts the part yet: this is only the reading, pure and simple, with no emphasis or modulation. It sounds monotonous— it doesn't matter, it *should* sound monotonous. Only occasionally does it take fire: a whole dialogue will pour out with a life which gives a pretty good idea of what that passage will sound like in the future. Experienced directors know that this sort of thing *can* be decep-tive. Sometimes it sounds so full of life and character just because one of the actors at the table is a typical "read-through actor": the kind that gives his best right at the start and will never get any deeper into the part during rehearsals. At other times everything sounds cut and dried because the play is a typical "read-through play." To this category belong, in Bergman's eyes, several of Ten-nessee Williams's full-length plays (not the one-acters); everything works out quickly and easily because there is no depth of dimen-sion; the actors soon start giving everything and keeping nothing back; the last rehearsal weeks get a trifle boring— if one excepts scenes like that in which father and son have it out in CAT ON A HOT TIN ROOF. "You can rehearse that indefinitely."

Yet it's understandable that film people don't read through the script as often as theater people. A stage play consists almost en-tirely of lines to be spoken (with a few meager stage directions in parenthesis). In a film script the "stage directions" have expanded into a special column, a picture column. Who is to read that? Katinka Faragó, our scriptgirl, reads this one for us. Her quiet, non-professional voice takes the place of the actors' professional mumbling every time something happens.

That voice could be used as a gauge: the more cinematic the script that is being read, the more that voice should be heard— and the actors' voices would merely fall like drops through the room. But descriptions of pictures are tiring to read, boring to listen to. To write down *pictures* in *words*— that is indeed a contradiction, a folly, a necessary evil that the writer of a screenplay is forced to endure in order to communicate *something* to those who are to bring the pictures to life. If he were to try to write down everything that the finished shot was to contain: details, nuances, light, and shade, moods, then the script would become so bulky that it would be unreadable (hence Bergman's dream of a kind of abbreviation system for writing scripts, "a sort of musical notation"). No, the script is indeed what IB calls it: "a semi-finished article." The other half is to be finished in the studio— but .... "how?" Even here in the read-through room the actors put their first questions. The director is landed with new descriptions of pictures, with a new search for words; he is miserably aware how meager and bony the stream of pictures is when it flows out of his mouth instead of out of his film camera, how expressionless and stunted. Sure enough: Ingmar never asks Katinka to read out what is pure picture description in this script— the communion service, for instance. He concentrates on that which is most easily accessible at read-through: the acting scenes.

"Supposing I outline the main idea of this film?" he begins. "You see, the first conception of this was a church play or morality play, but then I realized that *that* was theater."

I glance around the room. This is the first and only time during this production that the actors are working together in their everyday clothes and not those of the characters. Ingrid Thulin is wearing her grey-green khaki slacks and her green sweater (the one with a richly autumn-colored pattern); next time her lithe, actress-slim figure will have vanished into Märta Lundberg's lean schoolmistress body, and her long fair hair will be hidden under a half-wig. Max von Sydow will have disappeared into the fisherman Jonas Persson's pale-grey raincoat, Olof Thunberg into the alcoholic organist Blom's crumpled and stained suit, with sloppy galoshes and the wide-brimmed, black, flat hat so often worn by a man of the people who has managed to get himself some education. Gunnel Lindblom is wearing a lavender blouse under a brown corduroy overcoat. She is round and bulging with child, eight months gone, beautifully easy-going in her movements on the chair. Next time she will be the fisherman's wife, Mrs. Persson, with a flat straw hat— the kind everlastingly worn by Swedish workmen's wives— tipped over her forehead.

Gunnar Björnstrand lends color to the afternoon with a touch of pure bourgeois elegance. He is dapperness itself, in white shirt, blue tie and well-cut dark-grey suit— before he disappears into

69

Thomas Ericsson's cassock in order to struggle with Ingmar's settling up with *"the auto-suggested god image."* (The same evening I sit at home deciphering my own notes; this is what IB said:) *"the father-fixated god image* .... that which both *speaks and answers itself*; that which he, Thomas Ericsson, *has himself invented* ...."

"In some curious way this god image includes the hatred of Christ and a *father-and-son relationship between Thomas Ericsson and his self-made god*, so that there is no room for Christ. Quite simply, he has misread the gospels, something which Algot Frövik brings home to him at the end in a terrible way."

Algot Frövik? Yes, he's sitting over there: he is still dressed as Allan Edwall. Edwall is the least clothes conscious of the actors here today: a dark-green shirt under a threadbare jacket.

"Does Thomas undergo some kind of conversion via Algot Frövik?" Allan asks.

"Yes. No. Not *so* much .... I'll come to that in a minute. First we must go a little deeper into Märta Lundberg, because Thomas Ericsson is demolished right at the start of the film. He's an industrious and orderly person .... (and Ingmar searches his memory for his father's remark:) .... he even *writes* his sermon. With Märta Lundberg the position is this: in *her* is enacted the passion, in both senses of the word. Märta is a non-believer. The circumstances of her life are good and happy at first. She is shy. They take to each other, she and Thomas— this is how I've conceived the whole thing— because they have such a goddam *humdrum* time of it."

"How humdrum?" someone laughs.

"I'll show you when we go up to Dalarna," Ingmar replies in a flash. "I'll show you a church: the goddam isolation they live in there; it's beyond belief. It's a loveless affair, therefore. An attempt to get away from the isolation. And this goddam eczema is not invented— I've known it myself in someone close to me."

Ingrid Thulin reacts when Ingmar says *loveless affair*, the statement destroys something for her. What does he mean by that? Ingmar maintains that the affair from the start has been, well, loveless.

"In that case I don't understand the intercession," Ingrid says. "The intercession can't be loveless, surely? She must love him to be able to pray? And when she prays for the eczema to go from her hands ...."

"It's out of sheer spite that she prays *then*," Ingmar says quickly. "We must keep the prayers apart: the first prayer, the eczema prayer, and the second prayer, last in the film. The intercession."

"Intercession," Ingrid murmurs in her husky everyday voice, which is apt to sound rather rasping. "Intercession I thought was something catholic."

The catholic Gunnar Björnstrand and the protestant Ingmar are equally swift in their informative:

"Oh no!"

Ingrid is all opposition, hesitation and dejection; she still can't fit Ingmar's "loveless affair" into her conception of the part.* Unwillingly she asks how he is going to do the intercession in pictures.

"You just kneel down and read it. Then of course it can be done with one of those spirit voices behind. Your face, without the lips moving. But I can't stand that sort of thing. Just a lot of goddam bluff."

Her opposition eggs Ingmar on; he now has to convince her, win her over; he shakes the whole of his intensity when he analyzes the religious paradox in the eczema prayer: it's reeled off out of spite, in the conviction that God doesn't exist; but the answer is that the prayer is heard. "I prayed for a mission for my strength," Märta writes in the letter to Thomas, "and I got it. The mission is you."

"Do you see? Her prayer has been answered. She has prayed for a mission and been given it, but her problem is that she has not been given *the means* to realize her love, *has she?* She has not acquired knowledge of how she is to reach the man. She stands in her own light .... "

All these expressions like *has she? doesn't it?* are some of Ingmar's commonest working words, both in conversation and in direction. He doesn't expect an answer when he uses them. They are words of suggestion, electrification. An eager appeal to the receiver to meet him half way, to understand. If the receiver listens and nods, then the contact is made, the wires are alive.

Yesterday I borrowed a tape recorder which is so small that it can be carried in the pocket. It's a control: when I get home I can

—

*Not until a year later have I any idea of *how* she has reacted to the script: then she tells me that she burst into tears when she read the outpouring of hate in the classroom. See Friday, July 13th, 1962.

71

compare my notes with the recording and see what I've missed. I've not been able to warn anyone in the room; that would cancel out the effect of the experiment; I'll have to get their permission afterwards. But Ingrid's hearing is very sharp; when I put my hand into my jacket pocket, she reacts instinctively to the click as the apparatus starts: the deer at the edge of the forest which raises its head instantly, but without being able to identify the sound. The miracles of technology have their defects, however. The microphone is made in the form of a wrist watch, craftily enough— but that means that it picks up a lot of secondary sounds when I move hand and pen; sitting at home I listen to the voices through the rustle of my own shirtsleeve.

INGRID'S VOICE: Mārta has one thing to her credit, she sees through her own lies as well as his ....
INGMAR'S VOICE: Yes, she sure does!
INGRID: She won't let herself be taken in by anything ....
INGMAR: Then, you see, the line throughout is this, that after this hate scene [in the classroom], her resistance is broken down; she's not standing in her own light anymore. In this last scene she has the chance of making a real intercession, in which she doesn't even mention God's name .... She is serious and sincere here; no longer thinking of herself. She even forgets the address.
INGRID, not understanding: The address? [Pause.] Oh yes, of course. [Laughs at the misunderstanding.] I was thinking of the letter ....

The scraping voices on the narrow brown tape give a special atmosphere. The voices bump against each other, work on each other. It is a game. The director is the Persuader. The actress is the Resistance that must be broken down— but not until she has grasped just what he is driving at.

There's a sound like the rattle of metal in my shirtsleeve as we all turn the page in the script.

INGRID'S VOICE reads aloud: .... *leads him away from his lie-god* ....
INGMAR'S VOICE: *If I could lead him away out of emptiness, away from his lie-god,* that's what I consider her second prayer. This is the real intercession. When she prays that, she has put herself aside, do you see? She herself is no longer standing in the way. There's no longer any feeling of what is fitting, because all that .... [inaudible] that's all gone now, do you see? and so, as I see it, the intercession has a naturally effective power. He who was going to cancel the service pulls himself together and is given the strength to hold it after all.
INGRID'S VOICE, slowly: I don't seem to understand it all the same; not if her love isn't really sincere. I don't understand her development if her love isn't real .... all that with the letter. Though she can't express it. But that's one

72

thing, not being able to express it.

INGMAR: Yes, when she has written the letter, it's real love ....

INGRID: But this letter's written ....

INGMAR interrupting eagerly: Yes, it's written two days before, because she has been sitting there all alone and ....

INGRID: Yes, she's in the process of development, so you must see that she has loved him.

INGMAR, eagerly: Not all the time!

INGRID sticking to her point: You must see that she really loves him ....
[Pause. With another inflection:] Hmm, that's what you said at the start: that they had such a humdrum time of it ....

INGMAR: The affair has been going on for three years; it has been developing the whole time. And she is also losing him during that time, you see. It's only the time intervals one has to keep apart there, you see?

INGRID: Yes, I see.

GUNNAR BJÖRNSTRAND'S VOICE, very quick: In fact, it has become a dreary erotic affair which— without knowing it— has turned into a love story which has come as a surprise to them.

INGMAR'S VOICE: How do you understand? One sees two lines, as it were: there's Thomas Ericsson's line and there goes Märta Lundberg's line. The redeeming factor in the crisis is Jonas Persson; the revealing factor is Blom, when, with his afternoon hangover, he gives the background to the marriage, Thomas's marriage, that is. You see, the whole time Thomas has said of his wife: "I love her, don't speak of her"; you see: Märta is then faced with a gigantic mission. At the same instant she realizes that this wife has been a sham: to start then .... For say what you like about Märta Lundberg, she has an indomitable urge for truth. That's her immense strength all through. And Algot Frövik, you see, for me he's, I mean if you forgive the expression ....

Here IB casts a rather childishly embarrassed glance at Allan Edwall (so I've jotted down on my pad).

INGMAR'S VOICE: .... he's an angel. [Apologetic voice:] One feels so shy using the word, you see. Call it what you like— to me he's an angel.

ALLAN EDWALL: So pure in heart?

INGMAR: Yes, sure. He has understood. And it's a terrible moment when Thomas realizes that this man, Algot Frövik, in his naivety has understood Christ far more deeply. And understood something else besides: and that is that Christ has suffered in a very much more terrible way than Thomas Ericsson has ever suffered. He perceives that Christ has really taken mankind's frailties upon himself; he has suffered the suffering of all mankind. Except possibly that of marriage ....

Those words trigger off a violent change in mood: tense seriousness swings over to loud laughter. Ingmar starts the laugh; Gunnar takes it up; then the whole table is flung into full swing. (There I switch off the tape recorder.)

Only *now* does the actual reading aloud begin.

73

It begins with the end.

Allan Edwall has to go off to a rehearsal at the Royal Dramatic Theater; first he must plod through Frostnäs church, complaining that the new candles on the altar were hard to light— "presumably a flaw in the manufacture!" Allan Edwall finds humor in that line; he guesses that Algot Frövik is also poking fun at himself and his diseases when he speaks of a "flaw in the manufacture," in a rather veiled way.

"Do you think the audience will get it, Ingmar?"

"Well, if you can make something amusing out of it, all the better! This film needs all the laughter it can get."

They hope that the audience will at least laugh a little when Algot Frövik calls the gospels "real sleeping pills" ("the only funny line in the film," according to the author-director).*

"Where are they going to shoot the last scenes?"

"In Skattungby church."

Ingmar tells the story of the clever building contractor who has concealed an air-conditioning plant of teak behind the altar of this church. Olof Thunberg reads *his* last scene with Ingrid Thulin in which he breathes drunken fumes over Märta in the pew ("you see," the director instructs, "Blom the organist is one of those people who must always come *right up against* you"). Blom quotes the Rev. Ericsson's preaching. Then Ingmar and Gunnar exchange a smile of recognition: *God is love and love is god. Love is the proof of god's existence. Love exists as something real in the world of men*— those words which Gunnar Björnstrand had charge of in the last scene of THROUGH A GLASS DARKLY; they recur now in another actor's mouth, but with a mocking accent, so that we shall feel how inadequate they are.

Blom disappears; Märta Lundberg kneels down.

" .... here Märta speaks so softly that the words are lost .... It's hard to describe this in a script, but what we'll do is when Ingrid says the last words of her intercession, the camera is on Gunnar in the vestry. We see *his* face and hear *her* voice."

This piece of information fascinates me. Only in a film can you

---

*IB repeats it many times later; and I have further confirmation of the professional's ability to foresee the audience's reaction in a private letter from a friend who lives in a small Swedish country town: "Saw WINTER LIGHT on Friday, 23 people. Nice and quiet. Only one giggle: when Edwall says that the New Testament is a real sleeping pill."

74

do that: show the meaning of intercession, in fact show the intercession itself— with the aid of a technical dodge: "we'll put Ingrid's voice onto Gunnar's picture .... "

Before Allan Edwall goes off to his rehearsal he manages to make Ingmar happy with a reflective question:

"On the last page but one. There it says: *Thomas looks at Algot. Algot asks: 'Shall we hold the service?' Thomas nods: 'Yes'.* Then you write: *Algot looks at Thomas in surprise.* I was just wondering: Why 'in surprise?' "

Ingmar sits bolt upright in the chair, with a strangely grateful tone in his voice:

"Oh, how logical you are, Allan!"

Quick, happy explanation:

"You see, in an earlier version, Thomas Ericsson was made to say that 'we might as well hold the service.' So *then* it was no wonder that Algot Frövik 'looked at the parson in surprise,' was it? Algot is pious, he can never possibly think that 'one might as well' hold the service. But in this context it doesn't fit, you're quite right there. Not when I cut out Thomas's line."

This is the director's happiness over an actor who doesn't just skim through the script but thinks for himself (and who reads the whole script, not just his own scenes). His happiness is increased by the fact that the actor in question is one he admires very much— just as a teacher is especially pleased when a favorite pupil distinguishes himself.

Now they read the last words of the script. Ten minutes' break for a smoke; then they start at the beginning of the script.

Max von Sydow wants to know "how much of a churchgoer" this fisherman is. Ingmar answers promptly: " .... he goes to church at Christmas, at Easter, at Whitsun, at Midsummer. And on the anniversary of his parents' death." What's the point of Max's knowing this? Well, when three Amens are sung in church, "perhaps Jonas joins in the last two," Max guesses.

The actors work over the details!

Gunnel Lindblom:

"You haven't read Sandemose's novel THE WALLS OF JERICHO?"

"No, but I have it at home."

"There's a story in it of a parson whose health is ruined by all the coffee parties he has to go to, it's fantastic. It gives the whole atmosphere."

Märta Lundberg enters the vestry ("the fact that she doesn't believe in God is her standing provocation against Thomas," IB
points out). The organist Blom knocks at the vestry door, looking
for some music he has fogotten. ("Märta and Thomas are now so
irritated with each other that they can't stand one another. Blom
is the incentive. The whole thing has happened very quickly, yet
they must be nice to each other before they part.") Ingmar explains what a mercy seat is. Ingrid reads Märta's big letter. From
my notebook: " .... just now Ingrid is reading the letter right
through. Very quiet in the room. No interruptions. Ingmar follows very attentively, word for word, line for line, while she reads.
The silence is broken by a rustling when everyone turns the page
together— like in a school class, with an old-fashioned exacting
teacher." After that the teacher laughs:

"Ingrid asked me: How are you going to do the letter? I said:
The camera will be on you the whole time. Then Ingrid didn't say
a word, she was thinking of all the lines she would have to learn.
And then she said: 'You're not pulling my leg, are you?' "

Ingrid retorts that she learned the letter by heart a month ago,
before going to the USA and making a TV film there. "Since then
you've made a few changes, so I'll learn it again." A few moments
later we've reached the fisherman's second visit to Thomas Ericsson.

"This is the dream sequence, isn't it?" Gunnar Björnstrand asks.

"I'll tell you quite honestly," Ingmar replies. "When I wrote this
I thought— only in a dream can one speak as openly as this."

Then I switch on the tape recorder in my pocket; this is an important detail:

INGMAR'S VOICE: I don't know whether it has happened to you, but it has
happened to me very often that if I have a terribly difficult task ahead of me
— or something that is a great nervous strain— I can wake up in awful distress
and then suddenly I fall asleep again. And then I'm in the middle of this task,
taking it in an emotional way, in an awful nakedness and awful pain. And I
use up all my strength. Then I wake up, utterly exhausted and my whole
body tensed ....

(I note down that he says this "eagerly and laughing.")

INGMAR'S VOICE: It's something like that I had in mind. Let's both imagine .... well, like this: we are not to have the slightest suspicion of a dream
mood. We must see it exactly as a reality. The only thing is that Märta has
never seen Jonas Persson. Because that moment of sleep— it can just as well
have come after Jonas Persson's visit as before, can't it? So I mean: it doesn't

matter which it is.

GUNNAR'S VOICE: He has thought over this man's problems, and now he's preparing what he is to say?

INGMAR'S VOICE: This is a moment in terrible anguish. So that the whole drama leads up to this— the whole line, that is, leads inexorably from the very beginning of the film, over the letter, and here comes the climax, the drama's first climax. The line goes right to here.

Now at last I begin to understand why Ingmar won't make up his mind whether it is a drama or not. For me it is a mystification; for him a necessity.

INGMAR'S VOICE: .... dream or no dream, for me when I wrote it, it was an enormous help, otherwise I would have had to experiment with day-consciousness as well in the character.

VILGOT'S VOICE: Couldn't the parson say all this just the same?

INGMAR: No, as I see it, he's a man with no contacts who can't speak so plainly. That's why this dream sequence comes in. *And I want to try out displacements in time, mazes among displacements in time.* At any rate, it was an enormous help to me. The dream was an incubator. Now that I've lifted the baby out of the incubator, I can make it into a real episode, perhaps, and not a dream sequence."

GUNNAR BJÖRNSTRAND: Even when I read it the first time, it was so dreamlike, the fact that the parson said "Jonas" to the fisherman. After that there's so much "Mr. Frövik this" and "Mr. Frövik that."

End of the tape recording.

The fisherman disappears. The parson is alone. He experiences God's silence. God is dead.

"If you think that the line mounts and mounts right up to here, then this is an almost ecstatic moment. The sun comes into the hideous silence after God."*

"Up to now it has been a gentle light," he goes on. "It has had that leaden tone. Now all of a sudden the light crashes into this breathless silence. It's the only place where the film rises to a *forte fortissimo*, if you see what I mean— though soundless, of

—

* Noted down on Wednesday (1.10.62), when Sven Nykvist set the lighting for this scene: Ingmar experiences sunshine as horror, not as good, encircling warmth.

"I bet you anything that somewhere in my family there's a little Sicilian who has been shrivelled up by the Mediterranean sun. He sits here, right inside me: to me sunshine is terrifying. Always has been. Rain gives me a feeling of comfort and security, and so does winter sun and autumn sun. Spring sun at a pinch. But summer sun .... !"

(In the next film, THE SILENCE, in which God has vanished altogether, steady, stifling sunshine reigns.)

77

course."

Märta finds him there, by the altar rail, in the middle of a coughing attack. Ingrid Thulin begins to laugh at the macabre love scene:

"When *at last* she is going to show him *some* warmth, he gets a coughing attack!"

Gunnar Björnstrand sighs:

"Yes, it's madly dreary. No glamour."

They read Jonas's suicide. Max von Sydow is already half out of the door— he, too, has to rehearse at the Royal Dramatic Theater.

"Now you're dead. Now you can go to the theater. Oh, Max, if we have time and feel up to it, we'll shoot your scenes and Gunnar's in the vestry before we go up to Dalarna."

"Aren't we going to have some of those standing scenes too," Max says. "So-called refrain scenes. That we take over and over again. Like the grille scene in THE SEVENTH SEAL."

"Oh, we're going to retake a *lot*," Ingmar says.

Max goes.

They speak of Gunnel's lying-in. Laughter: "It mustn't come too early, you must keep to the date, Gunnel." They read the scene in the classroom— "the big hate orgasm," Ingmar calls it. Märta asks to be allowed to go with him to Frostnäs— "then her face is severe, it's the first time in her life she has *that* face." They read the parson's visit to the fisherman's wife— "that scene upset my father most of all, that's the one he kept coming back to."

"Is Thomas influenced still more by this visit?" Gunnel Lindblom asks.

"No. You see, he is beyond all influence just then. The visit to Mrs. Persson is only a station on the road of suffering, he moves as it were in god-forsakenness, there are spots of self-insight and despair."

Where is Thomas in the last scene, from a religious point of view? Here, Ingmar says:

"The looking-glass is clean. There stands a newly-scrubbed vessel which has the possibility of being filled with grace. With a new god image."

Then the read-through is finished, all are rather tired. Scraping of chairs and small talk. Ingmar tells of a man who called up the villa at Djursholm the other day after Käbi had played Beethoven's

78

Appasionata on TV. The big Bergman laugh, for the man had said: "Can we never be spared that Käbi Laretei on TV" and had grown more and more rude. "I was about to flare up," but then he hit on another means. With an icy voice he said to the telephone man: "Do you know that the police have their eyes on you?"

There was a deathly silence on the phone. "The man just slunk off." Ingrid laughs; she, too, gets persecution-like calls— "now I know what to answer." Tiredness, content, fading-out, going home: we are all agreed that we have something we want to keep from the police.

So ended the read-through of WINTER LIGHT in a mumbling, creaking, gay unanimity that the Swedes really are afraid of the police.

TUESDAY 3 OCTOBER 1961
Press conference today

The female source of primeval energy called Dagmar Snäcke, who is in charge of the restaurant, has taken out the sherry glasses. Her girls set a long table. Ingmar dominates the conference. Are the actors a support for him? At any rate, he appealed to them yesterday:

"By the way, there's a press conference tomorrow at four o'clock and I'd like Gunnar, Ingrid, Max, and Gunnel very much to come along. Pure and straightforward information. We'll all sit there, they'll ask us questions, we'll talk a little, eh? It's awfully simple. As long as you turn up and lend your support. It feels goddam awful being alone with them."

I was rather surprised that he needed to ask the actors to come along. Now, long afterwards, I understand better— I've learned what an ordeal press conferences are for film and theater people.

(Actually, I ought to portray the average conference— I've known for fifteen years how a journalist feels. Describe the actors' fear when they have to express themselves in words— their desperate feeling that it doesn't sound fine enough, what they manage to say. They smile faintly, cocktail glass in hand, but squirm inwardly like worms on a hook— well of course, an artist wants to give an impression, not a description. Good God, to stand here gelding myself with words, when my job is to portray! The journalists smile back, full of skepticism in the presence of the actors as a *species*: their friendly doubts as they jot down the platitudes.

Timidity, condescension, unfamiliarity hover in the air— but no one can tell the other to go to hell, for both parties are dependent on each other: the journalist needs copy; the actor, publicity. All the greater joy when the wall is sometimes breached and the two parties talk to each other like human beings: on an equal footing, with mutual respect.)

Today one of the journalists present makes use of a contact he has had within SF— and pretends he has had permission to read the script. Before the press conference he had skimmed through the script, written down certain speeches— then he goes home and concocts a wooden summary of what he has gotten out of the reading; and starts an article like this: "It is not granted to just anybody to take a peep at Ingmar Bergman's screenplay before the shooting even begins. I, however, have had that privilege ...."

A lie hardly conducive to improve the relations between film and press. Has the man any idea how much he destroys for his journalist colleagues, those who clearly and distinctly, without any extra gimmicks, have given an account of what was said here today?

The most important thing during the press conference is IB's declaration that he is trying to get away from "stereotyping."

"The aim is to make people, write people. To what extent I succeed, I don't know. But it's a striving I have had and have; instead of drawing construction designs to try more and more to draw a human hand."

"I mean: it stands out more and more to me, in this strange age of non-art, as being very important that we don't lose man out of the center, but keep searching for an expression by which to portray human beings— a personal form of portrayal. To what extent it succeeds and to what extent it is possible, I don't know— but that's the aim anyway."

("This strange age of non-art." As a guess I would say he has taken the term from that brilliant craftsman Hjalmar Gullberg, who persisted in writing *terza rima* in this age of non-art.)

This self-assessment also includes a comparison with music; after the big formats he is now interested in the small. After having tried his hand at the large orchestration he is now curious to experiment with the "chamber music format." There is as much violent tension and expansion in one of Beethoven's or Béla Bartók's string quartets as in the vast works of Wagner or Richard Strauss. In other words, after THE SEVENTH SEAL it is time for

THROUGH A GLASS DARKLY and WINTER LIGHT.

The press conference ends by everyone tramping down to the studios. Ingmar shows the Big Studio, where the actual church is being built— stone walls of wood and cardboard and plastic. But in Studio No. 5 it is pitch dark.

"Put on the ceiling lights."

Over there is the vestry by itself. And the "smoking slab" with its circle of small garden chairs, each with everyone's name newly painted on the back. So neat it all is. So clean and tidy. And with an atmosphere all its own.

The atmosphere of expectation.

Tomorrow work will begin here.

But Ingmar himself has the check to say (before the press conference) that he is already "done with" this film! He sat in his office putting the finishing touches to a program commentary on THROUGH A GLASS DARKLY.

"Tomorrow I'm starting on WINTER LIGHT. Hmmm. But it's always the way: long before you start shooting something, you're already done with it."

What is more, he knows of old that he will get half an hour's sleep tonight, if that: "The jitters always start then. The shivering fit before you begin." Then he laughed:

"This shooting is starting in the worst possible way. One star comes along in very bad physical shape. The other is shaken up after nine months with THE FOUR HORSEMEN in Hollywood. And then this idea that she— just before shooting begins!— should hop over to America for a few weeks and do this goddam thing for American TV .... Only running away, of course. Before she has to come to grips with this part."

Addition, eight months later, 31 May 1962:

Last evening I met Harry Schein, Ingrid's husband, at a spring party given by Inger and Roland Pålsson. A long talk about Ingrid's and his experiences in Hollywood; *hers* tasted bitter— "but I consider that she knows nothing about Hollywood and American shooting conditions; she only knows something of Metro-Goldwyn-Mayer and Minelli." Ingrid has just started learning her part for Ingmar's new film, THE SILENCE— "what do you think of it? I think it's the first good script he has written since WILD STRAWBERRIES. Just as good as the script of WINTER LIGHT was bad." Just the line about the Chinese and the atom bomb is so absurd

81

that it will become a classic joke, he guesses.

Harry laughs.

"I thought it was so bad that I tried to get Ingrid to turn down WINTER LIGHT. I was intrigued as hell, but I was caught in my own trap."

He tells the story like a good loser. And Ingmar loves tactics, he knows that. I don't remember the details of Harry's story; only that he used the clauses in Ingrid's USA contract as one of the pretexts.

This was the double pressure under which Ingrid worked when she started WINTER LIGHT: pressure from her husband, pressure from the director.

But she has strength. And an "almost Chinese capacity," said Gunnar Björnstrand the other day, of moving aside, out of the way— away from pressure.

PART II

THE SHOOTING

WEDNESDAY 4 OCTOBER 1961
The first day's shooting
"When did you think of this shot?"

"To tell the truth, in the car this morning. I sat working on the material yesterday evening, I knew that I wanted these three things in it: the Christ image; the grated window; the collection money. At first I thought of shooting each one by itself, in small shots and vis-à-vis .... "

(That's true: at the technical meeting the day before yesterday he decided that they would start the shooting with "close-up of the collection bag.")

" .... but this morning I thought: I'll lump them all together in one scene and give the audience something to chew on straight away. Make them work right at the start. It won't hurt them."

This is the first day's first camera angle: on the Christ image on the wall of the vestry. The collection bag is stuck in front of Christ and is turned up and emptied. The parson's hand puts a thermos on the wooden table. The churchwarden Aronsson comes into shot— he is played by Kolbjörn Knudsen. Behind him Thomas Ericsson sits down but is immediately seized with a coughing fit and goes over to the grated window, muttering: *If I could just go home to bed.* At the same time the camera pans sideways over to the window; then it follows Thomas back to the table. Small talk between the parson and the churchwarden. All this is taken in one shot, right up to where Algot Frövik knocks on the vestry door.

The whole morning is spent in technical preparations. (When you think of it, technical matters always take up a lot of time on the first day of shooting— before the crew have settled down together and everyone has grown familiar with the rhythm of the new film.)

Stig Flodin comes out of the darkness beyond the spotlight palisades, shaking his head.

"Trouble, Stickan?"

"Brian can't get the mike arm in for *If I could just go home to bed.*"

Stig Flodin, sound engineer, dark-haired, owner of a red MG, is in charge of the sound table. Brian Wikström, assistant sound, handles the mike. Sensitive work that calls for the light touch of an equilibrist.

Right at the end of the long arm dangles the mike; he has to find "a position." He must bring the mike as close to the actor's lips as possible but avoid the mike's being visible in shot. When he has found an ideal "position," there's always a spotlight in the way which casts a horrible shadow of the mike arm, which ruins the whole shot. Sometimes the shadows are so treacherous that they are not noticed until the next day in the screening room, when the shot has been taken and developed. "Hunting shadows" is therefore part of everyone's job— the sound and camera boys and the electricians. Now and then Bergman appoints one of them as a special "shadow hunter" which he pronounces in English (his worst school English) to give the title a dignified sound.

Stickan groans over the bad sound quality he gets on Björnstrand's line *If I could just go home to bed.* If he passes that, there'll be a hell of a row in the screening room tomorrow. Must Björnstrand say it over by the grated window? Yes.

"Then I'll have to take it wild and lay it on afterward."

K. A. has a moment of distress this very first morning. He has thought out very carefully what objects are to be found in a vestry — and procured them, with iron energy, on the principle: better too much than too little. Were Ingmar to use *everything* that K. A. provides, the set would be overloaded. But K. A. loves the things he procures— and suffers from Ingmar's weeding out process. The casualties this morning were a few bundles of pamphlets from the Central Board of the Church of Sweden; now they are lying untidily over by the make-up table. K. A. shows them to me with a gloomy shake of the head.

"Look, I wasn't allowed to keep these in!"

Ingmar opens one of the pamphlets, THE COMMUNION, by the former archbishop Yngve Brilioth, and starts reading aloud to Gunnar Björnstrand: "We have in our church begun once more to realize that our divine service is a costly jewel which we have inherited from bygone generations, a jewel to cherish and protect. We have begun to clean and polish this jewel with gentle hands, but we have often been blind to how the whole jewel is like a setting for a pearl of extremely great price ...." " and Ingmar tosses the pamphlet aside with distaste.

"What incredible language. So *highflown.* I'll be damned if they don't write like Selma Lagerlöf the whole bunch."

He goes out and walks up and down the corridors. He goes away to his office. He wanders around the studio, with Björnstrand, with Kolbjörn Knudsen.

"The first day you take such a hell of a lot of walks. You walk for *miles*."

I have started my Eckermann job.

"What are you writing?"

"I'm writing that 'the first day you take such a hell of a lot of walks. You walk for *miles*.' "

Lunch at twelve o'clock. I note down impatiently: "Still no take."

It *is* tricky taking everything at once. So before lunch Ingmar decides to divide the shot up into two camera positions; during lunch he reassures Gunnar Björnstrand of this decision; and after lunch he takes the whole shot at once, according to plan.

The subject finder is a splendid little gadget. The director can hang it around his neck like a necklace. When he holds it up to his eye, he can look through it and see what the finished image will be like. He regulates it to the same lens as the camera has and gets exactly the same cutting of the subject. Ingmar seldom uses it.

He uses his hands instead.

His hunger satisfied (with boiled ham and a fried egg, as always!) he crouches down in front of Knudsen and Björnstrand, holding his hands to one eye. With the aid of his thumbs and forefingers he forms a square in the air. The cutting is not exact, but he prefers this to looking in the finder. And it gives you just as much contact with the subject, perhaps more— if you know all the lenses of the camera, that is. He turns to Sven Nykvist:

"How would it be with a tracking-in here?"

"Where?"

"When the churchwarden starts asking about Märta Lundberg."

Sven nods and gives an order.

"Åland and Håkan, put down rails here, please."

"Åland"is called so in the studio because he was born in Åland; on the pay list he is down as Yngve Söderlund. "Håkan" is an abbreviation of Rune Håkansson. "Åland" is short, with peering, boyish eyes and charm in his Åland accent. "Håkan" is taller, more lanky, with hair like Charles XII. They form a working pair. They move the camera. They move the sets. They move the chairs, roof beams, cupboards, everything that has to be moved. They bear other people's burdens, all day long. Just now they're putting down rails. Their trade name is studio hand.

One of the studio hands is entrusted with looking after the clapper.

The good old hand clapper on which everything is noted: the film's production number (L-136); the date; the script number that Ingmar says the scene is to have; for which time in succession that scene is taken— all so that the laboratory can find the right spot in the film reel and print the take that the director has approved. The studio hand fishes a stump of chalk out of his dungarees pocket, writes the number and shoves the clapper in front of the camera, right under the nose of the actors who are just concentrating on giving their best. The director says: "Camera!"; Stickan answers from over at the sound table: "Camera running!"; the studio hand calls out: "76-83, take one," and slams down the bit of wood that has given the clapper its name (this slam which makes it possible to synchronize image and sound for next day's screening). Then he dives out of sight so as not to be in the picture himself, while the actors wait for the thin cloud of chalk dust to disperse before they start acting.

The first day of WINTER LIGHT begins with a revolution: the clapper has been abolished.

A new invention is used: a "light clapper" which is worked from the sound table. A shrill squeak instead of the slam of the clapper, a white frame on the film— that's all that will be noticed tomorrow at the screening.

"Wonderful, *isn't it*, to be spared the clapper!"

Ingmar draws Gunnar into his enthusiasm.

"Yes. Oh, yes!"

"To be saved that chalk spraying out," says Ingmar.

"And that goddam slam," says Gunnar.

"And the studio hand who sounds reproachful when you get to the thirteenth-fourteenth take," says Ingmar, mimicking a previous studio hand: "Take thirteen ...."

"Has it ever happened?" someone asks.

Ingmar smiles:

"That I've gotten up to the thirteenth take, you mean?"

Sven Nykvist announces that everything is ready for a rehearsal.

Knudsen and Björnstrand play the whole scene.

Then Kalle leaps to one side.

It looks nasty.

"Kalle," Gerhard Karlsson, is the chief electrician and resembles Joseph Cotton.

He got an electric shock.

"It must be the camera lamp."

A large, heavy, square metal frame equipped with a number of small lamps which can if necessary be hooked on to the actual camera. It is examined and lifted off.

"Not soldered," Kalle mutters.

Technical snag.

How do the actors react to these nerve-racking delays that always occur just when they are keyed up to play the scene? Gunnar Björnstrand can lean on his long film experience; he knows this muddled, troublesome studio world; he goes to one side and tries to relax. But Kolbjörn Knudsen has gained all *his* experience in the theater; he finds it hard to step out of character during all these pauses. While waiting for the take he rehearses on his own in the vestry set in the middle of all the noise from the workmen's voices; murmuring to himself, he goes through the whole scene, memorizing it. Ingmar pops up at his side.

"How does it feel? Troublesome?"

"Oh no, not at all."

They have known each other well ever since 1946-1950, when Ingmar was engaged at the Gothenburg City Theater.

New rehearsal. This time the technical side functions and the director can concentrate on the actors. There's very little he wants to alter with them, however. He subdues Kolbjörn Knudsen's tone a shade— but it's merely a question of polishing: degrees and nuances. Knudsen has the stage actor's fear that the dialogue will be expressionless, unaccented, dull, if it is taken as subdued as Ingmar wants it; but Ingmar reassures him, in a *film* this is exactly right, quite enough. Ingmar takes a lot of trouble over this, for:

"You have to get the actors to strike the right note the first day. If they do, they keep to it automatically."

Which note? Gunnar Björnstrand declared just now, out in the wings, that it was not "stylization and exactness" that Ingmar was after just here, "but mumbling."

Ready for the first take, at last.

Dead silence in the studio.   Björnstrand's and Knudsen's voices inside the vestry are approaching the end of the scene:

ARONSSON: You could ask Märta Lundberg to help you. I'm sure there's nothing she'd like better. I can ask her.

THOMAS: No thanks. (Loud knocking at the vestry door.)

"*Cut!* (Pause.) Oh, Gunnar, I think your *no thanks* was a shade too aggressive. Say it rather wearily. More or less: 'Oh, don't start all that over again!' "

Gunnar nods; he is still sitting at the vestry table with Thomas Ericsson's tired demeanor. Ingmar:

"Let's take it again, as we have time anyway."

Third time's the charm; the director's voice has a happy, contented ring:

"Thanks. Good. Excellent. That was something special, did you notice? (Happy murmurs.) A new creation."

Katinka from her chair;

"Which ones do we print?"

Ingmar promptly:

"First and third takes!"

Katinka, a girl who grew up in Sundbyberg. Born of Hungarian parents who came to Sweden with one of the refugee waves of the 30s. She sits with her pen lifted and her big metal cover on her knee, ready to write *Pr.* in front of the takes that are to be printed (and draw a circle around those that will not be used). The metal cover protects her big scriptgirl script in which she notes down what distinguishes the various takes (not only the judgments passed on them by the director, but also what she herself observes). A frightfully exacting test of attention which might be thought of as having been made only for people with a narrow, dry emotional register. But Katinka, who has anything but a statistical nature, has developed within a few years into one of the skilled workers in a profession swarming with awfully pleasant amateurs. She made her debut as Sweden's youngest scriptgirl at the early age of fifteen in THE ROAD TO KLOCKRIKE. It has given her an unusual feeling for the people in the studio and the needs of the actors: she is a seismograph for moods, pressures, happenings under the surface.

During the break Ingmar described one of his most usual directing knacks:

"Kolbjörn was inclined to tense himself; so he wasn't really very good in the first take. But I didn't want to go at him straight off. I sat groping about while they did the scene and thought: What shall I do now? That's why I was so terribly glad when Gunnar

92

made a little too much of his *No thanks*, so that I had an excuse to hang the retake on. In that way Kolbjörn grew relaxed and easy .... You see, you must never go straight at an actor. You must *carry* them ...."

And adapt yourself to the peculiarity of each actor, I think to myself. You can't expect the *same* qualities in different types of talent. The exuberant, improvising actor is not likely to be pedantic over details. The precision actor who loves delicate engraving work can't very well be spontaneous, etc.

But a film's demands are preposterous: it calls for *both* precision *and* spontaneity. The actor must open himself to the camera— quietly, nakedly, sensitively— and at the same time remember to stand on exactly the spot on the vestry floor that the director has shown him, in exactly the lighting that the cameraman has worked out for him, in exactly the right corner of the picture so that he doesn't upset the pictorial composition. Ingmar compares his two actors today on this last point, with the same warmth for both:

"Kolbjörn Knudsen is the most imprecise man imaginable. You can unload as much on Gunnar Björnstrand as you like."

So he made a simple plan of movement for Knudsen— so that his particular qualities would be seen to the best advantage. And did not hesitate to make things a little more complicated for Björnstrand.

Ingmar's own mood on this first day is a rather restless purring good humor. The crew have cream cake with green icing served to them with the three o'clock coffee; he himself has tea with Harriet Andersson (and plans out her immediate film future for her, I guess).

The first studio day ends with the usual giving of orders for tomorrow. Allan Edwall is to come in through the iron door of the vestry. Where is the camera to stand?

"*Here*. That wall is to be taken away! and that one put in!"

Håkan and Åland nod. And Sven Nykvist is already thinking out the lighting for tomorrow's first camera position.

The final thing is to look at the last make-up and costume tests: Ingrid Thulin's hair and Gunnel Lindblom's coat. Gathering in one of the pavilion's small screening rooms.

A compromise has been reached: Ingrid Thulin has agreed to shorten her own blond hair a trifle; Ingmar has given in on his previous insistence that she should cut her hair entirely; Börje Lundh has stepped into the breach with a so-called half-wig, under which Ingrid can hide her own fair hair.

"Shall we do Ingrid's hair like this then? With a half-wig? A diplomatic solution, I think .... (Ingmar yawns slightly, afternoon tired:) "A *praiseworthy* solution."

Gunnel Lindblom up on the screen displays three different coats for Mrs. Persson, all three of the type "Swedish country wife." One is chosen.

Last of all Ingmar pops his head into the cutting room and looks at the trailer for THROUGH A GLASS DARKLY in its almost final version.

THURSDAY 5 OCTOBER 1961
Allan Edwall provides a shock
Stravinsky's cannibal mouth and child's eyes
A director's disappointments and an actor's aloofness
"We must retake the whole thing"

Suddenly there he stood this morning: Algot Frövik, knocking at the iron door of the vestry.

"You're not feeling very well, vicar?"

It was a shock. We have grown used to the appearance of the two leading parts through a series of test films; Allan Edwall had the advantage of a surprise effect: one morning he's just standing there in the spotlight in Algot Frövik's clothes, and *is* Algot Frövik. It was uncannily genuine. I asked Ingmar whether he had previously rehearsed the scene with Allan.

"No. We've just talked a bit about it."

"The precision with which he strikes exactly the right note!"

"Yes indeed. He's a perfect instrument. Like the Virtuosi di Roma. They don't fumble for the note up here or down here, but hit it bang in the middle. *There.*"

(K. A. is sitting near me next day when we run the scene. K. A. is not so enthusiastic about Edwall's interpretation as we are, not so convinced. In an undertone he remarks that Allan Edwall holds his shoulder wrong. He would like to have put this fault right yesterday, but didn't want to interfere.)

Allan Edwall moves quietly around the table, smiling contentedly. He likes the little scene— "the sort of thing that happens to everybody: to find you've come in when you're not wanted." Algot Frövik is meant to be an "angel"— I can't imagine any smile

that can express more delicate shades of feeling than Allan Edwall's in that part: good-hearted, a trifle distrait, with a touch of
penetration.

I don't know whether Allan's kind of part gives rise to it: all of
a sudden, however, they have relaxed and are discussing childishness and maturity in different people. IB is reminded abruptly
of his meeting with Stravinsky last week.

"I've never seen it as it is with him! This cannibal mouth— and
child's eyes as clear as glass. With a heavenly light in them. A
great childishness— ruled by an absolutely strict reason."

IB describes it with a mixture of amazement and joy. No doubt
whatever that Stravinsky has bewitched him.

Meanwhile Håkan and Åland are putting down rails for a tracking-in on Allan Edwall— but it's a shot that is never seen in the
finished film. A subtle touch of direction (not until long afterward
do I realize what it is for): Ingmar gets two different positions by
this; two picture compositions: first Edwall is standing some distance away in the shot, then the camera moves up on him. Well,
why couldn't he break off the scene and move the camera nearer?
Yes, of course he could, but he gets a smoother, quieter and more
delicate tone in the acting if he lets the actors play the scene
straight through without a break.

Sure, it's fun to track with the camera— but this tracking is for
the good of the actors, nothing else.

Allan Edwall's little scene is shot four times; only the last is used.
After the first take Ingmar asks Allan to tone down his acting a
shade; Ingmar feels a certain stylization in Edwall's acting and he
wants to get rid of it.

K. A. spends the day hunting for a handwriting. He tries one person after the other to find someone who can write out Märta
Lundberg's long letter for him— "it must be real handwriting, the
letter is seen in shot." At last he finds the right handwriting: it belongs to one of the girls on the telephone switchboard.

A day of groping for contact. Ingmar bends considerably over
Gunnar Björnstrand, who is sitting concentratedly in the vestry:

"You're getting into it now, aren't you? Am I not right? Getting
a more comfortable, calm feeling?"

Gunnar nods. Later Ingmar says:

"To think we did get started after all. I never thought we ever
would."

No? It sounds odd to an outsider. Just what kind of positions *is* one to have in order to be sure of getting a response from one's fellow-workers? Isn't IB's enough? Apparently not. Response is irrational; and IB's September contained more disappointments than I suspected. To Gunnar:

"You were in the middle of shooting THE GARDEN OF EDEN, and it took longer than expected. Ingrid made difficulties over Hollywood. I very nearly couldn't get Max. Gunnel kept getting bigger and bigger. And no one was very enthusiastic. Those I wanted support from, dropped out; or kept their distance .... The same as when I made THE FACE. It's always the same. Films that are easy to do, everyone is enthusiastic about. Then you get all the response you want. But when you really need it .... well. I nearly chucked the whole thing, I thought: I'll just have to give up the idea of WINTER LIGHT."

Gunnar is anxious about the public: won't it stay away from a film like this? Ingmar answers with a loud laugh:

".... nothing in comparison with *my* anxiety! This morning I got stuck in a goddam great traffic jam. I sat there looking at the drivers in the other cars. And thought: *You* won't come and see WINTER LIGHT, and *you* won't come and see WINTER LIGHT, and *you* won't come and see ...."

Ingmar talks alone; Gunnar has a kind of aloofness: he *wants* to respond but can't— and nothing is easier to understand than Gunnar's state of mind these days. A film studio can impose a claustrophobic nervous strain on all who work in it; the heat from the spotlights; everyone's breath; no windows; all doors shut to keep the noise out. The nervous strain is all the greater for someone who has been given such a stifling doctor's report as GB— the whole time he is fighting a sensation of something being drawn tight, he is longing to get out of the studio, into the fresh air outside.

Åland does a good deed and opens the big drive-in doors of Studio 5: outside, on the sloping wooden ramp, the clear air of the fall is waiting.

The thin sunshine. The October colors. This ramp is for the truck that brings in the sets and properties.

Gunnar walks across the ramp in his cassock, 53 years old, slim as a young man. (The only peculiarity is that his shirt and clerical bands are yellow in color— for the sake of the film. Plain white

96

cloth does not come out well in a picture; so everything white out here is dyed yellow, from handkerchiefs to sheets and pillow-cases.)

We pace up and down on the transport ramp; on Sunday Gunnar tried to relax by driving out to his summer place; he describes his joy: the archipelago, the cottage, the boats— and I, who find it hard to express myself clearly, am amazed once more at his phenomenal verbal agility. He is a word-painter, skilled in the art of putting his thoughts into words, an aphoristic craftsman with no published collection of aphorisms; his literary talent is oral: he publishes himself in conversation, in relaxing talks, sometimes in interviews with dumb-founded journalists. His ironic knowledge of human nature is kindly and yet cutting— sharper actually than he cares to show, for fear of wounding and offending. He knows so well how restricted people's limits are; how little they can stand— and himself too, for that matter. His self-insight: "I like eating well, feeling well; in fact, I'm rather sybaritic." He smiles— with thin lips and those incredible peppercorn eyes. "And then I have all my channels cut off, right in the middle of my middle-aged muddle." Those peppercorn eyes that have suddenly vanished as he screws them up when he laughs.

The time is 4:45 p.m.:

An exciting and uncanny moment: we gather in the screening room to see the rushes. This will be a daily routine from now on. The laboratory has, as usual, had a day in which to print the material.

The lights go down in the screening room: the collection bag is stuck in front of the Christ image; Thomas Ericsson starts coughing .... but Gunnar Björnstrand is not there watching.

No actors are ever there to see the rushes, only the technical crew. Other directors perhaps let the actors in; not IB. If they see themselves they become self-observant in the wrong way; they stare blindly at the wrong things and are disturbed in the immediate work— that is the theory behind his refusal. Only in exceptional cases are they allowed to see themselves in the middle of the shooting: when he wants to retake a scene that was not good. "Go and see for yourself in this scene and you'll understand what I mean!" In that case, the picture tells the actor more than a long explanation from the director.

Screening over. Silence.

"What the hell's wrong with the sound? It sounds canned and stuffy. It picks up far too many sounds from the studio.(Happily:) Doesn't it? Now admit that it sounds goddam awful!"

Mumbled answers, deep thinking. Can it be the fault of the new light clapper? Maybe. Look into it then! We can't have it like this.

"But the photography is good, the light is good."

Pause while he thinks it over.

"We must retake the whole thing. There's nothing else to do."

FRIDAY 6 OCTOBER 1961
Less weight and more "outline"

When cast and crew drift into the studio in the morning, they find five men from the sound department gathered around the sound equipment. Someone says with a smile: "Technical snag, aha! Always the way with Ingmar's productions. Never with other productions"— unsuspectingly airing their ignorance.*

A moment later it is dark in the studio.

The only source of light is that coming from the parson's table in the vestry, where the fisherman and his wife have sat down to get help. Max with his silence, rubbing his forefinger against his cheek; Gunnel eight months pregnant. When *he* says nothing, *she* has to step in and explain matters to the parson.

"Something like this, Gunnel: at home he talks! He goes around all day talking about the Chinese. But when he comes here he won't open his goddam mouth, eh?"

MRS. PERSSON: Drive me home and then come back to the vicar. It's *much* better if you talk to him alone.

Ingmar to Gunnel:

"Here she is motherly and practical. A little more Ria Wagner, that's how you should be! (Laughs.) You see, we mustn't be too heavy here. The real unpleasantness comes later. This should be a mixture of embarrassment and lack of contact. People who misunderstand each other and say the wrong things. It's so important that it feel *real*. Completely ordinary and everyday. No acting. It applies to all three of you here. It's purely a matter of getting into —

---

* It *was* the light clapper that gave the "canniness" to the sound as a result of a faulty connection. The inventor, an engineer from AGA, came out at once and fixed it; after that the light clapper worked perfectly— but it took Ingmar a week or so to get over his mistrust of this novelty which had ruined the film's first two days' takes.

the mood of it."

Rehearsal. Ingmar:

"He's tired, Thomas, terribly tired. He's actually thinking of asking them to come back some other time. He has a service at Frostnäs at three o'clock."

Pause. IB goes on elaborating:

"Actually Thomas is irritated and wants to say this to them: 'If it's some marital trouble, then come back on Monday. No, on Tuesday— the parish office is open on Tuesdays and Fridays.' So that it's not too heavy at the start. Do you see? You're both pressing too hard now, you and Gunnar. Don't do that. Then the whole goddam play will sink too soon, like the *Andrea Doria*."

He praises Gunnel's strength and need of clear-cut instructions. If she gets them, everything's all right. I am surprised that he uses such abstract instructions as *more outline*. Does that tell the actors anything?

"Some. But I agree it doesn't tally with people's idea of what 'instruction' is."

"What *is* instruction then?"

"Influencing their feelings. The whole time: to influence the actors' feelings! And talking nonsense. Whenever you can. So that they don't get cramps from concentration. (Smiles.) They're so frightfully ambitious when faced with a scene like this. They take it so awfully seriously."

In Gunnar Björnstrand a counter-reaction has set in: he can't rest at peace with the doctor's report he received, he must do something to relieve the feeling of pressure and tightness— he has therefore contacted another doctor than the one he first went to.

Late in the afternoon there is a painful incident. Ingmar fires off criticism and a woman in the studio bursts into tears. I am not there when it happens. I merely see her crying, soak up the atmosphere and feel distressed.

SATURDAY 7 OCTOBER 1961
Examine the string quartet in THROUGH A GLASS DARKLY

Heard the Végh Quartet play Bartók's fifth and sixth last evening at the Museum of Modern Art; then I started trying out whether THROUGH A GLASS DARKLY really can be analyzed as a string quartet. In that case Harriet Andersson and Lars Passgård would represent the violins, of course. Max von Sydow would be the viola, Gunnar Björnstrand the cello. And the first of the four movements would end in a long drawn-out adagio on the cello: Björnstrand alone, smoking his pipe in the summer dusk .... And so on, in detail.

And what is the point of the comparison? Oh, one could for instance see the themes so much more clearly: Faith. Incest. Love. The artist's emotional coldness. How they pass from movement to movement. (Note, however, Ingmar's difficulty in keeping all four instruments going at the same time, as in a real string quartet! He is forced the whole time to break the ensemble playing up into duo scenes.)

Today the fisherman and his wife finish their talk with the parson. Conversation during the break is about bringing up children. Guessing what they feel when you speak to them like this:

"As long as you're eating our bread, you keep quiet."

Or:

"That's the least you can do for your mother."

It is only twelve o'clock when the Rev. Ericsson takes leave of the fisherman and his wife, and Ingmar is one big yawn of contentment at being able to go home and have a nap and enjoy himself "until two o'clock tomorrow morning."

"What happens at two o'clock tomorrow morning?"

"Then I start thinking of the film again. And then they come: the snakes in my stomach."

Tomorrow SF's Sten Lindén is going to drive Ingmar and Gunnar Björnstrand to Sigtuna. They will have lunch there before going off to Vassunda church, where there is a "duplication" of the morning service at two o'clock, "just as in our film."

"Like to come?"

Suddenly I go on strike. I don't want to, I'm not up to it. I'm dead tired after the first week in the studio, and down in the dumps.

SUNDAY 8 OCTOBER 1961
Blue Sunday

Long depressing Sunday. My thoughts just churn around the production and Ingmar.

When did these blues start? On Friday afternoon.

A man criticizes a woman, so that a woman starts to cry— does that frighten me so much? Am I *so* afraid of outbursts of aggression?!

Evidently I have a double reaction to this event. I am tormented and frightened by Ingmar's capacity to strike out, hard and suddenly, in criticism and attack. And envious: just think of being spared that ideal of kindness that coils around my feet.

(Experienced in January 1962, after a similar incident: Ingmar describes how his nerves lie just under his skin: lightning flashes that he *simply cannot check*. I describe my own fear of losing my temper, the always-be-nice-and-kind compulsion. "And I," he says, "I balance on a narrow margin of aggressiveness which it's so horribly easy for me to overstep"; and we look at each other in astonishment, like two different species of animals put by mistake into the same cage at the zoo.)

MONDAY 9 OCTOBER 1961
When Jesus saw the bearers' faith

Incredible; but one and a half day's takes with GB, Knudsen and Edwall in the vestry are now re-shot in half a day— because *now* everyone knows everything, actors and technicians alike.

"What was it like at church yesterday?" I ask.

"Oh," Gunnar replies, "it was desolate. Religion transformed into myth. The next step is Offenbach."

Only *four* in the congregation: two churchwardens and two old women. "Worse even than in WINTER LIGHT." But Ingmar was deeply impressed by the sermon. Jesus heals a man sick of the palsy, that was the text. When Jesus saw the *bearers'* faith he healed the lame man, that was the parson's theme.

" .... and that was fantastic *for us*, wasn't it, Gunnar? Just as in our film: Algot Frövik and Märta Lundberg, they are the bearers in this film. They bear the paralyzed Thomas, so that he can totter in and hold the service again .... "*

"What about the snakes?" I ask. "Did they come along at two o'clock?"

"No, not until five," Ingmar laughs. "How did you get along?"

—

*Ingmar often reverted to this exposition of the text during shooting. I guess that it resolved the religious difficulty that arose during the actual process of writing, when Thomas merely sank in dramatic activity and Märta merely rose. It also fitted IB's earlier thought that Thomas is "the pack donkey that keeps struggling on" (see Thursday, August 10th, 1961).

It was on the tip of my tongue to answer "I had a fit of the blues," but I pass it up:

"I always get the Sunday blues between three and five."

"Don't you think it's because when you were a child, you knew that school would begin on Monday morning?"

"No," I reply. "*My* Sunday depression is due to the fact that when I was a child, the matinée was over at three o'clock. And when I came out of that, nothing was fun anymore. Only lonely and empty and dreary."

Ingmar, brusquely:

"So for me it was school! We lived at the Sophiahemmet private hospital, Daddy was the parson there, and on Sundays there was always a funeral in Engelbrekts church at three o'clock. The funeral bells started tolling with a hell of a noise, and I sat at home listening to them and thinking of all the homework I hadn't done ...."

In the afternoon Ingrid comes into the studio.

I experience the same feeling of happiness every time a character takes shape and appears in all the studio clutter.

There she *is*, Mārta Lundberg.

"Not such a bad idea, is it, writing for particular actors?" IB says. "Then you know what you get."

But he's skeptical about those who write biographies about him and "lift the whole of my production work in the theater out of context."

"My films are only a distillation of what I do in the theater. Theater work is sixty percent, you see. Not to take up the connection between THE SEVENTH SEAL and my production of UR-FAUST (although they came about in the reverse order). Not to take up the connection between THE FACE and my production of SIX CHARACTERS IN SEARCH OF AN AUTHOR in Malmö ...."

In the afternoon he inspects the building of the church in the big studio. Isn't P. A. going to paint anything on the wall? The flagellants' procession from THE SEVENTH SEAL for instance?

"Sure," P. A. laughs, "nowadays they're always unearthing old paintings in all the churches."

TUESDAY 10 OCTOBER 1961
The art of plotting the moves
To direct actors is to go on making things up

102

Gunnar gets thin
"Skill" and "technique"
The frightful technical machinery

"Plotting the moves," what is that?

The Rev. Thomas Ericsson comes in through the vestry door, he goes over to the grated window, he puts his arms up on the window sill .... that is the beginning of a set of moves.

This is a problem that always surprises the outsider. For one thing, every move is planned. Every step the actor takes in front of the camera. Every chair he sits down in on a theater stage. For another thing: surprise that this planning can give rise to such arguments, to so much unpleasantness between director and actors. Is it so goddam important if the actor goes here or there?! Can't you settle all that quickly, so that the work can go on?

The director seems stubborn, intractable, as he walks about planning how the move will look from the stalls of a theater or the seat of a cinema. The actor seems hypersensitive, affected, awkward and fussy as he fights shy of a set of moves that feel unnatural to him. He can make faces as though he had put on an ill-fitting suit. It's tight in all the wrong places, it doesn't feel comfortable anywhere; and the director agrees to a little alteration: shall we let it out a little here? Is that better? Not that either? Heavens above, isn't there a suit in the whole stock that fits him?

This is the first time the actor is to put on the character: that is why plotting the moves is a tricky business, and an important one. When the director demonstrates to the actor what moves he has planned for him, it is a question of feeling that is decided: now it will be seen whether director and actor feel *the same* about the character.

IB takes Björnstrand by the sleeve of his cassock and leads him over to the grated window. IB puts his hand to his nose. Every person has his little stock of ingrained habits and gestures; IB canalizes his doubts in this way: he draws his thumb and forefinger down his long, prominent nose. An idiosyncrasy while he thinks something over: will this be good or not? Pondering, he goes back to Ingrid Thulin. He pulls his nose again. Then, making up his mind, he leads Ingrid over to the grated window and sets her moves.

There is very little discussion. The suits and dresses are cut to a classic pattern. And the experienced director knows that every move will be accepted more readily by the actor if he is given a reason for it.

"How ugly it is when Mārta snuffles and blows her nose! That's why Thomas goes over to the window."

From our talks over meals in Paris in 1949 I remember how Ingmar set up his colleagues Olof Molander and Alf Sjöberg as two extremes in this very matter of plotting the moves of a scene: Molander "is brilliant when he only needs to put two actors opposite each other at a table and devote the rest of the time to analyzing the characters"; Sjöberg, on the other hand, plays dazzlingly on the whole keyboard of conceivable moves— such a supreme talent as Sjöberg's in this respect seems incredible to him and almost unique; Ingmar described it with astonishment and a touch of envy. He himself has usually leaned more toward Molander's type of scene-setting than Sjöberg's.

The typical Bergman scheme of moves is simple. He has no time for anything fussy or complicated when sizing up the mechanics of a scene; the text of his sermon is always the same: Clarity. Survey. Order and method.

1. Thomas shivers with fever, yawns, sinks down in the window embrasure. 2. Mārta goes around behind Thomas's back, comforting him from the other side *as well*. 3. When Mārta is hurt, she moves away from Thomas, out onto the floor of the vestry. 4. Thomas goes after her a few steps— seeking her help. 5. She makes yet another attempt to comfort him: takes hold of him, turns him toward her, goes close against him. The kiss. Thomas gives her no response. 6. Then she goes out the door.

A strong human being seeks a weak one. The weak one cannot accept help, but repulses it. That's what happens in the moves— twice, what is more, in quick succession.

(Three weeks later, on October 28th, we are sitting in the canteen talking about the imminent journey to Dalarna: Ingrid thinks of cold and winter and fires— "in Hollywood," she says, "I had a gas stove in every room of the set." This makes Ingmar think of all the American films he has seen:

".... and then you leaned against the mantelpiece, *didn't you?* You or Glen Ford. It's always the same in American films. If Man loves Woman, then Woman loves Man, and then the moves are like this:

"Man comes into Woman's bedroom. Woman combs her hair at

the dressing table. Close-up of Woman as Man comes from behind. Woman says something cutting and goes out of shot. Man remains standing, looks after her, goes after her out of shot.

"Next shot: Woman leans against mantelpiece. Man comes up, also leans against mantelpiece. Woman says something cutting and goes out of shot.

"Next shot: Man comes up to Woman on edge of bed— they're getting awfully daring now. Woman says something cutting and goes out of shot.

"If Woman loves Man more than Man loves Woman, it's done the other way around. Fantastic isn't it?"

Ingmar's description makes a hit; he neighs loudly at it; then he yawns, a little tired after his meal, and adds:

"Come to think of it, we do the same thing in our film, when Ingrid comes in to Gunnar in the vestry.")

It interests me to include a detailed example of how Ingmar works out a key scene, so that I note down every detail I snap up. This is how it started yesterday afternoon:

Having given orders that the flat was to be sawed up, Ingmar left the field, taking Ingrid and Gunnar and Katinka with him to a corner of the studio and drawing up crates and stools to sit on. The window wall was sawed in two, so that Sven could stick the camera right into the window (from the side); the floorboards were torn up, nails screeched— in the midst of this noise from the other corner of the studio Ingmar sat on a stool analyzing the text with the actors.

Then, after the coffee break at three o'clock, he turned nearly everyone out of the studio. No more sawing and hammering; he needed the set himself now to plot the moves— and in peace and quiet.

The only ones left were Katinka, Peter Wester and Sven Nykvist. Katinka drew every move in her continuity book; Gunnar Björnstrand checked anxiously to see that she got everything down, afraid that he himself might forget something by today. Peter Wester, assistant cameraman, trotted around with Ingmar's own director's copy, "like a choirboy." Sven Nykvist checked to see how the actors' moves looked in the camera and what sort of light he would need. Ingmar's voice, eager, excited:

"Is this okay for you?"

Sven nodded.

"This too? When he crouches down here?"

Sven made a careful extra check in the camera before answering. Then Ingmar fired off the surprise, as a feeler to see how much enthusiasm or opposition he could count on:

"What do you say to taking the whole lot in one go?"

Sven returned Ingmar's enthusiasm with a:

".... one hell of a great idea ...."

But swearwords sound very strange in Sven Nykvist's mouth, they are said without the slightest emphasis. It sounded much more genuine when Sven added thoughtfully:

".... it would be *great* with one take."

By 4:10 p.m. they had gone through the moves four times; in the pause after the second run-through Märta Lundberg's spectacles were discussed; great thought had been given to these. Märta Lundberg is supposed to be very shortsighted. Ingrid Thulin does not wear glasses herself. If Ingrid uses ordinary windowglass, this will be noticed in the close-ups— but in order to be able to see, she has corrective extra glass (cornea glass). Ingmar had previously approved this arrangement, but now he backs out of it:

"No, not in this scene. It will be a bit too unpleasant. Too much of the invalid about it. We might need them in an extreme close-up, to get the full effect; but not tomorrow. We'll use ordinary windowglass."

This day's work does not begin until 1:00 p.m. The camera can now be rolled freely on plywood slabs, and Ingmar seats himself behind the camera, himself checking to see what the moves look like. The actors are told not to act, they are just to walk across the scene for mechanics.

"Not a speck of feeling now, or I'll stop at once."

Gunnar nods, with well-restrained gaiety:

"If a speck of talent creeps in— disaster!"

Just what does a director say when he analyzes a text? How does he instruct the actors, how does he explain the meaning of the moves? I write down every phrase of the instruction and number them like this: I (what he said yesterday on the stool in the corner of the studio); II, III, IV (said during the repeated rehearsal of moves yesterday); V, VI (today when they rehearsed with the camera, "with no feeling"); VII, VIII, IX (when there were complete rehearsals with lights, sound and acting).

... ...

106

He moves away from her. She goes after him into the vestry.

THOMAS: I'm waiting for someone who wants to talk to me. He'll be here at any minute.

Ingmar to Gunnar (IX):

"Gunnar! The line about expecting a visitor. Can't you take it a little more formally, brushing her off more?"

MÄRTA: Don't worry, I'm going now.

She puts the basket on a chair and unbuttons her sheepskin coat, fumbles in the pocket, takes out a handkerchief and blows her nose.

Ingmar to Gunnar (IX):

"How ugly he thinks it is when she blows her nose! That's why he goes over to the window."

MARTA: It's turning really cold.

Thomas goes over to the little prison window of the vestry, lays his elbows against the wide sill. She stands beside him, puts her arms around his shoulders and draws him to her.

MÄRTA: Poor Thomas.

The tenderness in her tone, the fever, the feeling of ill omen: his eyelids swell and flush.

MÄRTA: What is it, Thomas?

Ingmar to Gunnar (II):

"There he is touched that she is suddenly kind to him."

Ingmar to Ingrid (III):

"Here you almost grin. You put your arm around him. Nudge and poke him a bit."

THOMAS: It's all the same to you.

MÄRTA: Tell me anyway.

THOMAS: God's silence.

Ingmar to Gunnar (VII):

"Not so dramatically, Gunnar!" (I am surprised: to my ears Björnstrand's tone was very subdued. This toning down of the pitch! This constant scraping off!)

MÄRTA (puzzled): God's silence?

THOMAS: Yes. (Long pause.) God's silence.

She lays her head against his shoulder, her beret is knocked askew, drops to the floor. They watch the snow falling; it is getting heavier.

156-157

The edge of the forest on the other side of the road and the field is obliterated more and more.

158

THOMAS: Then Jonas Persson and his wife came.

159

He presses his clenched hand to his mouth and his body is racked with coughing.

THOMAS: I talked a lot of rot. Cut off from God. Yet I had a feeling that every word was— decisive. What am I to do!

Ingmar to Gunnar (I):

"He says this 'I talked a lot of rot' with a terrible feeling."

Gunnar (III):

" 'What am I to do!' Is it a question put to anyone?"

Ingmar, with tenderness (III):

"Oh no, not to anyone! You put your hands to your mouth. You almost bite."

MÄRTA: Poor Thomas, you should take some brandy and go to bed. You've quite a high temperature.

Ingmar to Ingrid (III):

"Here you cross to that side of him, so that you almost hide him."

160

Märta lays her big hand against his brow, he lets her, her hand is cooling if nothing else.

THOMAS: Why did you go to communion?

Ingmar to Gunnar (IX):

"A rather suspicious look there, Gunnar. More or less: What is she up to now?"

MÄRTA: It's supposed to be a love feast. (Pause.) Have you read my letter, by the way?

THOMAS: Your letter? No. I haven't had time.

161-165

Märta draws back her hand and smiles ironically.

MÄRTA: You're hopeless. When did you get it?

THOMAS (truthfully): Yesterday. I was busy writing the sermon and it was a thick letter. I thought in fact ....

MÄRTA: What did you think?

THOMAS: That it was something unpleasant. I brought it with me.

Ingmar (I):

"I've cut that about the sermon and being unpleasant. Put in a few words instead, Gunnar: 'I have it here, I was just going to read it ....' "

He puts his hand to his pocket, she shakes her head.

MÄRTA: No, no, read it later. Sometime when you feel like it.

THOMAS: Why do you write, when we meet every day?

MÄRTA: When one talks, one goes off on a tangent. Don't look so alarmed.

166-170

Thomas loses the thread of the conversation, can't be bothered to explain, every syllable hurts his throat, every thought has to be hauled up out of a deep well of fever. He yawns like a sleepy child and lays his head in his arms.

Ingmar to Gunnar (I):

"*Now he yawns, an enormous yawn.* (IV): *Like this. You lay your head in your arms. First you feel your throat .... There are three things:* 1) *that you want to leave,* 2) *that you feel your throat,* 3) *that you lay your head down ....* (VII, laughs, dissatisfied with Gunnar's yawn:) *Funny how actors dislike yawning! The only person I ever got to yawn properly was Eva Dahlbeck, in the elevator, in WOMEN'S WAITING. It should be a huge, repulsive, disgusting yawn ....*"

MÄRTA (with a smile): A Sunday at the bottom of the vale of tears.

Ingmar to Ingrid (IV):

"*Not so heavy, Ingrid. She's teasing him a little. Dear me, now. She doesn't believe in the vale of tears. Here we can have a little of that affinity between them.*"

THOMAS: I don't feel well.

MÄRTA: Do you want sympathy?

Ingmar to Ingrid (VII):

"*She says it quietly and tenderly. As though to a child. He has suddenly become a little child to her.* (VIII, reminding her): *Quietly and intimately fondling. After all, they have lain in bed and petted a few times.*"

THOMAS: Yes, please.

MÄRTA (smiling): Then you'll have to marry me.

THOMAS (sighs, shuts his eyes): Oh.

Ingmar to Gunnar (V):

"There should be a little sigh there from Gunnar. Is she starting that again ...."
MÅRTA: You could easily marry me.
Ingrid asks Ingmar (I):
"Is there any irony in that?"
Ingmar:
"She's bargaining: You'll get sympathy if you marry me."
Gunnar's comment:
"That's not like Swedish girls. It's something imported."
THOMAS: Why?
MÅRTA: I wouldn't have to move away from here, for instance.
Ingmar to both (I):
"This should be brought out rather slowly and naggingly."
THOMAS: Why should you move away from here?
Ingmar stretches out the line (I):
"Why should you ...."
Gunnar:
"It will be Martin Ljung, this."
MÅRTA: As long as I'm only temporary staff they can move me anywhere at all. Far away.(Smiles.) From you.
THOMAS (wearily): Well, we'll see ....
Ingmar (III):
"He couldn't care less! That makes her so goddam mad that she pinches his ear and makes it bleed, and leaves the room .... No, not like that. It's a need to torment him."
— —
180-181 cont.
THOMAS: Supposing he doesn't come. I mean Jonas Persson?
MÅRTA: Then you can go home and have a rest. (Ironically.) And read my letter.
THOMAS: No, you don't understand.
Ingmar to Gunnar (I):
"It must be scarcely audible. Then she answers: 'There's the coffee.' This is where the irritation begins."
MÅRTA: There's the coffee.
182-184
She walks towards the door, on the way she stretches out her hand and grasps Thomas's arm.
THOMAS: What do you want now?
MÅRTA: Poor Thomas. I mean it. Here I come worrying you.

Ingmar to Ingrid (V):
"She has thought: 'Now he has read the letter. Now I'll go to communion.' And he hasn't read it. So everything's more wrong than ever. And God doesn't exist."

THOMAS (impatient): Oh, not at all.

MÄRTA (irritated): Sometimes I've no patience with you! God's silence, god keeps silent, god has never spoken for god doesn't exist. It's awfully simple really.

Ingmar to Ingrid (I):
"She says the last tenderly."

185-187
She bends over and kisses him on the mouth and on the cheek. She is violently sad.

Ingrid to Ingmar (III):
"Is it all right for me to have my glove on when I kiss him? Is that okay?"

THOMAS: Now you'll get flu.

MÄRTA (ironically): I shall have to like it of course. As I have caught it from you. Shall I stay?

THOMAS: No thanks, there's no need.

MÄRTA: Oh Thomas, what a lot you have to learn.

THOMAS (ironically): You don't say so, teacher.

Ingmar to Gunnar (I):
"You must be awfully tired here. Almost no tone at all."

Ingrid:
"But she is pretty energetic? As strong as a horse."

MÄRTA (same tone): You must learn to love.

THOMAS (same tone): And you'd teach me, I suppose?

Ingmar to Gunnar (VIII):
"Gunnar, don't make too much of it here. It only needs so little. We're right on top of you with the camera. A sulky forehead is all that's needed."

Märta looks at him for quite a long time, then she shakes her head and gives a little crooked smile.

Ingmar, with a laugh to Ingrid (VIII):
"Actually it's all so dull that it's beyond words. (Big laugh.) Isn't it? So awfully, goddam dreary."

189
She leaves him, goes out through the church. He hears the doors shut behind her.

Ingmar, to both (I):
"Actually we ought to take the whole of this scene in one shot. That would be the most logical."

... ...

One thing I do grasp after all this: why Ingmar calls the script a "semi-finished product." All the rest is done here, now, in the studio.

Had IB been a novelist, he would have written: "There she stood, blowing her nose— it was so ugly that he had to turn away; he put his arms up on the window sill." Now he is a director; now he paints in words for the actors. He gives them something to hold onto: feelings, moods, atmosphere. "That makes her so goddam mad that she pinches his ear and makes it bleed ...." He adds something new, fabricates, improvises, draws on his imagination.

To direct actors— is to *go on making things up.*

"Why do you place Mārta and Thomas in the window?"

"I don't know. I just saw them there, the whole time I was writing. Those two, over by the window, looking at the snow."

The vision he saw at his desk is now brought to life in the studio. The moves are given fine shades of meaning. The actors give birth to new details. When he sits writing, experience tells him that the actors will suggest these details— but not when and how or what details it will be. Therein lies the magic of the studio work. Here, in this clutter of cables, lamps and technical gear, something can really be created. Sometimes it isn't. Sometimes something quite unexpected happens.

Why does Ingmar want to do the whole of this long scene in one take? Not for the sake of saving money— nowadays. Formerly, yes, when he made his first films, PRISON and THIRST : then he shot long, splendid chunks in a single camera position in order to get as much as possible done in one working day. Now he does a single take in order to strain every nerve and to stimulate everyone concerned into giving their best; everyone is forced to concentrate, technicians as well as actors.

"That irrational element that comes into the acting when they play a scene right through— you never know what's going to happen .... You just have to be careful *not to over-rehearse.*"

At 3:05 p. m. they shoot the scene for the first time.

"Cut."

He feels light-hearted and satisfied.

"Fine. Nice rhythm. Relaxed, calm and quiet. How many meters was it? I make a guess at 150."

The assistant cameraman checks.

"157 meters."

"There, I wasn't far off. Can we have quiet in the studio again!"

The concluding phase begins:

The camera is backed out of the way. The two assistant cameramen get ready with their stills cameras like two press photographers. Ingrid Thulin and Gunnar Björnstrand play right through the scene once more (exactly as if it were a take); but this time the clicks from the stills cameras smatter at them. Tomorrow these stills will be ready on the director's desk: a hundred or so small pictures for him to choose from.

There are other ways of taking stills. You can lift an instant out of the action and ask the actors to take up this position. You can arrange expressive situations, etc. IB's method seems to me much better. The cameras capture the actors *in full action*: by means of this, fine shades of expression are registered which the actors could not reproduce if they merely took up positions. This system is routine in the studio now: stills are taken after (nearly) every camera angle in WINTER LIGHT.

"I introduced this system of taking stills— well, you can see why. But it's no good going off and leaving the procedure to the actors and the photographers. Then they slacken in concentration. You must be there and keep an eye on things."

According to the script, the organist Blom is to appear in the vestry in the middle of the scene between Märta and Thomas. Olof Thunberg came to the studio this morning; there was a short, intensive rehearsal with him. He played an organist whom the chatter bubbled out of while he hunted about for some music he had forgotten. But the laughter? Last of all Blom is to grin "derisively" at these semi-old people hiding in the vestry with their love. I didn't think Olof Thunberg made enough of the laugh.

"No, that's true, he didn't. It wasn't very good. He has never understood that laugh. But he got such goddam *pace* in it from the word go. Made such a good entrance. With such a rush."

Maybe Thunberg hadn't "understood" the laugh— but neither had I ever seen IB go out of his way to direct Thunberg on that point. Why didn't he bother about it?

113

Sometimes I seem to see two figures struggling violently together in IB: a Pedant fights a Sensualist. The Sensualist in him says: "Hah, it doesn't matter ...." but then the Pedant gets furious: "It *does* matter!" The Sensualist laughs and yawns, feels tired, loses interest. Then the Pedant leaps up with pointer and pince-nez, takes himself and his co-workers by the scruff of the neck, and preaches Compulsion, Demand, Duty, Necessity.

Had I asked IB why he let Thunberg go uninstructed in the matter of his exit laugh, I might have had several kinds of answers: The laugh wasn't so important; "you must make the best of what you get"; "you can only drive an actor so far and no farther"; etc. Perhaps it was like that. Perhaps it was merely that the Sensualist didn't feel like it just then.

Later in the afternoon I see Gunnar Björnstrand deep in conversation with the make-up man, Börje Lundh. They are inspecting Gunnar's face. They look worried. WINTER LIGHT takes place during three short hours, and the Rev. Ericsson can't very well alter his appearance during that time. But the shooting is going to take a couple of months, and the camera is a sensitive recorder of facial changes. They call Ingmar, and Börje Lundh tells him his trouble:

"Gunnar's getting thin."

"Doesn't matter. On the contrary, we have the climax of the drama ahead of us, it doesn't matter if his face withers up."

But the communion service, the first half of the film. That hasn't been shot yet?

"It doesn't matter if he's a bit hollow-cheeked. Good thing, in fact. Lose a bit more weight!"

Gunnar Björnstrand answers with a nod, rather tired after the nervous strain of the day:

"Well, as it's not a *physical* part ...."

I go with IB into his office. Yesterday's crop of stills is lying developed on his desk. Unsorted. It must be sifted out carefully. Some stills are quite impossible to use: blurry, expressionless— but it's enough if two or three are good. And one must weed out the ones that are unfavorable to the actors. A short sermon on this subject: the director's duty not to leave his actors unprotected.

".... and you must take *damn* good care of your actors. The public are on them like vultures, laughing with malicious pleasure whenever they seem the least bit ugly or absurd. Just think how

114

actors are exposed! Take Bibi Andersson now, going to play in your film and leaving herself quite unprotected from you— you don't know anything but only have a feeling, a willpower to offer."

This afternoon, incidentally, he put forward a hypothesis about the difference between the actors who have "skill" and those who have "technique." I didn't grasp what he meant and asked him for examples of those who had "technique." He picked two out of many: Harriet Andersson and Bibi Andersson.

"As soon as they know up here (gesture to the head) how a part is to be played, they know also *how* they're to do it. "Technique" leads unswervingly to the goal. "Skill," on the other hand, can stand in its own light. That often happens with Gunnar: that he stands in his own light. Because he has skill. But not technique, in this sense. But Gunnar is a wonderful instrument that one must take great care of."

At five o'clock we see yesterday's rushes: suddenly there is a spot on half of the material! Discussion as to where the fault can be. "Muck on the lens," probably. The spot must have come there during reloading, it was not in the scenes 79-80, only in the subsequent ones.

"And the sound's not good. Just as bad now as at the beginning. That harsh metal tone. A goddam awful snuffly canned sound, Stickan. *Isn't it?*"

"Yes, in the bass."

"The *bass*, it's not only in the bass. The whole damn thing's wrong. It's not *quite* so bad as the first day, I'll admit. But the *freshness* isn't there. There's no freshness. The sound in what we ran yesterday was so awfully good, it was clean and fresh. I don't understand why you don't hear that in your earphones? A practiced ear like yours ought to be able to hear that."

When I write out these pencil notes from the screening room, I can see two or three different reactions in front of me. I remember a conversation with Carl Anders Dymling; it was when Ingmar made THE DEVIL'S EYE; Carl Anders groaned over how pedantic Ingmar had become over the years: " .... he makes such terrible demands on himself, on everyone .... "; in his voice I fancied I heard a longing for the years in the past when IB was a brisk young fellow who had no time for petty details; it costs the company money if the director makes big demands.

I see the reactions of the fellow-workers, in one long falling scale: from those who are stimulated by the demands to those who wearily shake their heads; and between the head-shakers and IB is a state of war which constantly explodes in unpleasantness.

I see IB's own impotent rage at the creaking, imperfect machinery to which he is exposed. Yesterday and today everyone has lived at high tension in order to give of his best in the vestry scene; tomorrow everything can turn out to be in vain on account of "muck on the lens." The painter needs paints, canvas and brush. The writer manages with pen and paper. But anyone who wants to create with film is dependent on a terribly intricate process of production in which nothing must go wrong— but in which a thousand defects can arise, starting with the raw-film supplier who sells a product with faulty emulsion.

This morning Ingmar and Sven Nykvist were down at Röda Kvarn at a check screening of THROUGH A GLASS DARKLY; both return in dejection; the copy was "goddam awful."

"It was lousy. Sven thought so too. Always the same old story: dust and scratches and muck."

Sigh; sardonic laugh.

"The only thing I can console myself with: If you think a film is good, you don't give a damn for the technical side."

UNDATED, OCTOBER 1961

Part of Katinka's job is to check every morning whether Ingmar has cut or altered any of the lines. His copy of the script is on his director's desk (together with a box of Droste's chocolate and a packet of stomach-soothing biscuits). I pick up his copy on one of the first shooting days; he stops me.

"This is nothing to do with you. It's magic. I don't want anyone to look at it."

But he makes very few notes in the script. Camera positions, moves— he has everything in his head.

UNDATED, FALL 1961

Ingmar about Gunnar:

"He has one of the strongest ambitions I know."

WEDNESDAY 11 OCTOBER 1961

During a pause between rehearsal and take in the vestry:

116

"These guys who are to write about my films and haven't the vaguest idea of what they're all about. They haven't even read Luther's shorter catechism!"

THURSDAY 12 OCTOBER 1961
"Bear pacing"

Wherever you are in the studio clutter— you can't mistake those footsteps. A quick clamping, sometimes like that of a happy child who is demanding instant attention ("here I am!"); sometimes motorially dark and commanding:

"Shall we assemble in the vestry?"

Gunnar Björnstrand nods at the thought of the feat of strength ahead:

"120 meters of private devotions."

The vestry resembles a cell. Or a cage. Thomas Ericsson paces about waiting for the fisherman. The camera is standing in the middle of the cage. It follows Thomas to and fro. So all the walls must be in place. This makes everything incredibly difficult: lighting, focus adjusting, schedule of moves .... "Well, *you* spurred me on to it!" Ingmar says to Sven. (Sven happened to tell Ingmar about a similar thing in a Kurt Hoffmann film called MAN HUNT.)

" .... there's just one thing I don't understand," Gunnar Björnstrand says. "Why does he open the cupboard?"

Ingmar:

"Haven't you ever done that? You just *do* things, to feel that you exist."

Gunnar turns this into something of his own with a murmured:

"Automatically, that is. Aimlessly."

In the end everything becomes unbelievably complicated. Ingmar, Katinka, Kalle everyone on the team clinging up among the spotlights and down in the cage Sven Nykvist and Roffe twist like worms around the camera, coiled up on their own cables.

(This "bear pacing" takes nearly the whole day to do and is not a success: on December 6th and January 12th, 1962, Ingmar retakes the lot and simplifies it.)

Last thing in the afternoon: final inspection of the big studio church, before they start using it tomorrow. Ingmar is delighted with the joy-in-handicraft with which the church is built— "because of that it is almost consecrated."

117

FRIDAY 13 OCTOBER 1961

Gunnel Lindblom's confinement is approaching— her close-ups will have to be taken quickly, to be on the safe side. So we move into the big studio church today and Gunnel is given the communion wine (Merlino drink) by the parson.

The handing out of the wafers, on the other hand, can be done later. It is a big long shot from the back; Gunnel's stand-in can be used in that: Sirkka Jehkinen, a Finnish girl whom K. A. found at a café in Falun last fall.

K. A. is stand-in himself today for Allan Edwall. He sits there silently, patiently waiting in his pew, in Edwall's overcoat, hymnbook in hand. He is so like Allan that someone passing greets him: "Hallo, Edwall!"

Late in the afternoon IB agrees to sacrifice five minutes on two American journalists and is away for an hour. Rushes into the studio in high spirits and, at a tearing rate and with a bad conscience, creates two entire positions in three quarters of an hour.

"I learned to do this in the days when I made films in thirty days."

UNDATED, OCTOBER 1961

Gunnar Björnstrand has done as he planned: gone to see another doctor, for a further check-up.

Doctor number two made the same tests as doctor number one, Gunnar says, but the result was quite different this time. Likewise the orders about his health. His blood pressure was found to be much lower than at the first overhaul— he was told to stop taking half of the medicines recommended to him before.

"After a week I stopped taking the lot, and then I felt quite well again."

The pressure of lurking fears lifted, the inner front strengthened— the visit to the new doctor has cancelled the effects of the first visit and psychologically has meant an enormous relief. He can go on working and feel that he is healthy.

MONDAY 16 OCTOBER 1961

First-night nerves

It never gets easier "with the years." The tougher your professional skin gets, the more sensitive you become to the Demands (your own demands, other people's demands, the critics' demands, the public's demands)— and the screw is drawn tighter.

Tonight it's the première at Röda Kvarn of THROUGH A GLASS DARKLY ; tomorrow morning the notices will be in the papers. So shooting is cancelled today and tomorrow.

TUESDAY 17 OCTOBER 1961
The convalescent
I have never seen IB so frail before— he looks like someone who is just recovering from an illness. No loud laughter at today's lunch table; only the softness of the convalescent. Success spreads all over the film town, I note with surprise: happiness expands in water rings out here, just like misery; nobody wants the company's films to be slated. If the newspaper critic only knew how his opinions affect the climate out here!

Wormwood is waiting outside the gates of the film town when IB jumps out of the car and buys the evening papers. ("Typical, isn't it? Anders Ehnmark writes about Antonioni's L'AVENTURA on the literature and arts page in *Expressen*, but Tjerneld's notice of Harriet Andersson is interviewed under headlines like these: "HEAVENS, THE FUSS THEY MAKE! I'M NOT ONE OF THOSE PROFOUND GIRLS." He reacts sharply.

"She shouldn't say things like that." (Shake of the head.) "Not good."

Incidentally it's a double première in the Bergman-Laretei family: this evening Käbi is giving a recital in the small hall of the Concert House— a program of German romantics.

WEDNESDAY 18 OCTOBER 1961
"Oh, how touchy I am today"
The Virginia creeper is turning red on the walls of the film town, and we shoot the visit of the fisherman and his wife in the vestry for the third time. Then we move over to the communion service in the church. At lunch it is the colleagues' day today. Sober, comradely group mood: they have all read Harriet's evening press interviews on the edge of the bed; they both joke and admire: "Isn't she fantastic the way she deals with journalists?!" Ingmar groans aloud to himself ("Oh, how touchy I am today"). Slyly, I decide to experiment with him:

"Do you think Harriet's interview answers can hurt your film in any way?"

119

He rejects the idea with both hands:

"Not in the slightest!"

How can he have swung around so completely since yesterday? Oh, some departmental head out there has criticized Harriet's interview answers; this immediately aroused his defensive instincts:

"They think out here that it's not good for the film, but it's only talk. No-o. Harriet must be Harriet!"

Gunnel lifts her coffee cup gently:

"I think Harriet is never so much Harriet as when she is interviewed."

The touchy mood lasts all day (" .... oh, how I'd like to do something else today! I hate the very thought of work"). But Kābi's notices are dancing around with his own in the pit of his stomach:

"If you only knew what a lesson in indifference I got this morning! I was nearly sick with excitement as I sat waiting for the papers with Kābi's notices. Then I went in with them to her. She half woke up: "Aren't you going to kiss me before you go? I shall sleep till one o'clock," and didn't give a damn about the notices! That's a platform artist for you. She just goes on to the next concert. I'm so envious of that indifference! Me with my dependence on the critics— and it's so goddam humiliating. Did you read the notices? They were mean and nasty. On top of a brilliant concert."

A "coldly charming" concert, someone thought: "brilliant," "chilly," "dazzling emptiness," while someone else found "an inclination for the sentimental." But in the afternoon comes Alf Thoor's notice in *Expressen*:

In really fortunate cases what happens with musicians is that the natural need to impress is slowly ousted by the need to be true — — — Kābi Laretei is one who ought to be able to tell us quite a lot about this. — — — Her concert was like a demonstration against what is out-going and full of effects, a demonstration in favor of simplicity and honesty and directness, a demonstration for bread and against stones. This artistic simplicity often has a deceptive tendency to seem quite obvious.

IB has a favorite word; when he says it, his eyes narrow gravely and the sharp eye-teeth appear:

"That's it *exactly*. He has got the point exactly. You see, five years ago Kābi would come on to the platform like a whirlwind and it didn't matter if her technique was not perfect and she played wrong notes, she captivated everyone with her passion and vitality and charm and all the rest of it. But now. Now she's a meticulously working artist who polishes and polishes and purifies her playing. Ah, he has understood that .... "

Few know the price Käbi has paid for her artistic readjustment: she has lost her joy in playing; at present she does nothing but (I recall her disconsolate smile last summer:) "just work." It's no good assuring her that such a thing is necessary and usual in an artistic development: she mourns the loss and cannot believe that the empty vessel will be filled again.

But the pious (so it is said) can never imagine *either* that "the dark night of faith" can ever end. The night of non-inspiration. Such is the condition of silence: to work in spite of everything. To work *just the same.*

THURSDAY 19 OCTOBER 1961

The autumn rain pours down over the subway. I get off the No. 16 bus at the film town, but over by the newspaper kiosk the indefatigable production manager Lars-Owe Carlberg signals to me with his thumb down:

"Cancelled today. Ingmar has gastric flu."

Someone immediately suspects the worst (" .... I don't think Ingmar *wants* to do this film"). I get a lift home with Börje Lundh in his red Saab; on Karlbergsvägen there are pails with gleaming asters.

FRIDAY 20 OCTOBER 1961

Cancelled today too. What more tangible proof could you have of the film director's key position? Other work can go on even if the boss is ill— here, no one can take his place.

MONDAY 23 OCTOBER 1961

Work again: Gunnar's scenes at the altar. At 9 o'clock he reads *Lift up your hearts to God*; at 11:25 he reads *Our Father*. After lunch he reads the blessing, at 4:05 he gives Märta the communion wine. (But all day long Ingmar is like a schoolboy who keeps looking at his watch; not an exciting school day today.)

TUESDAY 24 OCTOBER 1961

Ingrid does not take communion

At 9:25 Märta Lundberg is given the communion wafer by her

parson and lover. Ingmar asks her to smile.

"She gives a little smile of secret understanding, eh? She has written the letter and thinks he has read it."

K. A. comes in with the Merlino bottle, and now Mārta is given the wine. The time is 10 o'clock.

"This time the smile has faded, Ingrid. Hasn't it? No more expectation. She feels suddenly that it was melodramatic: that wrought up feeling when she decided to go to communion."

(Long afterwards IB told me that Ingrid had spat out the wafer after the take— she doesn't believe; therefore one shouldn't swallow it. Ingrid is not one of the lukewarm uninterested non-believers: she has left the state church, and Ingmar is convinced of her "religious talent.")

WEDNESDAY 25 OCTOBER 1961

When the rushes are shown, Ingmar finds fault with a shot that is too light. I get a lift into town with Sven; it is raining cats and dogs in Valhallavägen:

"Oh, this film that is so sensitive to light! It calls for such a *balancing act* that you ...." (Sven stifles an oath.) "That shot which Ingmar faulted— the electrician had moved a lamp four inches. Just think: four inches!"

"You could have explained it?"

"No, I hate making excuses. Anyway, I should have seen it myself. One should be 100% on one's guard *just* before a take. I know. The slightest bit lax and ...."

The garden of Sophiahemmet private hospital is dark and covered with sodden autumn leaves. Sven sighs.

"Oh, what a profession to have chosen!"

THURSDAY 26 OCTOBER 1961
Stand-in plays the leading part

The press's knowledge of films is really incredible. What do the people who devise the headlines think a stand-in does? Sirkka Jehkinen, to her own astonishment, finds out today from the front page of *Aftonbladet* that she is "playing the leading part" in WINTER LIGHT.

(And Ingmar's fingers are itching. The communion service is going to be an editing adventure; he purrs every day at the thought: "I'd like to get at it immediately.")

122

FRIDAY 27 OCTOBER 1961

Remark after today's rushes:

"They have all sunk into their parts now. Suddenly it's *there*. It can never be explained. But it's always like this. Actually we should retake all the scenes in the vestry from the beginning. They are good as they are, but the difference would be noticeable."

The journey to Dalarna is imminent. But the scenes in the church have not been finished yet.

"Supposing we were to let the church stand until we come home from Dalarna? They would be mad at us, of course. But we have six studios and only two films being made just now."

The other film is Sandrew's VITA FRUN (THE WHITE LADY), one of Arne Mattsson's thrillers. ("They've been out in a swamp, standing in water up to their knees for several nights now," someone said the other day.)

SUNDAY 29 OCTOBER 1961

The loneliness of the director

Only now do I begin to realize how lonely a director really is.

He has his vision. The collective works hard to help him give it visible form, he is dependent for his life on its support. But hardly anyone on the team sees the inside of his vision.

Not so strange perhaps, when an artistic vision has so many different layers. It has intellectual layers that can be presented in words. But it also has emotional layers that become flat and lacking in dimension when they are communicated in words— in fact the author himself is sometimes only half aware of them.

Therefore this gratitude when someone suddenly *has understood.*

A chink of light in the loneliness.

MONDAY 30 OCTOBER 1961

In the midst of the laughter at stories: sudden silence, Gunnar Björnstrand's voice: "Christ's blood shed for you." (Then the same relaxation chatter again.)

Ingrid likes it because there are big, proper acting scenes in WINTER LIGHT, she says. And because Märta Lundberg is a distinct type.

"And of course the fact that she has something in her head! In WILD STRAWBERRIES (and in THE FACE too) I knew so little about what I was really supposed to do."

At 3 o'clock they take down the gallery barrier to shoot a scene with the sloppy organist Blom. A mild delight plays across Ingmar's face when he sees Olof Thunberg work out a sketch of the organ playing. Oh, to have his revenge on all the apathetic, uninterested organists he has known!

"You see, all my childhood I sat on an organ stool in my father's church! I know what I'm talking about."

Meeting at 4:55 in "the Opera" screening room about the trip to Dalarna. Is the lighting plant coming up on Monday? Is the sound bus ready? When will the cutting table be loaded? Will Duvner be there, so that he can mend anything that gets shaken to pieces? Will you arrange for police who will hold back curious people at Finnbacka and the scene of the suicide? Shall we get a snow sling and plastic snow, in case "Our Lord has got the wrong idea about this and gives us fine weather?!" K. A.:

"How has the fisherman shot himself? Through the mouth?" Ingmar:

"I haven't thought of that."

P. S.

Gunnel Lindblom has been delivered of a daughter. We sent our congratulations and her thanks arrived today in the form of a cake for the 3 o'clock coffee from "the youngest communicant."

TUESDAY 31 OCTOBER 1961

Asked IB yesterday about "the loneliness of the director." He responded eagerly. "You'll write about that too, won't you, if you ever do your book? Don't forget!"

WEDNESDAY 1 NOVEMBER 1961

Ingrid does the letter (first time)

Ingrid's day today. I curse myself for not bringing along a tape recorder when I hear the *tone* of his instruction today. Gentle, cautious insight. And the quietness around the letter rehearsal. Only Sven and Katinka are there in the studio.

Ingrid is worried about her enormous speech. (She vanished into the pews for the whole of last week and sat there learning her lines.)

"Little heart, let's take it very easy. This isn't an audition, you know. An engagement doesn't depend on this. We consider you've already been given that."

124

During the take Ingrid is to look straight into the camera, but during the rehearsal IB wants her to say her lines to Gunnar Björnstrand.

"You see, there's a slight danger here .... No, we won't talk about it now. But there is a slight danger that you won't feel it is a face you are talking to."

His voice grows very soft:

"You see, when she gets to that bit about the eczema .... that's the nail through the hands. It hurts her terribly to have to say it. Only an awful tenderness in it. No reproach. And an icy clarity: What for her— if *he* had got the eczema— would only have made her love him still more, makes him love her still less, not at all. Then the bit that she doesn't believe— she says that tenderly."

Ingrid is afraid the reading will be monotonous. Does she vary it enough? She is worried the whole time.

"Remember now one thing, Ingrid. All this about variation, let's forget it. (Laughter.) Let's go for simplicity, stripping down to the bare bone. Let's trust the mental forces within us. The only thing that lasts. You have *everything*. All the technical knowledge— you have only to trust those forces. The moment you start thinking "this is going to be boring," it *will* be boring. Don't you agree, Gunnar? Mediocrities must fall back on technique, eh? and tricks and "variation"! We don't need to. (Laughter. Seriousness:) That's the way with *all* art."

The Museum of Modern Art has a Buñuel week, and over lunch Ingrid asks me what is being shown this evening. Her eyes light up as she remembers:

"NAZARIN?! I've already seen it! I so liked the dwarf and the woman six feet tall. He didn't have a spiteful dwarf-face, but a wonderful goodness. Oh, I remember how that gigantic woman lifted him up .... *like this*. (Gesture, display, she laughs at herself.) But I do everything over again in my imagination, so perhaps it won't be like that at all this evening if you go .... "

Take at 1:50. The camera starts rattling. Ingmar breaks.

"Ingrid, you can go and lie down."

"No thanks," Ingrid replies, and remains seated at the table.

Deep sigh from Bergman's breast:

"One thinks it *couldn't* be simpler: from straight in front and a stationary camera .... Goddam paraphernalia!"

How is it abroad? What about the Germans? Don't their cameras rattle just as much? Yes, replies Sven Nykvist. But they don't care."*

During the coffee break I go over to the stores, in accordance with orders from Carlberg. Lovely thick fur coat, two pairs of boots, rain clothes— it feels like signing for winter gear in the army (though much nicer). It can be cold in Dalarna.

When I get back the rattling camera has been covered over with large quantities of quilts. It looks like the protective measures of a rock-blaster before the explosion.

Time for explosion then.

How beautifully Ingrid does her letter!

THURSDAY 2 NOVEMBER 1961

Three gloomy men go into a huddle up at Filmteknik's super-modern laboratory. As if the sound problem was not enough— there are sparks at the edge of Ingrid's letter! A sort of flaring, veiled effect. A riddle what could have caused it. Sven Nykvist shakes his head. "What *can* it be?" in a persistent murmur.

And in *that* of all scenes!

FRIDAY 3 NOVEMBER 1961

Darkness sets in during the car drive and between Falun and Rättvik wet lumps of snow flicker in the beam of the headlights.

IB arrives late in the evening, happy:

"Exactly the right weather."

SUNDAY 5 NOVEMBER 1961

The military atmosphere increases: at about 5 o'clock the column of SF cars swings around outside the entrance of Siljansborg Hotel. The tires of the trucks scrunch on the frozen gravel. The darkness is perforated red with the rear lights.

The troupe installs itself, occupying room after room. Room No. 3 is turned into dressing rooms. No. 4 into make-up room, No. 5 into editing room; another room is the darkroom.

—

* By degrees IB's despair over the camera rattle grew to such a pitch that in the next film he decided to keep on experimenting. First, every scene was shot as usual, with picture and sound. Then it was shot again, with sound and without picture (the sound was taken "wild"). It fell to the editor's (Ulla Ryghe) lot to fit the sound to the picture. This tedious technique was called "hush-hush." Ulla spent innumerable hours "laying hush-hush."

126

IB returns from a car trip to the shooting locations.

MONDAY 6 NOVEMBER 1961
Dependence on women and dream interpretation
Car to Finnbacka, getting the feel of the classroom
Tension Ingmar-Gunnar

Seldom have I so clearly seen the duplicity in a dependence on women. On the same day, what is more. Right through work and off-time chat.

The Siljansborg Hotel serves a very late lunch; we have a special lunch at 12 o'clock and are alone among rows of white tables. Ingrid Thulin arrived late last night, she lunches with Gunnar Björnstrand at the table behind us. I sit with Ingmar, Ulla Isaksson and Lena, age 17, Ingmar's daughter by Else Fisher in his first marriage. Through the window we see Lake Siljan evaporate in the sun haze.

"Isn't it fantastic up here?"

The serving dishes are passed around, we talk of "slips of the tongue." I relate a typical example from my own experience and am rewarded with disbelief from Ulla and eager assent from Ingmar. (But perhaps he overestimates the individual's capacity for converting psychoanalytical theories into practical self-therapy: "You need only have read a psychology book at some time and then you can put it into practice.")

"How are you feeling? Slept well? No dreams?"

Ulla loves dreams; they open a big, rich, magic world for her, just as they do for Ingmar; he promises to relate a long dream he had last night— but later, this evening; he's unwilling to relate the whole dream when Lena is there. So we get everything in reverse order: the interpretation first, the dream material afterwards.

"In the dream I'm working to .... or rather: the dream is working *for* me to separate my mother and my wife. I've muddled these two up for years and years. And this is depicted in completely clear dream situations— it's fantastic."

For him it is a struggle: in dreams he "fights out" all that "anguished mix-up between wife and mother"; I am struck by the word *anguished*. "But there's a vast difference between perceiving something intellectually and realizing it emotionally"; not until you realize something emotionally does the air go out of the problem.

127

"I suppose that's why for a time I unconsciously sought out younger women: merely in order to get as far away as possible from that tendency to mix things up."

He adds with a smile that he has always been so "goddam frightened of women." The smile grows into a burst of laughter:

"But enthusiasm has always got the better of fear."

We speak of fidelity. We speak of male and female.

"I am female on that point: I must have a mental complication, I must be able to exchange souls with my partner in order to get excited. The ones I've merely been together with for the other thing— well, I can count them on the fingers of one hand. And deep down I am faithful— though no one will believe it. My being is actually fidelity: all those whom I have grown fond of in some way, I am faithful to afterwards."

I'm in no position to check this except on one point: in his way of speaking about people who have meant something special to him. The fact that he hits out bitterly in some directions doesn't surprise me in the least; but this warm loyalty which he *also* shows, that does surprise me— especially when I see how consistent it is, how active, supporting. Often it is a loyalty with quite a bit of professional admiration in it. And a dash of paternal pride.

Lunch is finished. Over coffee Ingmar tries to force Ulla I. into agreeing with his hypothesis that all women *want* to be martyrs— before he hurries out to the SF car.

At the Rättvik Diocesan Center they are flying the flag for the Sixth of November— but along the highroad the atmosphere is one of late winter. The sun is shining on bare ground covered with patches of snow. Ingmar purrs with the feeling of being at home: this Dalarna, full of the smells, sights and discoveries of childhood. Ingrid Thulin is still some distance from *her* childhood, up north in Sollefteå; but she feels something homely in the air and tells a long north-Swedish saga about a remote village with a lot of inbreeding in the cottages:

" .... and when someone died, they buried him and stuck a pipe down to the coffin, so that the parson could pour sand down onto the coffin when he came in the spring to hold the funeral service for the man ...."

Ingrid never ends her stories in the usual way, but with a laugh. Then she is Beauty who turns herself into something else and speaks with an animal voice out of the pile of stones, harsh and laughing. She loves black fairytales— the blacker the better.

The road climbs through the forest.

A sudden huddle of cottages.

Our own cars are already there: the lighting van, the transport vans, the sound bus.

We have come to Finnbacka.

A village stripped bare of all tourist attraction, hidden away and genuine. A slice of Swedish country everyday life, dreary and honest, with TV aerials on the roofs— washed around by this time-less blue haze.

For the view from this height is fantastic: the line of the horizon as far as you can see.

"Just think: to buy this house and live here for a month every year .... "

Steam rises from our mouths in the November cold. Gunnar Björnstrand looks in silence at the solitude around us (I've an idea he shivers inwardly at the thought of having to live here). Not even Ingrid, a north-Swedish girl, seems enthusiastic. Does Ingmar really mean that ugly old two-storied house in front of us? Sure.

"It's the old schoolhouse. It's used for village meetings now."

In there we are going to shoot all the schoolroom scenes.

I remember that when reading the script for the first time I thought the schoolroom was a clever idea for a setting— easy to build in the studio. What's the point of coming all the way up here? Ingmar is no friend of the neo-realism principle that every-thing should be shot in so-called genuine settings.

We enter a schoolroom that bears the stamp of the genuine article. The organ and the blackboard. The notice board with the schoolchildren's drawings. The worn seats and desks. A fire is crackling in an old stove.

This is no ordinary schoolroom. P. A. and Blomkvist have made it genuine like this, with great love of handicraft. What appears to be neo-realistic is not neo-realistic after all— if anything it is an offense against neo-realistic principles. Then why not build every-thing in the studio, just like the church?

Because of the light. And the atmosphere.

When Sven Nykvist and Ingmar eventually see the takes, they do not regret the expedition here. The November light streaming into this schoolroom has a softness and refinement that is superior to anything that can be produced in a studio. The mat sheen over the seats. The whole scale of nuances. And then there is the view through the window thrown in: no backcloths with enlarged photographs of the November landscape. No problems either in getting exterior and interior shots to fit.

"But there's a withered old rowan tree out there that I'd like to get rid of, have you heard? Well, at first the villagers were quite willing to cut it down. For nothing. It had to go anyway. Then they got drunk that evening and asked 500 kronor for the tree. I've sent back word that they can have 75 kronor, not one öre more."

Ingrid and Gunnar move about the schoolroom making themselves at home. The three of them sit down in the seats. Two actors and a director: three grownups with their overcoats on, in the schoolchildren's seats. The logs crackle in the iron stove. I am naively surprised that Ingrid and Gunnar already know their lines so well, they hardly need to look at their parts as they go through the scene.

This is the first run-through: Ingmar just listens. He listens whether they have struck the right note. Feels the atmosphere, watches their bearing. Only a couple of directions from him, now at the beginning. Ingrid reads: *Thomas my dear, it's so hard to stick up for oneself.*

"This is where she starts to cry."

Gunnar reads: *Now Märta, please don't get hysterical.* Ingrid replies: *You always say that when you see me cry.* Ingmar asks her to make the most of the pause. Ingrid nods and goes on: *And I suppose I am a little hysterical.* Ingmar comments:

"She says this very quietly."

The three grownups stand up from the school seats. Now for the second run-through.

Ingmar:

"What about a few moves?" (Pause. He looks around. Pulls his nose.) "Gunnar, if you sit *there*." (He points to a certain seat.) "And Ingrid. Let's see now what you've brought when you come from auntie. Tray. Glass. And the wonder-working pills." (Pause.) "The whole of this scene begins almost with two backs, we're standing over here with the camera." (He goes to the door and shows where the camera will stand. He goes up to Ingrid.) "Märta stands here. And Thomas is nothing but one goddam sullen back."

They start to read the scene. This time directions come thick and

130

fast. Ingrid reads Mārta's line: *Sometimes it sounds almost as if you hated me.*

"She's standing quite still. She has never said this before."

Mārta goes on at him about accompanying him to Frostnäs; Ingmar goes over to Gunnar Björnstrand, who still has his back to Ingrid. Ingmar puts his forehead on the back of Gunnar's neck, begging affectionately; showing Ingrid how to do it.

Mārta is about to ask Thomas if he wants to get rid of her. Ingmar:

"Then you sit down and start touching him."

Mārta asks if she fits "all too well" into the rest of the picture of a parson who has failed.

"Then, Gunnar, you look at her. And laugh."

Mārta says that she "could have been nicer."

"You see: The whole time *she* is the one who is submissive and imploring. And he is the capricious child who hits out all the time."

Mārta apologizes for talking so much.

"You say this eagerly, Ingrid. And give a little laugh."

Thomas starts blaming all the gossip in the village.

"Don't look at her then, Gunnar. He never looks at her when he's lying."

Mārta wonders doubtfully whether *that* is his real reason?

"That's it, Ingrid: make it coarser from the start. *Then* he gets out of his seat."

Gunnar:

"He has finished lying now, and here, when she says *Is that your reason?* he can look at her?"

Ingmar nods:

"Then she starts crying. Though restrainedly. She keeps biting her hands. You, Gunnar, are standing over by the window."

Thomas tells Mārta not to get "hysterical."

"Then, Gunnar, you turn around. And you. Do like this."

Ingmar shows Gunnar how he has pictured the next sit down.

"Not like this. Like *this*."

A mere shade of difference: Ingmar draws back on the seat and sits down with his hands on his knees.

Now comes the hate catalogue: *I'm tired of your fussing solicitude, your twaddle, your good advice, your small candlesticks and tablecloths.*

131

"Say it without emphasis, Gunnar. Look at your hands."
I'm fed up with your short-sightedness ....
"Don't stress 'fed up'. He says it almost kindly."
And Mārta just listens. Ingmar:
"*At last* she hears the Truth. Woman's sensual pleasure in having everything reduced .... "
Thomas says he is "well brought up," Ingmar wants a cutting tone on "well brought up":
"His aggressiveness increases! He's ready to strike her .... this face in which pain lies bare."
Mārta takes off her spectacles.
"She rubs her eyes so that you can *hear* it. She almost presses her eyes in. She doesn't cry *now*."
Mārta realizes that she has "done wrong" to Thomas, the whole time.
"Are we agreed, Ingrid, about playing it like that— the whole time she has used the wrong tactics with him? Instead of resisting him and being his opposite, she has always gone along with him, put up with everything .... for fear of losing him. She has put herself first. Egotistically. For fear of losing him."
But when Mārta gives way to her distress and anxiety for Thomas, he loses his temper: *Can't you be quiet. Can't you leave me alone.*
"That's where it breaks loose! You take hold of her. Like this!"
Ingmar grips Ingrid's arm roughly. So roughly that he is instantly afraid he has hurt her:
"Did I grip you too hard? Forgive me, Ingrid."
Ingmar takes a new grip. More carefully. Shows Gunnar.
"Then he moves away here, eh? So as *not* to hit her."
Thomas goes right out into the hall before turning back to ask Mārta to go with him to Frostnās after all.
"Cut his *I'll try to be nice*, we'll cut that out. Then she looks up at him. She's quite different now. And Gunnar! When you stand out there in the hall, let's *see* quite clearly that he's not equal to being alone. (Pause.) Shall we run through it once more?"
This third time Gunnar and Ingrid start using the moves. Mārta says: *Sometimes it sounds almost as if you hated me*; Ingmar whispers:
"Then a smile, Ingrid: surely it can't be as bad as that?"
Ingmar interrupts Gunnar in the hate-catalogue:

"Don't rush it, Gunnar. That speech will *hold* as long as you like. It's like retching. He has *never* said this before."

Ingmar himself is violently emotional when he explains this; he strikes the desk with his fist; *your weak stomach, your eczema, your periods, your frostbitten cheek.*

"You just reckon it all up, bit by bit, as you think of it."

Mārta wonders what will "become of" Thomas without her. *You'll go under, Thomas my dear.* Ingrid ponders:

"Shouldn't there be a little aggressiveness in that line?"

Ingmar, gravely:

"None at all. She just knows that separated from her he *is* lost."

Sten Lindén pops his head round the door:

"Like some coffee?"

His whisper is extra distinct in the silence and crackle from the fire; and Ingmar declines with extra eagerness, extra pleasantness:

"No thanks. Thank you. Thanks awfully all the same, but .... "

Ingrid grows thoughtful and regretful:

"Then I did the letter wrong. The end of the letter. She should still be ruled by an egotistical love."

"No, you did the letter absolutely right. You see, that letter was written in a moment of clear sight. Then reality rolls back over her. But here, now, the clear sight has returned. And it *remains*, from now on. There's a straight line from here up to the intercession at the end in the church. In the letter it was an *intuitive* clear sight. Here it is a clear sight that has come true, if you understand what I mean. Not until now does she get the strength to give up everything."

Ingrid ponders, listens, takes in the explanation bit by bit. And once again Thomas is standing out in the hall, asking Mārta to go with him to Frostnäs.

"Gunnar. Don't look at her now. They're so severe with each other now. Be quite bare about it."

End of the third run-through.

The tension resolves itself in a typical Bergman-Björnstrand ping-pong match: the sarcastic remarks bounce to and fro.

"It's not so goddam easy," Gunnar says about the exceptionally difficult scene.

Ingmar gives him a piercing look.

"Isn't it?"

"For you, yes!" Gunnar says, knowing what hard work writing

can be. "You wrote this in a morning, of course! It practically wrote itself."

Ingrid sits down at the organ and plays. Gunnar and Ingmar look at the children's drawings. They wander about the classroom, relaxing. The stove crackles with burning wood. November closes in outside the windows. Ingmar talks to someone about the stove:

"Use coal in it tomorrow, will you, because of the sound. The wood crackles too much, we can't have it like that."

I could feel how everyone was affected during this rehearsal hour. The atmosphere in the house. The scene that came alive, in here, between these school seats. And Ingmar's female ambivalence, which I recognize so well from myself.

How he defended men and attacked women's qualities today, during lunch: mothers who demand everything for themselves, women who cultivate their masochism— but just now, when he was directing Ingrid, it is the woman who is big and deep and genuine in her feelings, and the man who is little, pitiable, because he cannot love. *Ever since I was born,* Thomas groans, *I have learned that women are higher beings, creatures to be admired, inviolable martyrs*; and Ingmar tugs at the halter like a tethered animal: at one moment he kicks out at this faith in women's exalted position; at the next he accepts it, as if he thought it was true, and lives with it.

Darkness has set in when we drive away, down the long slope from Finnbacka village. Tiredness and small talk. The work has taken about an hour. Ingmar mimics the villain in Japanese films, Ingmar mimics the Japanese heroine who "should preferably cry the whole time." Ingrid speaks of Glenn Ford, who was her leading man in THE FOUR HORSEMEN. She liked his professional know-how. She went to dancing classes in Los Angeles. There she learned the best things during her time in America. She describes the dancing teacher. The Sixth-of-November flag is hanging slack in the dusk outside the Rättvik Diocesan Center.

So this day ends as it began: with women, and dreams about women.

Over dinner IB analyzes a best-selling woman writer: her particular form of "deceitfulness," the "iron-hard intuition" with which she steers her life— he does it with a brilliant bias.

We slip into the library with our coffee. Books from the 1920s are resting in a locked glass case. No one borrows them. The room smells mahogany brown: dark walls, dark furniture, leather sofas. The coffee cups clink against the thick glass table top. In the evenings you see a bridge group or two in here. A cozy room? To me it is uncomfortable in its bareness, with its flavor of tired, old, well-worn middle-class respectability. Ingmar loves it and closes the door so that we can be alone. Ulla is to have the dream he promised her.

"Actually it was two dreams. In the first I was together with a woman whom I knew once. And the room we were in .... well, it was a mixture of the nursery at the Sophiahemmet rectory and my present home at Djursholm. I heard my mother's voice and was furious— couldn't I be left alone now?"

As the dream goes on he runs down the stairs, back up again, throws his arms around a woman's knees— and this woman at one moment is his wife Kābi, at the next his mother. Then she's Kābi again. And then his mother again.

"If anyone told this dream people would say that it's too much arranged. In a novel it would certainly seem too neat and smooth. But I can swear that it *was* like that."

Ingrid keeps away from the dining room and the public gaze: she hides in her two rooms, has dinner there, spends whole evenings by herself. But Gunnar is with us in the library, drinking coffee, listening. Ingmar tells his dream No. 2, in which he found he had been locked up in a prison— "for some idealistic reason."

"I'm in this prison. I am to be there for three days. When I entered the cell .... oh, I forgot that in the corridor there's a fountain splashing. But in the cell are three women: Bertha Sånell (who is in charge of the clothes in the film); someone who resembles Kābi; someone who resembles my mother (or grandmother). I decide to conquer them in this one way: by keeping silent. They are not going to get *one word* out of me."

That dream sticks in Gunnar's memory. He thinks it has a striking symbolism. We have a sandwich late in the evening; this is how he regarded it:

"Has it occurred to you what it was about? About someone who is watched over from all sides: by an SF representative (Bertha Sånell); by wife; by mother .... But in the corridor is a fountain. And that fountain splashes quite freely."

There is a tension between Ingmar and Gunnar. It has evidently increased the last few days. What it consists of I don't really know yet. With Gunnar I notice a feeling of not being free; an idea that Ingmar has a deep contempt for actors, "and when you've done a good job, you still don't get the credit for it yourself." With Ingmar I notice an aggressiveness which he cannot camouflage: his tone is sharp, and Gunnar tightens up still more. Gunnar is silent or aggressive in return. Ingmar seems disappointed. Gunnar too. How is that tension going to affect the film?

Sometimes I get the idea that this is a familiar state for them: for years they have been used to living in this kind of tension with one another. It appears so from the outbursts: they argue together with a terrible routine and drill, with the brilliant gaiety of two who have seen through most layers in each other. A friendship of twenty years lies behind this. And during the last ten years GB has been in nearly every one of IB's films— often in a leading part. (And not just *any* leading part: almost always Gunnar has had to play the parts in which Ingmar has portrayed himself. Through Gunnar, Ingmar has lashed himself time after time.)

I make a note of the matter now, but I don't know what I shall do with it. I shall have to ask Gunnar and Ingmar if they will agree to my mentioning it. In one way it's a purely private matter. In another way it is part of the work. I wouldn't have thought that a couple of years ago.

This is the side of theater and film work that is the most difficult to describe. Workers in the theater are convinced that the public will only stand the front view; and when the interviewers come from the weekly press the actors have a modest new part ready: they act the private version of the picture the public has of them, of their image. They know an awful lot about each other's private ego. In the hotel room on tour when the performance is over, in the dressing room while the radio churns out music— then they dissect their colleagues with a knowledge of human nature which is often brilliant, with a professional eye which swings between what is ice-cold and what is indulgent. That is then. But outwardly they defend themselves and each other. Outwardly they build a barrier. Actors display so much else to the public: body, voice, appearance, talent, lack of talent, the entire physical person with all its charm and blemishes and easily-parodied idiosyncracies— so can't they have their behind-stage problems in peace? Their rehearsal conflicts? Their internal worries? I can well understand their need of protection.

But some of the greatest achievements in theater and film have grown out of a violent conflict between two parties— more often than not a director and an actor or actress. In Swedish theater there are a couple of such relations at least: they have lasted for years and years, and had all the characteristics of love-hate— but out of *that* conflict some of the greatest performances have been created. Each has done great things on his own, but when they have forced themselves to work together the great creative tension has come about: two poles— and an outburst.

It is one of the most fascinating and private aspects of this work. It would be a pity to have to gloss over it and pretend that the torment, the nerves, the tension were not there.

TUESDAY 7 NOVEMBER 1961

Nerves on edge and comments in the screening room
"Theater in the room"

"Good advice to observers: don't neglect any one part. The two hours you're away are always the most important, because that's just when they take the scenes you're most anxious not to miss ...." writes Lindsay Anderson in his film diary, *Making a Film*, 1952; the best reportage that has been written on this subject.

Sure enough; at dinner today Ingmar says:

"Pity you didn't come along to Finnbacka today!"

"What happened?"

"Hard to describe. But Ingrid and Gunnar were to go through the beginning of their scene. I let them act the whole scene, so that everyone could see what the moves were. They all stood around the walls in the schoolroom, watching— the studio hands, the electricians, the sound technicians. And then: when Ingrid and Gunnar felt that they had an audience— then they acted for all they were worth. It spurred them on, it gave them something extra .... and you know, when Gunnar has to go out into the hall at the end, they automatically gave way to let him out. I looked at Lennart Nilsson, the photographer, he's up to make a reportage about us for *Se*: he was so moved that he cried. That was really 'theater in the room'."

Ingmar's eyes light up.

"And, you know, that's all that's needed to perform a play."

Why, of course. That's how he began a lecture at the University of Stockholm a year or two ago: he asked the students what was needed to perform a play. An old device that he had formerly used on the pupils at the Malmö City Theater. The result is always the same: all come with their "spotlights," "cyclorama" and all the other modern theatrical equipment; and when the list has grown long enough, IB says stop and begins a process of elimination. Is a cyclorama necessary? No. Etc. Finally only three things remain which are essential for the performance of a play.

A place to act it on— if only a stage of planks on trestles.

A text to act.

An audience to act for.

That trinity exists today, in the schoolroom at Finnbacka.

Not until towards the end of the meal does Ingmar bring out the day's good happening. First of all the bad has to come out, the irritation that has been piling up during the day: "Gunnar and Ingrid are quite crazy now." Ingrid is having dinner in her room as usual, but Gunnar is sitting just behind Ingmar, can overhear everything if he likes; and Ingmar certainly doesn't lower his voice: "My own nerves are all on edge now."

He makes his way through the asparagus soup and the fish and reaches the apple dumplings. Then he stretches, tries to laugh:

"The worst of the nervous tension is beginning to relax now."

I can see how the sense of well-being spreads, especially when we have looked at the rushes of the last few days at the cutting table.

"To think that no one has ever had the idea of bringing along a cutting table on location! And that it took me such a long time to get the idea!"

Room No. 605 on the groundfloor hotel corridor (the corridor to the TV room) has been turned into a cutting room. A neat row of reels, with a plastic cover spread over them— the editor Ulla Ryghe has arranged her room in perfect order.

"The trouble is," he sighs, "that once you're used to running films like this, you never want it any other way. You don't want to let it go."

The blind is drawn down. Ingrid's face appears in the little projection frame of the cutting table. She is Märta Lundberg, reading her letter. Gunnar's face appears: Thomas Ericsson listening to Märta's letter.

"Isn't it fantastic, Gunnar's face? How intense he is at first, and is the actor ...."

Ingmar demonstrates.

" .... and then it is filled from within. Gets more and more bare, filled with shame. That transformation, eh?! In the first take it didn't come until I had said *cut*— only then did he drop all acting. That's why I retook it. And got this!"

After seeing the rushes over the coffee cups, he imitates his English distributor, Cy Harvey, who has criticized his present pictorial language:

"Ingmar, why don't you move your camera anymore?"

These fixed positions, with very few trackings and pannings, are evidently not to Cy Harvey's taste. Does Ingmar resent such criticism?* Somewhere, perhaps— although the criticism is superficial. Here is yet another person who doesn't understand what he's aiming at and who thinks that an itinerant camera would be an improvement.

"I like Cy very much. He doesn't know anything about art, but he's a wonderful businessman."

The strained nerves have relaxed; well-being spreads in rings around him; he says that the American publishers Simon and Schuster have come with a new offer. The first book, FOUR SCREENPLAYS, was so successful ("guess what I earned on the USA edition alone? 65 000 kronor!") and now they want to follow it up with another volume. This time they want six of his screenplays.

"Are you going to?"

"I don't know."

He is proud of the offer, happy, attracted— it is a little more balm on old wounds that have not yet healed. But as always he is ambivalent about the actual publication. Is it wise to bring out old scripts? And does he need any more balm from abroad?

WEDNESDAY 8 NOVEMBER 1961
Ingrid weeps in the schoolroom
"Chinese torture"
Ingmar's self-destruction

Morning at the hotel: eggs, toast, porridge. Cornflakes with stewed apples or prunes. Wine party in a room last night— I am limp and sluggish. Ingmar's footsteps down the hotel staircase seem all

—

* But examine the difference between the use of the camera in WINTER LIGHT and the next film, THE SILENCE.

the more violent, thundering out his morning energy. " .... But none of the women I have lived with has ever been at her best in the mornings. Only myself. I'm always in a hell of a good mood."

The technicians have already left. So have Ingrid and Gunnar. Gunnar has a cold coming on. Ingmar, with sober sympathy:

"You know how it feels for an actor if his throat and voice don't function? What shall we do if he gets ill? Everything depends on that. He knows that we must call it off if he does.

I go with Sven Nykvist and Ingmar. They speak of Lennart Nilsson, the photographer. It turns out that Sven has some adventurous memories in common with Lennart Nilsson: ten years ago they endured hardships in the mountains and both nearly collapsed. Two photographers, both stubborn by nature— under their reserved Swedish exterior. Ingmar loves that obsessed trait in Lennart Nilsson:

"You'd never think he was such a passionate type. But he is. Once he gets an idea, he never gives it up .... And so goddam generous."

With that obsession Lennart Nilsson threw himself into the study of ants and published a wonderful picturebook about their life. Now he is photographing the development of the human fetus. He has a couple of series with him and shows them to Ingmar. "Incredible pictures!" Man's first nine months; all stages, right from the recently fertilized egg.

We rush past a black car. It is old-fashioned, and bounces along like a horse carriage. The driver has our hotel badge on his uniform. Sometimes he forces the car to a dizzy pace. A museum piece of a car to belong to a modern hotel. In the back seat Ingrid and Gunnar are sitting, enjoying the slow tempo. They give a dignified wave to our racer.

An hour's drive through the November morning. Pulp wood, dark and damp, is stacked up beside the ditch. Some workmen are busy with an unloading crane which, with a claw-grip, lifts the wood onto the truck. The huge grab-claw suggests all sorts of things: it is a striking vision. Ingmar gazes at it with all his hungry interest in reality. Leans back and yawns pleasurably at the thought of last night. He has rented a TV set up here. ".... Oh, it's so nice to have your own TV in the room. To sink down after the exertions of the day and relax in front of the TV. Last night they showed a terribly boring propaganda film from Angola, made by the Americans.

140

Blacks rushing out of the jungle and pressing the Americans' hands and shouting: FREEDOM, FREEDOM. Oh dear."

We have reached the turn off to Finnbacka. SF has put up a temporary green signpost, so that all our cars can find the way. The road climbs up through the forest.

"We're driving straight up into the clouds."

Yes, everything is in cloud today. A mist is trailing its fringes over the heights of Finnbacka: the schoolhouse is hidden inside it. But the inside of the cloud is a hive of activity. Electric cables coil across the wet grass. One of our men is patching up the artificial tree that P. A. has had set up. The workmen have grey SF overalls. Field equipment is good to have now.

"Why, look! The rowan tree has been cut down!"

The peaceful schoolroom has been changed into a film studio, the entire house is full of cameras, sound and light equipment. Handkerchiefs and talk of colds. The black car drives up with Ingrid and Gunnar.

"How's the invalid patrol?"

The mist has consequences for the day's job. Just now, in the car, Ingmar and Sven agreed to retake yesterday's first shot, "the one against the window." It's no good. There's a thick mist outside the window. The light will be all wrong. And the shot won't fit in with the others.

"We'll have to take a close-up instead. Until the fog lifts."

Ingmar sits down in Ingrid's seat, thinking. Shall he have a track shot? No, he rejects the idea: "It'll be too hard to cut it in." So they'll have a fixed position on Ingrid. A close-up as she listens to Thomas's sudden hate-catalogue. She has her eyes towards Gunnar Björnstrand— that is, towards the camera. How much is the close-up to comprise? "Either an extreme close-up, Sven, or else we'll take a Bergman position and cut here." He gives a little laugh as he says "Bergman position." I ask Sven why Ingmar likes just that cutting of the picture? "It gives balance to the shot— not to cut here, in the middle of the breast, but here, just under the edge of the desk. Have a look for yourself in the camera."

At 9:40. IB has decided to give up the Bergman position in favor of a more extreme close-up of Ingrid Thulin, with the 35 lens. Ready for the day's first rehearsal: from Now Mårta, please don't get hysterical, to Mårta's smile I can hardly see you without my glasses. A good four pages of the script! Gunnar sits beside the

141

camera and gives Ingrid her cues.

After the rehearsal:

"We won't have you beside the camera, Gunnar. You can sit a little farther away. Otherwise Ingrid won't be looking in the right direction, her gaze will rove in your direction, it's better if she does the scene straight into the camera."

At 10:00. Another rehearsal. I'm astonished. Ingrid weeps this time too. The tears glisten under her eyes. I ask Gullan Westfeldt, the make-up girl, if she has put anything on.

"Nothing," Gullan whispers. "And what about yesterday! When she did one retake after the other, and cried every time! By herself."

At 10:05. Ingmar talks to Gunnar, quietly, very subdued:

"Gunnar, he just sits there *brooding*."

"You mean, I must keep it almost at the read-through stage?"

"Yes, it's so important that this scene is not *acted*, you see. That he just sits like this and has the hatred *inside* him. Then it will come of its own accord, the whole lot, in the skin and in the eyes."

At 10:20-10:25. Take 1 (with the 35 lens). Incredible shades of expression in Ingrid's face— and the tears just pour down. When Ingmar says "Cut!" Ingrid mumbles that she has missed a pause. Her face is wet with the tears— she herself is the actress who knows that she missed a pause.

She searches for a resting point in her nervous tension; finds it on the floor, between the teacher's desk and the organ. Spreading out her sheepskin coat, she lies down, with lamp stands and cables right against her. Just now Ingmar was fiddling with the geography globe and it came apart; Åland is mending it, right against Ingrid's feet, with K. A.'s help. Lennart Nilsson discovers what a picture is waiting for him: tall enough in himself, Lennart grows up to the ceiling when he climbs to a seat to get a glimpse of Ingrid down on the floor.

At 10:35. Take 2 (now with the 50 lens). Ingmar calls for silence — and K. A.'s voice rumbles through floorboards and up steps: "*Silence up there!*" Then the whole house falls silent; even the mice stop nibbling down in the cellar; it's so quiet that I can hear a knee joint creak when someone changes position.

In this silence the only sound is a soft hum; what is it? Oh yes, the camera.

When Ingrid reaches the point in the scene where the tears should come— well of course they come. How many times is this?

What extraordinary demands filming makes on the actors. Now Ingrid sits there playing a difficult scene with Gunnar— but it's not him she is looking in the eyes; it's the camera. (She doesn't look straight into the camera, however, but at the edge of the frame that surrounds the camera opening.) It must be done like this during the shooting; otherwise it will look peculiar on the screen when the film is shown.

At 10:30. "Right. Now let's have the equivalent on Gunnar Björnstrand." The camera on Gunnar; Ingrid's turn to sit behind.

Big regrouping: everything has to be moved, lamps, cables, camera; but the mist has lifted so much that it is *too* light outside now. Sensitive adjustment. Gunnar's black figure has to be outlined against the schoolroom window— and Sven Nykist asks for yellow filters. Åland and Håkan bring armfuls of filter material, they climb up and stretch it between the double windows, so that the entire panes are covered with filter.

Lunch upstairs. One great big table for the crew; a small room for director and actors. Ingrid looks for a new floor to rest on: the wooden floor downstairs— she likes to have something hard to lie on when she relaxes; in the church in the big studio she could lie for hours on one of the pews, as invisible to the world around her as at Siljansborg, where she always disappears into her room (rather Garbo-ish). Ingmar:

"Ingrid is like the beaver at Skansen. Everyone stares at it but can never catch more than a glimpse. It doesn't even appear at feeding time."

At 12:30. Take 1. (Börje has butterflies.) Gunnar stumbles slightly over *anxious tokens of affection* in the hate-catalogue; Ingmar breaks off the shot and retakes the beginning. Before, it began with Gunnar sitting down. "But there's something that doesn't hang together here, and Gunnar doesn't get the right start to his scene." Better to begin with Gunnar standing over by the window: that will be a better start. "Can we take the whole walk over to the seat?" Sven nods and begins to reset the lights.

At 12:40. Now Sven has reset the lights so that the scene can begin with Gunnar by the window. GB rehearses the new beginning, so that Sven can check whether he can follow the walk in the camera. (Sven is working with the Newall camera today, the one that

143

has the least motor hum. But the Newall has a side viewfinder—with parallax adjustment; it calls for enormous skill to decide by means of the side viewfinder whether the actor is right in picture or not.)

Thomas Ericsson leaves the window, on the way to tell Märta Lundberg that he doesn't love her.

"When you've sat down, Gunnar: sit without saying anything at first. Then comes the hatred. You know, it's the hangman setting about the execution. That's it! *Now* it feels right."

Rehearsal. Thomas leaves the window, sits down, starts talking. IB breaks off:

"Now you've started reckoning up in the Gunnar way. If you kept your hands in your pockets, you'd have the right abstraction.

Typical IB detail: hands in pocket— in order to release the right inflection. Practical behaviorism in the film studio: make the movement, then the state of feeling will come.

GB starts again, bearing in mind not to make a reckoning up this time. IB breaks off just as brusquely:

"No, now you're *preparing* a reckoning up. If you just started, and then let your rage carry you on .... do you see?"

This time GB is allowed to go on undisturbed until *Have a look. I can stand it.* Ingmar corrects the inflection:

"*Have a look.* All the hatred of a bad conscience in that look! And you look away when she starts talking. All you think is: to hell with it all, to hell with her, to hell with .... Now let's try and take this."

At 12.55. "Silence!" IB tries to relax his eagerness and create calm: "And, Gunnar! We'll take this scene a couple of times— so take it easy .... "

Take 1. GB begins. I hear Gunnar's voice, he's in the middle of the hate-catalogue now, but I also hear the motor hum of the camera. IB breaks the take with a tired, tense, angry voice:

"The camera's rattling enough to wake the dead."

Sven:

"Sometimes it makes a noise, sometimes it's quite silent."

Ingmar, sourly:

"I think it makes a noise all the time."

Sven:

"Change the magazine."

144

Peter Wester, assistant cameraman, changes the magazine.
Ingmar:
"What is there to guarantee it's any better? It's been out in the cold."
Sven:
"It has been inside."
Peter is hard at work.
Ingmar:
"Hurry up now. No time to waste."
I look about me. Åland is sitting on a chair, rubbing his chin. Gerhard Karlsson, electric foreman, looks over his shoulder at the children's drawings on the wall. Börje Lundh asks Sven Nykvist "What happened to Roffe?" Sven says: "I'll tell you later." Ingmar sits beside Ingrid near the camera, talking to her. I go down to them.

They are talking in a low voice, discussing one of Märta's last lines in this scene: *What's to become of you— without me?* Ingrid is sitting in her typical way, thoughtful, introspective, groping for a firm hold on the line. (When she is tired and relaxed, her voice has a kind of hoarse lack of expression, a raspiness all its own.) Evidently Ingrid wants to say the line more sharply than Ingmar had thought of it: perhaps she has a woman's desire to strip the woman? I ask Ingrid afterwards: Well, she finds it hard to make the line express what Ingmar means— whichever way it is said, she thinks, it sounds feminine and egocentric. *What's to become of you— without me?* It can easily sound like feminine self-pity in all its glory, she thinks of it as "harsher," she says.

But this is how Ingmar explained it, while they were waiting for the magazine to be changed: he spoke quietly, with an undertone of great gravity:

"She sees into hell, you see. It's more of a horror, you see: an awful horror. She doesn't even have to turn to him as she says it .... this is no longer a question of 'her' or 'not her'. She is outside it. She merely sees that he is heading straight for hell. The real, ghastly hell. Damnation— loneliness."

Ingrid demurs, in a drawl:

"She may feel that there are other women who are just as good for him as she is."

Ingmar:

"That thought is unrealistic. No, it's like this: in a moment of

145

love's insight she *sees* this— he *is* heading for absolute damnation. Do you see what I mean?"

Ingrid, hoarsely, tonelessly:

"But I'm not sure I know how it's to be done. (Smiles.) Come to think of it, I never have known how anything is to be done."

Ingmar:

"One surely has to have a little confidence in the creative forces within one?"

Ingrid:

"I have no confidence."

Ingmar, moved, quietly:

"No, I know."

Now the magazine has been changed. A blanket is wrapped around the camera against the hum. In addition they borrow Ingrid's sheepskin coat and lay it on top of the blanket. In these few moments the feeling between Ingmar and Ingrid changes into growling laughter which relieves the tension.

Ingmar:

"In the words of Torsten Hammarén: 'I don't give a damn what you think, as long as you have voice and gesture.' There's a lot in it. You can think *pancakes* if you like."

Ingrid laughs:

"All right, I will. Because I feel hungry when I look as if I'm suffering."

(In the afternoon when I get back to the hotel and write out the day's notes: This weighing and balancing! If you put so much fear of women into one scale, then of course you must put an enormous weight into the other scale: only *she* can save him. The more disgust Thomas pours out, the greater is Márta's task of salvation. How inextricably this belongs together: the compulsion to debase what one exalts. Shame, guilt; and the new compulsion: to exalt what one has debased. Typically male or not, from *this* pendulum movement IB directed Ingrid Thulin today. But perhaps it is foreign to her? Perhaps *that* was why she never quite understood IB and was very little helped by his explanation?)

At 1:15. Take 2. Once again IB interrupts GB in the middle of the hate-catalogue. Gunnar sits there in silence. I imagine I can feel the tension that GB finds himself in. Ingmar says:

"You must feel the weight in it. You must get away from being alert. From articulating it. (Nicely:) Otherwise it's absolutely

146

right. You just pick up the lines a little too much; you make them *alert*."

Gunnar answers heavily:

"I can't get the hang of this. I can't do it."

His voice is depressed, deprecating and appealing.

Ingmar looks grave. He scowls, but controls himself. Pause; then he hands out the rebuke, like a schoolteacher making a particularly grave criticism with an extra-light, reproachful tone:

"That's surely not the thing to say, Gunnar?"

Then he repeats what he said just now; more calmly:

"You're doing it exactly right now, rhythmically and everything. But you're making it alert. A little accent crops up just as you start to play the scene. It's as if that hum from the camera put you on the alert. (He gives a little laugh. Restrained, rather appealing to GB:) I did say we'd take this several times, didn't I? Let's take it now – and maybe in a day or two we'll retake the lot."

New take.

This time IB does something unusual. He gives an instruction during the actual take. While the camera is running he says to GB: "Take that last line again— with pause and everything!" GB does so. Technically this gives rise to no difficulties; the scene is going to be cut to pieces anyway later on, with cut-in shots on Ingrid; then IB will cut out his own words of direction. And both actor and director gain a great deal by not having to retake the scene from the beginning, again.

"There, you see, Gunnar! Now it was suddenly quite right!"

To Sven:

"But why was the camera suddenly quiet, and running without a sound? All of a sudden it's *dead quiet*."

Sven:

"It has been overhauled mechanically .... "

Ingmar:

"I don't give a damn if it has been overhauled or not, it just shows that something *is* wrong, somewhere, however many times it's overhauled."

Sven:

"Here in Sweden the Newall hasn't the service it should have."

Ingmar:

"Then we'll retake this with the 50. And now Gunnar, go and lie down for a bit."

Gunnar, relieved after the tension:

"I'd rather not."

Ingmar, more kindly:

"That goddam camera!"

Sven:

"I think the Americans are right to have a camera specialist with them every day of shooting."

Börje Lundh takes part in the conversation; they start discussing the Mitchell cameras.

Ingmar:

"Sven, let's not forget when this film is finished, we'll never do anything more with this camera."

Sven:

"It will be sent away to the factory."

Ingmar laughs; the tension between him and Sven has slackened now:

"It must be sent away. Not to the factory. *Away*."

Sven:

"It gives me a duodenal ulcer."

Ingmar:

"It gives me *one* of my duodenal ulcers. I have the sound too. That makes two ulcers."

I speak to Börje Lundh, who is seismographically sensitive to atmosphere.

"It's as if the mood of the scene itself were infectious. When the content of a scene is unpleasant, it can be felt in the air all over the room."

At 1:40. Take 4 on GB, now with the 50 lens: no walk from the window, Gunnar sits in shot from the start. He has hardly begun—this time a distinct drip-drip-drip can be heard on the window pane. It ruins the whole scene and Ingmar has to break.

New take.

"No, stop! Heavier, Gunnar. And calmer. And more naked. You must articulate the lines *inside* you— before you say them. You did it so well when you walked into the shot— it was like a heavy hammer."

New take. A successful one.

"*Good*, Gunnar! Do you know the nice thing that happened now? The bit that sagged in the middle of the first take (with lens 35) was nice and taut here. Now I have both takes to choose

148

from."

IB stretches.

"Let's put an end to the agony for today. There are limits to Chinese torture."

He stands up.

He gives a laugh.

"Even my sadism has its limits."

At 2:00. Oh, outside the schoolhouse .... On the sloping meadow is an empty hay-drying hurdle. It is rain-black against the wet grass— and with the thin, Japanese line pattern of the electricity wires above it. The sky now is as overcast with grey clouds as when we came this morning. The drizzle *splashes* in our faces.

The car moves off down the hill. An afterbirth of sighs:

"No, I don't want to practice any more Chinese torture. There are limits to what you can subject an artist."

The delicate tracery of the birches has a purple tinge, but not like that in the spring: this bareness is heavy with rain, autumnal purple. On Ingrid's way of saying her lines:

"She says her lines so naturally that she can get monotonous, that's her danger."

The conversation comes to a standstill. Sven Nykvist says a few words about the camera, that is all; I have never known him so silent. The car is splashed with mud from the puddles in the road. I look at the heavy veils of rain between the trees of the forest. Fantastic, really, what colors the rain entices out. Patches of snow, black stacks of pulp wood, pale-grey lichen.

I jot down what I see through the window of the car. That is my relaxation and flight from the day's conflict.

I don't know whether Ingmar finds this day one of defeat for a director. In one way, however, it is. Ingmar feels GB's reaction today to be "lack of loyalty" ("to make a fuss as he did today"); but he doesn't feel that he is pinning GB down on all sides.

The fault is not in the demands on the actor. But in the way they are made. The contact with Ingrid causes him very little difficulty: he makes a warm, reassuring bed around her work; then the demands are productive. Is it easier for a male director to have a creative effect on an actress than on an actor? IB touches Gunnar's talent with irritated fingers— then he is inflammable, incapable of controlling himself and of calming down. The demands then become a vice with tightly gripping jaws. I see Gunnar's performance

149

in WINTER LIGHT growing into a great performance— but it is growing out of a press of anguish.

It is a quiet drive home. Somewhere behind us Gunnar and Ingrid are driving along in the old black taxi. In the back of our car Ingmar starts humming a tune. He hums for a long time, in an undertone; *O sole mio*, of all things.

The afterbirth comes in the evening when IB has coffee in the library with Ulla, Lenn, Lena, Börje Lundh:

How difficult actors find it to put off themselves. Hard to make GB put off GB. "Still harder to get Max to put off Max von Sydow. But Ingrid can: put off herself. But it was a hell of a job with her too, at first."

Börje Lundh is sitting at the other end of the table in the library, opposite Ingmar. Börje gives a laugh:

"But you control yourself much better nowadays. Now you take a biscuit instead."

Börje mentions a young actress who he thinks is charming. Ingmar cuts in:

"No, she's not. She's untalented. And hysterical."

Suddenly he smiles and switches over to himself; sharply sarcastic at his own expense:

"But even *we hysterics* can have our charming sides."

Further description of himself:

"I am resentful. And suspicious. I am .... Oh, I'm everything that Kābi is not. When we've had our rows, it's all gone next day with her. But I *remember*. I *never* forget."

Ulla chuckles:

"I remember times when someone has hurt you and you've said: 'I won't forget *that*'."

IB goes on reckoning up his faults of character, ends with a sigh over one in particular: "God knows what's the cause of that. Yes, I do know .... " And a few words about his childhood when he was forced to fight for his "innocence," among other things. And his right.

The day's mail has brought the latest issue of the weekly magazine *Damernas Vārld (Women's World)* in which are published some opinions on THROUGH A GLASS DARKLY. Lenn goes up and gets it. Reading aloud. Ingmar reads himself.

Oddly (and typically) enough, he passes over Gunnel Vallquist's perceptive article with a few words to the effect that she "has understood what it's all about." Instead he devotes all his time to the medical professor Gudmund Björck's rambling emotional outburst against the person Ingmar Bergman. (The professor talks idiotically about affection, the tender affection of a father with five children; and doesn't even notice that IB's film is about three men who, in helpless affection, gather around the woman Karin.) My thought is that if the article were about me, I would put it down, as unread as possible— my self-defense. But IB reads it thoroughly. Line by line. With clear voice and strong, deeply-felt comments. Obstinately he plods through every line, swallowing it— then spits it out.

We make a move; it's bedtime. I've half a mind to stay at home at the hotel tomorrow and work at my typewriter; but Ingmar checks the plan:

"I think you ought to come along tomorrow and see the end of the drama."

Undated, May 1962:

Today I was out at the Djursholm house and handed back the script for THE SILENCE; IB asked if there was anything I wanted to cut or alter in the dialogue. Yes, I wanted to cut the line "Why do we have to hurt each other?" which from a literary point of view was rather hackneyed. But Ingmar shook his head vigorously. He would not even discuss the existence of that line. It *had* to be there, and that was that.

THURSDAY 9 NOVEMBER 1961
Ingmar's morning vitality
Last night he dreamed about unruly supers
Ingrid's final scene in the schoolroom
IB's problems as supervisor

When Gunnar enters the dining room, made-up, wearing his cassock, a fantastic morning light covers Lake Siljan. The clouds are dragging themselves along, low-lying; all the light is concentrated on the lake, with a color of pewter; it is as if Siljan radiated a strong light of its own. I tell Gunnar that Ingmar is going down to Stockholm for the weekend. GB answers curtly:

"What a relief. The pressure will let up for two days at least. The parrots can do what they like for a while."

Ingmar can be heard far off: he comes bounding down the stairs— humming, whistling, with the terrible vitality of someone who is at his best in the mornings.* He climbs into the car with Sven and me. Grey outside, several degrees above zero— not a vestige of snow! The time is 8:30; and last night Ingmar had a dream which he thought was fun:

"I dreamed I was going to direct a Strindberg play. They had made a hideous decor: a landscape with real waterways, etc. I had called a whole crowd of pupils, I was to start the rehearsal by rehearsing the supers. I told them all to keep quiet, because I wanted to tell them what this Strindberg was about. But the supers went on chattering: one was playing with a fishing rod, and so on. I said: 'This is the only Strindberg play that is to be done quite realistically.' But the supers still went on talking and making a noise, I couldn't make them shut up; so I lost my temper and roared: 'Rehearsal over!' and walked out. Nice dream, eh?"

His laugh shows that he too associates the dream with yesterday's events in the schoolroom. The point of his comment:

"Actually in the dream I was glad to break off and leave the whole thing. I didn't really know what I was going to say to the supers!"

"Didn't you? But in the schoolroom yesterday you knew *what* you were going to say, surely?"

"Yes, I did. But I didn't know *how* to put it."

I give myself up to a little private interpretation of dreams as I sit there in the car. The super with the fishing rod— that's Brian Wikström, I think, assistant sound engineer, with his long mike boom. What I especially like is the phrase: *This is the only Strindberg play that is to be done quite realistically*. Märta's and Thomas's settling up scene has a distinct Strindberg flavor— but it is to be played from outside Ingmar's artistic principle in this film: in as bare and everyday manner as possible. As close up to Swedish reality as possible.

Ingmar and Sven discuss practical worries. The snow problem, for

* Addition, in January 1962: It took me in, as it did many others. I thought it was natural. Today, over dinner, Ingmar gave his own version of his morning torments: Waking up early; the heaviness; feeling out of sorts generally; the need of being alone and of getting the better of one's inner tensions before facing the outside world. Slowly he starts up the wheel of activity, through all this resistance; the wheel is not going full speed until he gets out to SF. Then, to make up, the belts are whirling at a terrific pace .... and he rushes into the corridor and meets all these morning people who are doing many fewer r.p.m.s than himself.

instance.

"I think I've solved it, Sven. Let's do it like this: We'll take all the exteriors even if we don't get snow. If the snow does come, then we'll retake the lot, and it will be awfully easy, because we'll all know how it is to be done; and the first time will be like a dress rehearsal."

Sven is pondering on the shot of the altar candlesticks in Frostnäs church. Allan Edwall is needed for that shot; but he is inaccessible on weekdays. In the evenings he is playing Ionesco's THE CHAIRS at the Royal Dramatic Theater; and now he has started to rehearse Max Frisch's ANDORRA for Olof Molander in the daytime.

"But K. A. can do that," Ingmar replies. "K. A. can light the seven-armed candlestick."

That moment fascinates him, he adds: how the light flares up over the figures on the reredos.

The shot is to be taken in Skattungby church. On its altar is a seven-armed candlestick.

"It's terribly ugly, that candlestick. But it appealed to me. It looked so horribly poor."

Suddenly he embraces the candlestick with all his affection. (These opposite poles in his emotional life: the aggressiveness, swift and blind— and then the tenderness. Sometimes I seem to have seen him so overcome by emotion that it makes him helpless with compassion.)

The bit of road up to the schoolhouse has been churned up by all the cars; SF's men are repairing it and laying down new sand. Ingrid and Gunnar are already warming themselves upstairs beside the glowing little electric fire; they entertain each other with chitchat about foreign artists. Gunnar has seen what a fantastically good stage actor Jean Paul Belmondo is; Ingrid is talking about how different the working rhythm is in foreign studios. Ingmar goes up to them, it's the first meeting since yesterday, but the tensions never appear; the three of them soon fall to talking about Swedish provincial characteristics: people from Roslagen, Värmland, Dalarna; Ingmar tells a long story about an old Finn. Katinka knocks on the door:

"Ready now."

Ingmar goes down and admires Sven's lighting and picture composition.

"What a lovely picture."

Sven thinks he is being sarcastic.

"No, I *mean* it. So nice and desolate, with her sitting with those goddam children's drawings behind her."

An hour is taken up with rehearsals. Ingmar moves his chair over to Ingrid's seat. He props his arms on the desk; they have another quiet conversation about the difficult last passage. Ingmar asks her:

"You'd like to cut *Thomas, my dearest?*"

"No, I'd like to cut *without me*, when she says *What's to become of you— without me?*"

"Cut anything you like. The main thing is that you isolate yourself from him, that you are wrapped up in yourself now."

Ingrid, lingeringly:

"It's easier for me to think that her grief is so great that she isolates herself because of that. When one has heard so many hurtful things as she has heard from him, it's natural for her to turn away."

"No, *that's* not what I mean. Not *that* loneliness. You see, Ingrid: She is a *visionary* for a moment. She is beyond all remonstrances— all *external* remonstrances— there is nothing of personal feeling, personal sorrow about her anymore. She has turned right away. (Pause. Consolingly): You *have* everything. I'm only talking about the technical side. And don't worry about the camera being so far away— keep that intimate feeling just the same. I'll cut in close-ups later. (Gently): What is it, my dear?"

Ingrid makes a shy movement with her head:

"There are so many standing over there," she says quietly. "Where I am to fix my eyes."

The cramped schoolroom is packed with people around the teacher's desk. It's not easy to be an unwordly visionary when you meet dozens of eyes that automatically stare at you as you act.

Ingmar interrupts her in a rehearsal:

"Give the pause its full value, before you say *You'll go under, Thomas, my dearest.* She sees a horror, you know."

They go on rehearsing.

"And Ingrid! You can raise one hand there, when Thomas loses his temper, *Can't you shut up!* She thinks he is going to strike her."

Pause. Ingmar wants to make himself still plainer to her.

"This can be taken in two ways. Actually it's written like this:

154

she is seized with a mad, expansive despair. Hysterical, is what I thought when I wrote it. That's why he gets so goddam furious with her. But it's better to do it like this, as you do it, I *feel* it."

"Don't you want it done that way then?"

"As I wrote it?"

"Yes."

"No," Ingmar says, "I'm grateful if it's like this instead."

Light, laughing inflections, half serious.

"I never know what to make of written words," Ingrid says deprecatingly.

"Actors never do," Ingmar consoles her. "They understand only the spoken word."

Ingrid laughs in her typical way:

"And not always that," she says with a kind of stubborness in her tone.*

Ingmar:

"No, actors are like dogs: they listen only to the tone of your voice. Actually."

Gunnar's look at Ingmar: the look of one who thinks he has heard a typical expression of contempt for actors.

Now they play right through the final passage. One of those present, Bertha Sånell, turns away; I ask her why, curious.

"Horrid scene," she whispers. "I can't bear it."

Isn't Bertha's reaction representative of a big Swedish movie audience? The aversion that Bertha feels here, now, during shooting– a whole lot of spectators in cinemas at Gislaved, Strömsund and Umeå are going to feel the same. Our Swedish fear of outbursts of aggression.

New rehearsal. Ingmar to Ingrid afterwards:

"Don't stress *all the time* when you say *I've done the wrong thing all the time.*"

Ingrid changes it.

"Fine! You give it quite a different inflection. More surprised."

The shot is taken twice; after the second take Ingrid remains sit-

---

* Actually, she explains long afterwards, her obstinate laughter was an aggressive I-don't-understand-your-goddam-text, aimed at the line "What's to become of you— without me?" For *her* it would have been simpler to take a critical stand from such a femininely-self-centered line than to give it "visionary" feeling.

ting, rather unhappy. Ingmar gets up, potters restlessly around her, notices her discontent with herself:

"No, why? It was fine!"

Ingrid complains introspectively, rather huddled:

"It was too much acting. The inflections were too deliberate."

Ingmar leans over her, propped on his elbows, consolingly; Lennart Nilsson thinks the situation is expressive and takes a series of pictures. Ingmar explains, murmuring in a friendly way, how he is going to edit the sequence.

"And you see, if you think of the audience too— towards the end of a long scene like this, a climax is needed. Don't worry! Otherwise it can easily be monotonous. Do you see?"

I jot down *monotnous*, remembering what he said on the drive home yesterday about Ingrid's danger in this kind of acting.

Lunch.

New camera position after lunch. New shade of color, moreover, in Ingmar's direction of Ingrid:

"Close your eyes there, when you say: *No, I've done the wrong thing* and open them on *What's to become of you— without me?*"

I guess that Ingmar resorts to the eye-closing as a direction knack in order to bring out an expression of surprised perception in her: Mãrta who sees a vision of Thomas's hell. I check afterwards that my guess is correct.

Rehearsal. Ingrid, afterwards:

"Now I forgot when to close my eyes."

"No. You did exactly right."

The scene is taken four times. During the second take Ingrid fluffs a line and breaks off herself; Ingmar thinks that that particular take has "quite an unsentimental intensity" which he asks her to try and recapture. (Every time the outburst of hatred comes, Bertha Sånell looks away.) After the fourth take Ingmar lets out an encouraging:

"You see!"

"There was a noise outside," Ingrid mumbles.

"Yes, a car. But it doesn't matter. It came in the pause, so I can cut."

The camera is moved, Ingrid's key lines are shot against the window— but the time is 2:40: the dusk is creeping up and Ingrid is on the way down the curve of fatigue. Just as well to call it a day.

Ingrid has every reason to feel limp after the day's effort. They have been doing the schoolroom scene the whole week; today Gullan had to come to the rescue with glycerine; for the first time during all these takes, Ingrid failed to produce any tears of her own.

Ingmar is a contented director during the drive home; he describes how he has "coaxed and bullied and joked" with Ingrid until this afternoon, at last, just before they parted, she said:

"I don't want to do it my way at all."

(Did Ingrid really say that? I was standing beside them at the schoolroom window; as I remember it Ingrid merely said, with a tired little laugh: "I'll do it your way.")

The car sways gently.

"In the end you can get her to go the way you want to. She had some vague idea of how she wanted to do this scene; then I said: 'Well, let's do it that way then!' So we did it her way and she could see herself that it wasn't good like that."

(This is just to show that you can't go by what Ingmar himself says about something. He likes the forceful, the drastic, anything that shows up well; when he recounts an incident he simplifies it violently and makes it superficial. The reality which he moves in and creates around him is far more varied and differentiated.)

Another worry for Sven Nykvist: the laboratory has reported a fault. Is Sven to blame? Sven knows that he *isn't*. In order to be 100% sure and to have arguments against possible criticism, Sven has carried out a series of controls on his own work. Sven has all the Swedish professional tradition in his blood—this professional tradition for which skill and pride in good workmanship is a matter of honor; for men with that background a reproof for neglect or carelessness feels like an attack on their good name. He has brooded on the matter the whole afternoon; back at the hotel he calls up the laboratory. His worries are unfounded. The laboratory was too hasty in reporting a suspicion that turned out to be unjustified. There was no fault.

I am wondering whether this can be a result of Ingmar's demand that all technicians, at the laboratory and elsewhere, shall instantly and in advance report all faults they discover. He loathes this sort of thing: He, Ingmar Bergman, discovers a fault; the person responsible excuses himself— and the excusing leads to an unpleasant and irritated discussion on how the hell the fault could have come about. Therefore all mistakes are to be reported in advance,

157

before Ingmar himself has had time to discover them. Out of the demand there can arise premature reports like the one today— out of anxiety.

Ingmar's own problem in such a context is, I think, this: he is weighed down by a burden of suspiciousness. In labor conflicts of this kind he is all too often driven swiftly towards a point that alerts this suspicion. The other person is vague and uncertain, speaks with a stammer, afraid of meeting this keen, narrowed gaze; the fear seems to Ingmar like a guilty conscience, as if the person concerned had something to hide— and suspiciousness clutches at him in a split second. He makes an effort to be clear, factual and matter-of-fact, but once his suspicions have been aroused, he cannot lull them; the discussion takes on a cutting undertone from their presence.

Gunnar's mood today is hard to describe. More or less making fun of the whole situation. At the moment there is nothing in the work that gives him stimulus or creative desire— everything is so awkward and trying that he seems to want to laugh at it.

Outwardly, however, the only thing that happened today was that Ingmar roared at him soon after lunch. Gunnar said nothing.

Yesterday's outburst was their most violent during the whole time of shooting: the climax in the tension between them. (After that outburst their relationship alters in a marked way.)

UNDATED, NOVEMBER 1961

The other evening in the bridge room Ingmar started talking about Alf Kjellin's good qualities as a director (Alf's capacity of creating a pleasant, friendly atmosphere, his endurance, etc.)— "whereas I .... "

From this he developed a terribly clear-sighted picture of his own weaknesses: "his moods," "his suspiciousness," etc.

UNDATED, NOVEMBER 1961

A writer's everyday life

Hard to combine everyday life and writing— "but in recent years I have really *tried*, so that I don't have to go away, or so that special arrangements don't have to be made in the house just because I'm about to write a film script."

Ulla I. nods at the dinner table: she knows only too well what Ingmar is talking about (she, who, moreover, is a slave to her

158

housewifely ambition when she is going to write).

"Last summer, for instance, when we were staying at Torö, Käbi, Lenn and I. It went awfully well. I wrote away at WINTER LIGHT in the mornings, drove down to the village store with Lenn, drove home and worked for a few hours in the afternoon .... It went awfully well."

I had no difficulty in joining in that conversation. It was worse the other day when Ulla and Ingmar plunged into the meaning of Swedish poverty— the absence of a feeling of kinship, "the lack of warmth," our spiritual meanness. Ingmar spoke enthusiastically of the atmosphere of Russian life that was so close to Käbi in her childhood (they try to keep something of it by reading Russian classics aloud to each other). He rapturously described her generosity, her desire to keep open house for friends and relations. Suddenly I realized that it is by no means as natural to *him* to throw wide the doors of his home; on the contrary, it would go very much against the grain .... he gives an amusing picture of his own reluctance; that's how Swedish *he* is.

But he struggles as well as he can to overcome that trait in him.

I wonder whether he doesn't criticize it also, indirectly, in Märta Lundberg's letter: *"Thomas, I have never believed in your faith. The main reason of course has been that I myself have never been plagued by any religious obsessions. I grew up in an unchristian family with lots of warmth and affection and loyalty— and joy. God and Christ didn't exist, other than as vague concepts."*

(Märta's letter was too long, so he shortened it before shooting. In the Torö version Märta also wrote this:

"Yes, we've had our religious discussions, you and I, but I've always thought we have touched only the fringe of the problems. I don't understand why. Perhaps it's merely because of my insensitivity and indifference. Perhaps I don't listen with sufficient interest to your explanations.")

UNDATED, NOVEMBER 1961

Another standing theme of conversation at dinnertime with Ulla and Ingmar: "cannibalism" in artists. They are flung into a crisis. Or they see friends and relatives torn apart by conflicts. But the cannibal in them is always ready waiting to note down, to observe: What a theme! I could make something of that ....

But supposing the artist is tormented by the cannibal in him and

159

is seized by a sense of guilt? Then he can make use of *that* conflict too and turn it into a film, for instance. (The writer David in THROUGH A GLASS DARKLY who exploits his daughter's madness in his novels.) The cannibal in the artist is a lusty devil. Always knows a thousand expedients.

I am astonished to hear how *early* Ulla and Ingmar confess the cannibal inside them (I myself kept him locked away in my subconscious for years). They discovered him; they made use of him; he caused a feeling of guilt, sure, but it never occurred to them to deny his existence.

With Ingmar, evidently, direction also functions on this plane. It's not enough to stop at what the actors can achieve as actors. It's a matter of probing deeper, down into their private lives— and of making them canalize their own conflicts in their acting. (Some actors help him gladly, they know how fruitful a conflict can be; others shy at it or refuse point blank.) Always to work with eyes open for the point of intersection between the artist's private problems and his objective talent: there, surely, is one of IB's cunning qualities as director.

TUESDAY 14 NOVEMBER 1961

Shooting inside Skattungby church: the final scenes. Algot Frövik walks up towards the vestry. IB checks me suddenly; he heard me swear.

"Not in here, if you don't mind."

The forest ridges around the church turn blue; one can see for miles; Ingmar points out to Ulla Isaksson:

"Down there lay Master Töre's house in THE VIRGIN SPRING."

Ulla has seen the house in her imagination (when she wrote the film) and in the finished film; never in reality. It was pulled down immediately after the shooting was finished.

Allan Edwall has travelled up for today's take; yesterday K. A. was stand-in for him. The same strange interaction between him and K. A., especially when they wear the same clothes.

"Do you know what the parson here said today to Allan Edwall? 'But you said yesterday that you were a stand-in. Are you going to *act* today?' "

THURSDAY 16 NOVEMBER 1961

The car scene is shot at Skattungby

160

The punitive silence: God's silence and father's and mother's
Reconnaissance at the scene of the suicide

Early in the morning Sven Nykvist comes tramping across the
gravel in front of the hotel, cold and shivering and furious. The
stuffing in the seat of his car has been eaten by mice: "big holes!"

The morning above Skattungby church. The parson's car has
stopped at a level crossing; he recounts a childhood memory. A
few loose firs are stood up behind the car; our big trucks are used
as a shield from the sun, which is breaking out of the clouds and
threatening to ruin the November atmosphere. All the trucks and
gear on the slope give the place the air of a circus.

During the breaks we get warm down in the church. Ingrid is
learning "Foreign Words" by heart, she walks about holding the
little book. Under the letter A alone there are many odd words.

On her forehead, just below the hair, is something scabby: a
scarcely perceptible paste-like flake against the skin. I imagine it
to be something to do with the half-wig she wears in the part, an
imperfection of make-up technique. Not at all! It is a finesse
which Börje Lundh has produced: the "scab" is intended as a re-
minder of the eczema that Märta Lundberg has had "on her forehead, just at the hair line."

The other day Ingmar said in passing that Ingrid was so much
better and more sure of herself in everyday details nowadays, he
thought. Her stay in the USA had taught her "contour," that was
the word he used. That was a small acknowledgment in favor of
Hollywood at any rate.

The whole film team is permitted to have lunch in the rectory.
Over the meal we suddenly begin to recount childhood memories. I recall a summer in Småland when I fell into the brook and
dared not go home with wet clothes. It revives a similar childhood
memory in Ingmar. He relates it with violent intensity. The prelude I don't remember— only the aftermath: he comes home, is
questioned, punished. The punishment was carried out quite sys-
tematically— that was the horrible part of it.

"Everyone thinks it's horrible *now*," he says. "They didn't think
so *then*. My parents kept abreast of the times, they were modern,
acted according to *that* age's ideals of upbringing, which stipu-
lated that you should *not* let your feelings be involved when you
punished children. You must not show that you yourself were upset or influenced; you should be sober and matter-of-fact, the

161

children would be all the better for such a punishment, it was believed."

The punishment is associated with a green plush sofa in his childhood home; that was where he was given it. Afterwards, repentance was to follow, redress, a resumption of the affectionate relations that had been broken by the offense he had committed.

"It's a wonder it didn't make me homosexual or a masochist," he adds.

Then comes the surprise.

This method of upbringing included something else: the punishment was to be accompanied by silence. The grownups should not speak to the child until it had shown contrition.

There is a glint in his eyes as he speaks of this silence. And then it comes:

"That really was God's silence."

At first I wonder how on earth he can combine the ancient concept of religious mysticism, "God's silence," which is the main theme of WINTER LIGHT, with his own childhood experience.

Then I feel as if I had found a key to a central theme in his private biography.

Addition, summer 1962:

There's to be a press conference on IB's new film, TIMOKA— but he doesn't dare to call it anything too mystifying and difficult to pronounce. What is he to tell the press that it's called then? He tries different suggestions for a title out at SF.

Actually it should be called GOD'S SILENCE, he says. That's exactly what it is about. But you can't call a film that!

"Call it THE SILENCE then."

That title appeals to him. He says it over, getting the feel of it; and decides on it.

Addition, Thursday 4 October 1962, Siljansborg.

He says that he sometimes gets a touch of claustrophobia; that's why he must have two rooms here at the hotel. He associates the claustrophobia with the memories of a dark closet in which he had to serve his punishment as a child sometimes (just as in Hjalmar Bergman's GRANNY AND OUR LORD). And then this about the "punitive silence":

" .... They didn't speak to me when I had done something. Even today I can still lose my temper for no apparent reason when someone consistently keeps silent and turns away from me— then

162

I kick and keep at them until I get an answer."
God's silence.
Mother and father keep silent.

After lunch we leave Skattungby for reconnaissance. The road
twists and turns along a chain of lakes: the scenery down here in
the valley gets more and more wild and desolate; up on the huge
ridge long lines of pines march into the light on the horizon. This
is the wild Dalarna which tourists never reach. Ingmar begins pour-
ing out his love of this landscape: we pass an old iron-foundry
estate, he tells of the days when pig-iron was transported down
this chain of lakes. To Sven:
"We'll remember this when we make our FOLKTALE."
He points to a part of the ridge full of atmosphere: "Look at
that! The entire scale of grey!" and they both sit for a while looking at the light over the landscape.
I first heard THE FOLKTALE spoken of a month ago. He is
thinking of doing it next summer. A burlesque film with lots of
Swedish fairytale material in it. Naima Wifstrand would play the
Princess who has grown old waiting for all the dull suitors, Ingrid
Thulin would play an amusing forest sprite, Gunnar Björnstrand
would be Old Nick. And three brothers lost in the great Swedish
primeval forest: Max von Sydow, Allan Edwall and Martin Ljung—
"you only need to put these three one behind the other and let
them tramp through a forest, and it'd be funny, don't you think?"
The pines thin out on top of the ridge, the chain of lakes grows
narrower, the valley gets more and more cramped ("that's where
the trolls live," Ingmar can even point out the exact spot). Then
Sten Lindén brakes— the last lake in the chain squeezes itself
through a sluice-gate and becomes rapids.
This is where the fisherman Jonas Persson is to commit suicide.
In the script it says that Jonas's body lies "half sprawling in the
ditch"; here, on the actual site, Ingmar decides instinctively that
Max is to lie under a tree.
Planning for tomorrow's work:
Ingmar points and Blomqvist, the master carpenter, makes a
sketch of the place. "We'll build a small wooden platform here and
put the camera on it .... And see if you can get permission to cut
away some of the bushes towards the rapids." The bushes are too
pretty and lend a romantic air to the spot, Ingmar wants "a coars-

er contour to the shot." Sound bus and food bus can be parked in a gravel pit on the other side of the road— "but check the times when they come to load gravel!" (It turns out that gravel is taken only four or five times a day. Fine! Then the trucks can be stopped during the final takes.) At one point Blomqvist wants to put up a screening stack of timber, "but it musn't look too arranged."

IB darts about the scene of the suicide, dressed in a dark-grey coat that Käbi bought for him in Switzerland. It is smart, and suits him. He looks like a raven in it.

"How did you find this spot?"

Hmm, how does one find the right spots? This doesn't look anything like its description in the script, no "landing jetty" for instance. But it's not easy to find landing jetties when you transfer shooting from a coastal landscape to Dalarna.

Often you come across them by chance.

"We had chosen quite a different suicide spot from the outset. Then one day we happened to drive past here, Sten Lindén said we'd better take this road back to Siljansborg because it was a short cut .... and that's how we found this. The river is called Nightmare Point River, don't they have fantastic names up here? One place is called Death Village, another Gravemount ...."

That is how it came about that Jonas Persson took his life at Young Lake Home dam.

We climb into the cars.

"That was a good haul, eh?" IB purrs contentedly. "But perhaps we'd better place the body nearer the camera, so that everyone moves up towards it? I'm thinking of that shot, right at the last, where the parson is alone .... it's so terribly important."

The darkness deepens over the ridges as we drive home, the same way back.

"In one way it's creepy with a thing that is lying far away in the shot."

Sven wonders whether it can be seen that it is a body; oh yes, no doubt about it.

"And everybody knows in any case what it is."

Ingmar, suddenly:

"What about shooting it in one take?!"

Sven looks a bit turned off.

"It'd give the whole thing a feeling of authenticity, it would be something objective, don't you think?"

164

(The camera would be like a recording eye. Slightly from up above, raised above the scene of acting.)

Then they start talking about doing the whole thing with *three* cameras, in one take.

"Then we'll get perfect continuity with the light, for one thing. And if there's a dull patch, we can cut in ...."

I sit with the notepad beside Sten Lindén and look out of the car window.

The forest undergrowth is lovely in its frozenness, freshly brushed by the November frost.

Back at Siljansborg IB collects those immediately concerned in the library. Tea drinking and organization of tomorrow's rehearsal. First of all he sketches out a detailed schedule:

1. The parson comes on road A, stops, gets out, goes up to the body.
2. Assistants take picture with flashbulb.
3. The chief constable lifts up the gun, takes it over to his car, the parson follows him. START OF THE CHIEF CONSTABLE'S LINES.
4. Meanwhile assistants who have finished taking pictures of the body come up to the car. The parson goes over to the body. Meanwhile the chief constable talks to assistants: CONT. OF CONSTABLE'S LINES: *Friberg has a van and we can take the body in that, so that we can get him to the cottage hospital and arrange for the death certificate.*
5. Assistants take a tarpaulin out of the car, go back and straighten out Jonas and lay tarpaulin over the body.
6. Constable goes up to guys on bridge, says: *Come on, guys, we'll get out of here.*
7. Dialogue between constable and parson and departure on road B.
8. Close-up of Jonas (Ingmar himself put a ? here).
9. Märta comes on road A. Has to go back to parson's car (= out of shot).
10. Soon afterwards the van backs in and assistants and driver, with Thomas's help, carry the body to the car, after which the car drives off.

FRIDAY 17 NOVEMBER 1961

The scene of the suicide
Light conflict brewing

A somewhat extraordinary working day.

Long, calm preparations. The whole team stamps about, hour after hour, trying to keep warm. Cameras are mounted, walks and car-backings are rehearsed, and Börje Lundh comes trudging along with a 5-liter small beer bottle filled with a liquid that is meant to be blood. Ingmar has decided on a radical measure: he will *not* have any close-ups. It is otherwise the obvious thing to do: the parson beside the fisherman's body— the torment in his eyes. But no, he will shoot the whole thing in a single, coherent long shot, with two cameras.

Sven Nykvist is in charge of the A camera, of course. The assistant cameraman, Peter Wester, is in charge of the B camera.

Surprised, I notice that IB is ashamed of having "two cameras." Why, in heaven's name?

"A sort of strange professional pride. It feels a bit like faking, not to manage it with one camera."

It's certainly cold today. But Ingmar is curiously calm. Don't rush things! Take your time over the preparations. And we might as well have lunch before we take the shot.

So it's nearly one o'clock before everything's ready for a take. Then comes the extraordinary change in the weather.

The air thickens, raw and biting, the cold increases, the landscape darkens a few shades, and something is whirling in the air.

Lumps of wet snow!

It lasts for half an hour. Just right for the two takes. Then the sleet is gone, and doesn't return for that day.

" .... As in THE SEVENTH SEAL when Bertil Anderberg collapses screaming in the forest glade and dies in torment of the plague, I let the camera run for a little longer than usual. Suddenly a ray of sunlight broke over him .... grace."

Ingmar doesn't mind your cultivating a little natural magic— or black magic— around him. He does it himself. What was it Ulla I. once told us? Oh yes, he had confided to her that in WILD STRAWBERRIES he had gone to one side and promised the Evil One a year of his life if only he would give him fine weather on that particular day; for the position was desperate and the whole production team had to go home the next day.

Yes of course it was a fine day.

He stamps around after the takes, enormously satisfied with the sleet. Now it's there! He has caught it on the film strip.

Lars-Owe Carlberg, the production manager, has one of the heaviest jobs during the shooting. Constant organizing and planning: detailed work of the most unrewarding kind— nobody outside really notices when the machinery runs smoothly. Today he has a short respite from the nerve-racking practical routine: he is playing the part of the chief constable. He learned the lines he was given yesterday in case they were needed. But the mike could not be placed

.... so that it reached far enough to catch his words. Besides, the rapids were roaring below the scene of the suicide, the sluice gate had been opened especially for the day's shooting. All that was heard of his lines was an unintelligible murmur. One noticed *that* he spoke, but could not hear what.

During the drive home about three o'clock.

"Did you notice that the scene went just as well *without* lines?!"

I nod, thinking of the roar of the rapids and wondering *when* you can make lineless scenes in a sound film. When you have a long shot, as today? When you have *another* sound which draws all the attention to itself (the roar of the rapids)? Every effect has its conditions, it's just a matter of finding out about them.

When the rushes are shown that evening at Ulla Ryghe's cutting table four light tests from Skattungby church are discussed: it's a question of capturing the dusk inside the church. The fourth and last test is very dark. When it was taken Sven Nykvist was convinced that the picture wouldn't expose— not even the new kind of film could cope with anything so dark.

"But it did!" Ingmar says. "And the fourth test is the *only* one to be accepted, Sven. It was exactly the right atmosphere of expectation of dusk and burial vault."

Ingmar attacks a shot from the altar. He wants Ingrid's kneeling down and prayer differently (it has too much "glamour" and "pang pang" in his opinion). Sven, the extremely conscientious photographer who has been at the game for twenty years, feels it as a blow to his professional pride. Half an hour's conversation ensues in which Ingmar's to begin with is heated and uncamouflaged. Sven broodingly turns the criticism to himself. He is making his forty-third film.

Then Ingmar notices just *how* hard his criticism has hit home.

"But this business of changing technique, Sven! The old technique is ingrained in one, it won't budge. One can't shift it right off, it must be done slowly. Look at me: I relapse into extraordinary old moves and groupings I have had before ...."

"But it's terrible that not a single picture in the whole sequence is good enough," Sven says.

When the shooting of WINTER LIGHT is over and all this conflict has been happily settled, it remains merely as an amusing memory that Sven could remove all artificial light sources and illuminate one of the shots with nothing but a seven-armed candlestick. It becomes the great story: a proof of the enormous light-sensitivity of double-X. But today we are in the middle of the conflict; and it annoys Ingmar that he will have to retake the intercession. Sven has Ingmar's unbounded confidence; Sven should be able to do anything.

"Ingrid does the intercession so beautifully .... it will only be worse if we retake it."

Compromise:

"We'll retake the intercession," Ingmar says. "If it's worse as regards the acting, we'll forget about the photography and keep this take, eh?"

I can guess how that compromise is going to keep Sven awake tonight.

One evening last fall I drove into town with Sven in his car from SF. It had been one of the most successful days up to then. We crossed the yard in the dark, to Sven's car; he was bubbling.

"From now on this is for me!"

He would refrain from all extra effects with light and shade, "all that sort of thing one did before"; he felt how right the line was along which he was working, and that he had mastered it. This is the first difficulty he has encountered during this production; he has cleared all hurdles up to now.

SATURDAY 18 NOVEMBER 1961
The tragicomic chain reaction
Ingmar discovers the stigmata spots

This morning we had not gone far along the road to Finnbacka before Ingmar started discussing yesterday's conflict:

"I've been thinking it over, Sven. We needn't retake the whole thing, we can solve it like this ...."

He puts forward a new compromise solution to Sven: they can order darker copies of Ingrid's shot.

In the Finnbacka house Ingrid is lying down, reading the literature and arts page of a newspaper, waiting for the sunlight to abate — at present it is too bright. They are to take a shot when Märta and Thomas get out of the car in front of the schoolhouse, and it must be a dull afternoon light on that shot. A cold wind is blowing, and suddenly Ingmar starts growling.

"I'm in one hell of a mood today."

"Why?"

168

"I don't know," he mutters like a sulky child.

He tries to laugh off his bad temper. Silence for a time.

"I know what it is. It's this business with Sven."

I find it hard to understand that a crisis can blow up out of this. Surely Sven has the same right to a margin of error as everyone else, including Ingmar himself? And he loves Sven: Sven's colossal craftsmanship and tough, stubborn endurance. But the few people who gain Ingmar's confidence *must not* fail. (This readiness to feel "let down" by one's fellow workers!— is it one of a director's "occupational diseases?" Because it is by no means peculiar to Ingmar, I notice as time goes on.)

But Ingmar often gets let in for emotional chain reactions of this type (he can relate them afterwards at his own expense and analyze the tragicomic element in them): He loses his temper with someone; this someone is hurt; Ingmar feels compelled to cover up his aggressiveness; and he is angry with the other person because of that *too*. (Compare the childhood situation: transgression; apology — followed by the necessity of reconciliation and amends.)

During the drive to Finnboda we talked about Federico Fellini (LA DOLCE VITA .... "a baroque wallpaper." How he admires Fellini and the Japanese Kurosawa, two of the few great directors in the world.). The papers today report the clearing up of a rape and murder case in Gothenburg: the murderer has confessed. ("I wonder how the guy feels. I wonder so much how he feels right inside.") At Finnbacka there is talk of the theater: "Today Ebbe Linde has written a notice for a play and on nearly *every* point I think differently." (Ebbe Linde has reviewed last night's TV performance of Musset's DON'T PLAY WITH LOVE.) There is also talk of psychoanalysis; Ingrid perks up and displays an intensely interested skepticism— she could never go and be analyzed.

It would mean, she thinks, giving oneself up to another person and relying on his authority. Katinka knocks on the door and says everything's ready for shooting, but Ingmar is reluctant to leave the subject: "It's damned interesting, this resistance of Ingrid's to authority; we must talk about it." But Ingmar doesn't talk about it; he confronts Ingrid with a statement on her real nature: "You are a veritable religious talent," and it's a serious and important statement for him. Gunnar Björnstrand touches on the question whether neuroses can be artistically creative; *No*, says Ingmar, they are *not* creative:

169

"As long as I tried to create on my neuroses, I got nowhere."

In the afternoon he tells Lars-Owe Carlberg how to deal with a small-part player who must be called for a retake:

"Don't say a *word* about his not acting well. At all costs he must be made to think it was a technical fault, otherwise he'll be nervous."

In the evening there's Saturday dancing at the hotel; but he does not like dancing or dance music and doesn't quite know what to do with himself: run a film? or go to bed? Rather at a loss and restless; suddenly he tells of a discovery he has made:

"Guess what has occurred to me! Märta Lundberg's eczema— it's placed on *the stigmata spots*. The hands and forehead, the hairline."

So he wasn't thinking of that when he wrote down that detail? No, he simply took it from a real case, in which the eczema was placed on those very spots.

He is happy as he tells us this. Happy as the artist always is when inspiration has preceded calculation and confirmation.*"You see, this film is starting to get a third dimension now," and his voice purrs with both well-being and restlessness.

MONDAY 20 NOVEMBER 1961

They've been working on the church today too.

"I think Sven Nykvist has produced an excellent lighting today," Ingmar says with satisfaction when they get home. "It was so dark that we needed a flashlight to see the actors. We groped for them."

(Gunnar blows his nose all the way through the film and Ingrid weeps— so it has been called SNOTTY JOHN AND CRY-BABY. We are wondering whether there will be a sequel: SNOTTY JOHN AND CRY-BABY IN TROUBLE AGAIN.)

TUESDAY 21 NOVEMBER 1961

The new number of *Chaplin* contains a taped interview with IB; but he thinks that the most important middle links have been cut out in the editing:

—

*The critics who mentioned the matter took it for granted that the eczema had been deliberately placed on the stigmata spots by IB.

"That bit about Picasso's centaurs at Antibes .... What I mean is this: the important thing is that Picasso *first* made them plump and full of detail, then he simplified them. Step by step! While still retaining the feeling. *That*'s the point: to simplify in that way. The whole time retaining the complete emotional content."

When he sees Ingrid Thulin's scenes in the schoolroom:

"Oh, this mixture of saint and hysteric ...."

His description of Märta Lundberg.

WEDNESDAY 22 NOVEMBER 1961
The lighting problem solved: retake in Stockholm

Ulla Ryghe has cut and put together all the shots from Skattung-by church which have been taken up to now, so that Sven and Ingmar can run them this evening and check them.

"All that brilliance! That charming quality of the light, don't you think it's wrong, Sven?"

"Of course it's wrong. But the studio church in Stockholm? Is that okay?"

"Sure. There the light had a chill, grey quality that was exactly right. What do we do now?"

Sven:

"This is a failure."

Ingmar:

"A failure all the way through, *isn't it*?"

Sven, patiently:

"Actually we should retake the whole thing."

Ingmar:

"What do *you* think we ought to do?"

He bores his gaze into his opponent Sven (as he usually does when he has already thought out a solution of his own).

A feeling of imminent departure has spread through the film team. All the technicians not needed for the remaining shots are ready to leave for home. Then are they to get Olof Thunberg up for a retake? And Allan Edwall? Wouldn't it be better to reconstruct the lower part of Skattungby church in the Råsunda studio?

Yes, of course.

Ulla Ryghe says afterwards that during this conversation she sat quiet, keeping her fingers crossed: "Oh, I do hope they decide on retakes! Otherwise Sven and Ingmar will only sit there during the rest of the work on the film, suffering and groaning and worrying

171

about these scenes that they were never satisfied with!"

When we come out from running the film, Britt Arpi, the owner and manageress of the hotel, tells Ingmar how sorry she is that he didn't get the weather he wanted; but Ingmar won't hear of it:

"You see, Britt, that thin covering of snow has more effect than deep layers of it .... it gives a bare, bleak atmosphere, stripped of all but the essentials ...."

He runs a substandard copy of Jacque Tati's WEEKEND SABO-TEUR. Afterwards a new discussion starts with Sven Nykvist. This evening IB is so done in that he's almost dotty with fatigue. A wisp of the thin hair hangs down over his brow, it gives him an air of worn-out middle age as he explains to Britt that he "must stick to what he saw when he wrote it."

"Once you start making compromises and concessions, then you are on the wrong track. Out in a bog .... it would be the same as if you lowered your standards here at Siljansborg."

Afterwards, when Sven and Ingmar had struggled through the conflict and decided on reconstruction and retakes at home at Rå-sunda, I wondered how this misunderstanding could have arisen in the first place. Was it Sven's fault for not realizing just how dark Ingmar wanted to have the church? Or was it Ingmar's, for grad-ually insisting on more and more burial-vault gloom in the church, as he discovered how much the new kind of film could take? I can-not tell which explanation is the correct one.

FRIDAY 24 NOVEMBER 1961

In the dusk they drive down and take all the shots with a puff-puff steam locomotive (in quick succession, with three cameras).

What ages they spent searching for this level crossing!— until they found it only a stone's throw from Rättvik's shopping center.

MONDAY 27 NOVEMBER 1961

The old film THIRST is run this evening, IB's own substandard copy. And Lamorisse's children's tale THE RED BALLOON. A film "about the artists and the critics," IB asserts! The boy with the balloon is the writer who has had a vision; then along come all the boys of the neighborhood to steal it .... these awful critics, envious and vindictive!

IB persists in his interpretation, in a wonderfully good humor:

"They're disorganized too, isn't it typical? The only thing they

172

have in common is *hatred*."

Now the young ruffians shoot down the red ballon. It crumples and dies. But then thousands of other balloons come sailing along instead, as a consolation.

"That's it *exactly*. When they've ruined one idea for you, you get a thousand new ones instead .... The symbolism holds! You must admit!"

TUESDAY 28 NOVEMBER 1961

IB himself owns the old silent film FAUST. He runs it this evening. The devil, Emil Jannings, has something white, glinting like a coin, in his eyes when he appears at the crossroads:

"We'll remember *that*, Sven, for THE FOLKTALE!"

After the film is over Ingrid slips quietly into her room; Ingmar laughs.

"Look how she dematerializes herself."

Today they've taken car scenes. IB would like to have put them off, but Carlberg kept on: "Well, seeing we're so close ...."; Sven hung outside the Rev. Ericsson's Opel with the assistant cameraman Peter Wester. Ingmar checked everything from his car, Carlberg at the head kept oncoming traffic out of the way, the SF truck drove last— and so the caravan advanced.

FRIDAY 1 DECEMBER 1961

We did nothing but stamp our feet about on the ice today, for the sake of one little car shot. Cold, boring, the batteries so run down that the camera went too slowly.

Evening, the warmth of the hotel again. Spirits rise, start to bubble. Ingmar cannot stop loving his ten-year-old Volvo.

Gunnar smiles, coffee cup in hand:

"Yes, you have a kind of paradoxical loyalty."

(Undertone: which affects even me, GB).

But women have an alarming desire to change their men. Ingmar:

"One of the big battles I had with Käbi was about my beret. And my leather jacket. I compromised and sacrificed my beret. But not the leather jacket. It contained my past; she took it. But I'm not letting the Volvo go, I'll hold onto that to my dying day."

SATURDAY 2 DECEMBER 1961

Departure for home.

Sven will be thirty-nine tomorrow.

TUESDAY 5 DECEMBER 1961
Home at SF again. Yesterday they rehearsed, today they took Märta's and Thomas's meeting in the vestry for the second time. (The first time was October 10th, when I kept track of all the instructions.)

The scene was shot in two halves. The first half was started ten times: seven takes were cut, three were complicated. The second half was shot three times. (One of these three was used in the finished film.)

WEDNESDAY 6 DECEMBER 1961
The cramped scene in the vestry is reshot: a wall is lifted out to make more room for lights, sound and camera. (Compare October 12th!)

THURSDAY 7 DECEMBER 1961
Ingrid is all keyed up for a retake of the entire letter at 12:15 today— but IB cancels it: fear again for "flariness" in the picture. Sven Nykvist does technical tests instead, and IB goes down and "relaxes" Ingrid.

FRIDAY 8 DECEMBER 1961
Ingrid does the letter (for the second time)
Technical meeting at Filmteknik at ten o'clock about the risk of flariness. IB and Sven decide to shoot the letter scene notwithstanding: any flariness that occurs can be "camouflaged" by increasing the light on Ingrid's face and softening it in the background (where the flariness is most noticeable). The letter is shot in two sections.
FIRST SECTION:
Take 1 is cut at 12:50 because of camera hum. Explosion between director and assistant cameraman Peter Wester in the firing line.

Take 2 is completed despite doors being banged outside the studio, but is not printed.

Take 3 is approved and printed. (I make a note to jog my memory: "Brilliant. The shimmer over her cheeks— the tense, rather hysterically shining and sensitively soft expression around the mouth. Shall I notice those nuances tomorrow also, when I see the rushes?")

SECOND SECTION:

Take 1 is no good, Ingrid gets a tickling in her throat and has to cough.

Take 2 is upset by the same throat trouble, plus the noise of an airplane.

Ingmar orders half an hour's break, so that Ingrid can have something hot to drink and rest her throat.

(I write: "IB wants the last lines quite bare. Märta must give in completely; but is Ingrid really up to it? Won't it be a bit too dry and tense like this?")

Take 3 is stopped right at the start.

Take 4 succeeds.

Ingmar, very gently:

"Now it's right, Ingrid! It's just that you chop it up a little too much. Let's take it once more, eh?"

Ingrid nods. Technical pause. IB finds that she is sitting rehearsing quietly to herself.

"Don't rehearse, Ingrid!"

Ingrid:

"I was only thinking of what bits I chopped up .... "

Ingmar asks her to take the final appeal even more gently.

"I'm afraid of its being a bit ingratiating then," Ingrid replies. "Too much film-acting, you know."

"You needn't be. I'll stop you if it is. It's better for you to put more into it, and I can check you if necessary."

Take 5 is a complete success and is printed.

"*That's* it! Just right. Let's call it a day." The time is 2:25.

(After that they run the new vestry scenes. Still not right: the lighting and trimming of the pictures could be improved. "Let's retake it, eh, Sven?")

SATURDAY 9 DECEMBER 1961

"One shouldn't use old jasmines"

In the morning Märta Lundberg walks forlornly down through the church, the empty church, leans her head against a wooden pillar, moaning. At 11 o'clock or so she has on a summer dress and is arranging the confirmation flowers. Suddenly she gets bloodyminded and asks Thomas whether he believes in intercession.

Just then I discover that Ingmar has cut a long bit in Thomas's conversation with the fisherman.

THOMAS: You must go on living, Jonas, the summer's coming, the darkness doesn't last forever. You have your strawberry patch and your flowering jasmine. Just think of the scent! Warm, long days. That's the earthly paradise, Jonas. It's something to live for.

"Much better without it. Much more desolate and awful. Thomas sits there and is to console Jonas, but all he manages to do is to take God right away from him. 'It's like when you were small, and were to look after another small child,' Ingmar says. 'So you carried it about. And then you dropped it and it hit its head on the radiator and started to howl, and then you got so scared that you spanked the child. And that only made it howl still worse ....' "

"You cut Märta's line outside Frostnäs church too. The one about when 'the water glitters in the sun. And the grove of birches. And the scent of the jasmines.' "

"Mmm. I had those jasmines in THE MURDER AT BARJÄRNA too. The old married couple sits there in the winter cold, thinking of the summer and the jasmines .... but no, away with them now."

He goes over to Ingrid and checks her eczema bandage.

"One shouldn't use old jasmines."

SUNDAY 10 DECEMBER 1961
Five ways of making actors crazy
"Director's psychology" department:

It must be hard to know what to *say* to actors when the take is over. "Cut!" is certainly not enough. They must know whether it was good or not.

If you say *good*, then why retake it?

If you say *not good* you must have some reason, so that they can do it better.

If you hesitate, a feeling of uneasiness spreads. What's this? Doesn't he know what he *thinks*?!

The moment when the director says "Cut!" is the most tricky moment of all for actors. That's when they are most vulnerable. Anyone wanting to hurt them should do so then.

During a pause in the letter shooting on Friday Ingmar did a couple of excellent sketches on the theme: "Five ways of making actors crazy."

1st way: The director mumbles nothing but nice things to the actor ("No, it was fine. Nothing wrong at all. Very good.") but in such a way that it sounds like veiled criticism. This convinces the actor that he has failed utterly.

2nd way: "Cut. Good. Let's take it again." The actor (anxiously): "Was there something wrong?" The director (brightly and amiably): "No, not at all. Oh no. But I think we'll take it again."

3rd way: Just before the take the director whispers to the cameraman in a suitably semi-audible tone: "Must she really be lit like that? It makes her chin so big. Oh, it doesn't matter. We'll take it like this!"

And so on.

IB acted the sketches well: distinctly and with telling mime. (But he didn't include his own most usual diversion stratagem: to blame the camera hum, lighting etc.— in order *not* to make the actors feel insecure. He lays the blame so often on technical faults, however, that there's a risk of the actors not believing him when there really is a technical fault.)

MONDAY 11 DECEMBER 1961

Today work begins on the big key scene when Thomas Ericsson tells the tormented fisherman about himself

I borrow a tape recorder from the sound department, get a mike installed in the wings of the vestry before work begins and make myself scarce in a dark corner of the studio behind protective screens. I made the decision after hearing Ingmar's careful way of instructing Ingrid before the letter reading: I cursed myself for not having thought of procuring a tape recorder. What kind of documentation is this— just serving up my own notes but never statements that can be checked?

The matter is made worse by my having to get IB's permission: he can suit his words to the microphone. But he doesn't let the mike hamper him, I can see that. He gradually forgets its existence: he lets himself go, just as usual. The unfortunate thing is, I can't say anything to Gunnar.

But who can hide in a film studio? Before long, everyone has discovered my hiding place and what I am up to. Someone asks: "What are you lurking down there in the corner for?" "I'm recording atmosphere sounds for the TV series." An unbelieving: "Oh, I see .... " and then I get hush-hush and silencing on the tape. ("Ssh, careful what you say .... he's taking it all on tape down there.")

The hardest thing for me to stand is GB's glance as he passes my corner. I can imagine how it feels to play an uncommonly difficult monologue scene and *at the same time* to know that someone has a mike switched on during the rehearsals; but I try to shake off the thought of the extra pressure I am putting on his nerves.

It's this very atmosphere of nerves that I want to get hold of—the emotional tension connected with a difficult scene.

GUNNAR'S VOICE: *Listen to me now, Jonas. I'll speak quite frankly and quite without reserve.*

INGMAR'S VOICE: Take the chair with you, Gunnar. Don't lift it up, just slide your way nearer. *Listen to me now, Jonas.* That's it! And put out your hands. That's it!

GUNNAR'S VOICE: *You know that my wife died four years ago.*

INGMAR'S VOICE: You don't look at him when you say that, because you know it's the most sensitive thing you have.

GUNNAR'S VOICE: *You must understand, Jonas. I'm no good as a parson.*

INGMAR'S VOICE: There you glance up at him, that's the crux of the whole thing. It comes out so terribly, as though you were retching ....

GUNNAR'S VOICE: *Supposing it's true that god doesn't exist. What does it matter?*

INGMAR'S VOICE: Slowly .... Clasp your hands *tight* there. *That's* where the whole tension must be .... And your voice quite calm and cold, suddenly.

GUNNAR'S VOICE: *Life makes sense. What a relief. Death is a snuffing out.*
   – – – There is no creator, no maintainer, no thought dizzy and unfathomable.

INGMAR'S VOICE: Long pause. Then you look up at him. (To both Max and Gunnar:) You both look at each other for the first time, a good long look. *That's* it. Then suddenly you get *deathly* scared, Gunnar. You know what you have *done* to him, you see. Then you say appealingly—

GUNNAR'S VOICE: *I don't feel well ....*

INGMAR'S VOICE: With a *horror*, suddenly, at what you have done ....

Gunnar asks whether Ingmar is going to take the *whole* scene in one camera position; but Ingmar reassures him. He only went through it once in order to feel on which side he would be with the camera. Discussion with Sven Nykvist about possible panning.
   Ingmar:
   "It's just that if we pan, we won't get the eyes right. I'd like to have the eyes of *both* of them, both Max and Gunnar, looking

almost straight into the camera .... Hah, we'll cut in! (Change of mood, recklessly): We'll cut in. Fixed positions! Never mind the expense."

(Here the tape is filled with chat about a remarkable homemade pipe that Stig Flodin, the chief sound engineer, is whittling for himself. Gunnar B. inspects the pipe, K. A. likewise.)

During the day they shoot the beginning of the scenes between Max and Gunnar when the parson offers the fisherman some coffee out of his thermos. Gunnar's big, difficult monologue is still a long way off.

TUESDAY 12 DECEMBER 1961
Thomas goes on confessing

The time is 9:45 and Gunnar is sitting with his back to the camera. He asks Max, the fisherman, how things are with his wife, the new boat, whether he's still brooding over the Chinese, whether he's managing to make ends meet .... IB:

"It's always the same when you sit with your back to the camera— either you overplay or else you get a bit outside the part. All actors do it. It's much more difficult to turn your back."

The scene is now divided up. Max von Sydow has to go off and act in a performance for schools, the bastard in Shakespeare's KING JOHN, at four o'clock. So IB devotes time first of all to the shots that Max is in. There's the close up of Max when he listens mutely to the parson's confession. There's the final shot with both of them in it: *Supposing it's true that god doesn't exist?* The beginning of Gunnar's monologue is kept until tomorrow; he has to do the end first, the entire questioning of God's existence.

GUNNAR'S VOICE: *No, no, don't go .... I want you to see what a miserable person, what a ruined wretch is sitting here opposite you. I'm no clergyman. I'm a beggar in need of your help!*
INGMAR'S VOICE, soft, appealing: "Don't stress *ruined* and *miserable*. (To Max): Don't look at him now, Max. You hide your eyes the whole time until .... "

If god doesn't exist, *there is no creator, no maintainer, no thought dizzy and unfathomable.* Ingmar probably senses that *dizzy* and *unfathomable* are not such good literature. He cuts it in

179

any case. The last words are: *no thought*.

Suddenly Ingmar gives this type of instruction:

INGMAR'S VOICE, very quiet: Don't rely on yourself, Gunnar. Rely only on your .... (inaudible owing to working noises from those around). You're no longer an actor. You see, this is beyond anything that can be expressed by voice or inflection, because the only thing that really can give a truth is .... (inaudible). Fear— the great fear— can never be expressed except with the eyes. Do you know what I mean?

MAX'S VOICE: So what's the last thing you say?

GUNNAR'S VOICE: .... *no thought*.

INGMAR'S VOICE: Exactly. (To Max:) Then you stand still— one, two, three, four— exit!

Later, after the take:

INGMAR'S VOICE: That was fine, Gunnar. Very good like that. Perhaps you used your voice a shade too much just now. Well, you didn't use your voice, you didn't do that exactly, but it was a little .... You must have a tiny bit more contour in it, I think. Also you took it much more softly this time, but I think it'll be all right.

At the day's rushes they run the first retake of Ingrid Thulin's letter reading. Discussion about flaring and camera buzz. Pause, silence for a while. Ingmar mumbles:

"The next film will be nothing but a close-up."

"Another ROPE?" asks the chief sound engineer, Lennart Unnerstad, referring to Hitchcock's THE ROPE.

"Well," IB says, "there were no close-ups in that. That's what was so tedious. Only trackings and pannings the whole time."

Börje Lundh has made a test with Gunnel Lindblom. At the beginning of shooting she was genuinely pregnant; now, after her delivery, a pregnancy has to be faked with make-up and padding for the scene that hasn't been shot yet when Pastor Ericsson goes to tell her that her husband is dead. Ingmar is not entirely satisfied with the test:

"Well, I don't know," he says, going all out for modesty. "I've only had six children. But I don't think the padding looks quite right. And the cheeks .... "

"Gunnel is rounder in the cheeks now," Börje Lundh says.

180

"Though in a different way."

Ingmar:

"The hair's too black, also. And she looks more exotic in this version."

Afterwards Ingmar, *en passant*, reveals how happy he is about Ingrid's new reading of the letter.

"And when Gunnar offers Max the basket with the coffee in it. Isn't he splendid? So touching."

He is bubbling with pleasure and delight. But that sort of thing isn't shown at screenings. That's when people are brought to book for technical faults— period. Never show how happy you are about your own pictures.

WEDNESDAY 13 DECEMBER 1961

Thomas concludes his confession

Today Gunnar is alone in front of the camera; Max is not here. Ingmar takes Max's place.

I have the tape recorder on today too; but the fine introductory conversation between Gunnar and Ingmar is drowned by carpentry noises. It's always the same: the best discussion blossoms out, suddenly and spontaneously, in the middle of clatter and muddle. Two voices acquire intimacy and a confidential tone in all the surrounding noise (while Sven Nykvist asks Åland to put a quilt over the camera). Ingmar speaks extremely softly, almost in a whisper, when he describes how Thomas has an unspoken request for forgiveness to the fisherman, in the middle of the actual confession:

INGMAR'S VOICE: .... understand me! The whole time: understand me, forgive me, help me over this, *don't you see?* But do you see the eyes, the whole time you must allow for the eyes ....

GUNNAR'S VOICE, rather muffled: I'd rather not do it so awfully hard ....

INGMAR'S VOICE: You needn't either, because now it holds. — — — Do you know what you have? You have the comedy habit of seizing on the main words, but here every little thing .... here it must be in the eyes .... it must come through the thought in order to come in the feeling .... (inaudible).

GUNNAR'S VOICE: .... and then if I can take it a couple of times, Ingmar, may I? You see, this is the most difficult thing I have in the whole film, I've been thinking of this for months. I do so want this to hold, you see.

INGMAR'S VOICE: It does. (Indecipherable) .... the strong feeling you have .... holds .... all your despair is there: in the shoulders, the way you hold yourself ....

They rehearse quite impromptu in the middle of the clatter: Gunnar takes his long speech in a whisper, goes right through it for the listening Ingmar. At one point Ingmar reminds Gunnar of a gesture he made before— and in the finished film Gunnar makes a touching little movement with his hand. He pushes aside a boyish lock of hair (which immediately falls over his forehead again) when he says:

"I had big dreams, let me tell you. I was going to be a remarkable person .... "

Then the tape is filled with talk between Ingmar, Stig Flodin and Peter Wester about post-synching (lines laid on afterwards). Ingmar:

"Our post-synching is worse than the Italians'— for some extraordinary reason."

Ready?

Not for a take, but for rehearsal:

INGMAR'S VOICE: Silence please! Action!

GUNNAR'S VOICE: *You must understand. I'm no good as a parson.*

INGMAR'S VOICE: Appeal more gently.

GUNNAR'S VOICE: *You must understand.*

INGMAR'S VOICE: That's it.

GUNNAR'S VOICE: *I'm no good as a parson. I have believed in an unreasonable ....*

INGMAR'S VOICE, checking: Er .... sorry, just one thing. Stress the word 'good' a little more.

GUNNAR'S VOICE: Yes, of course. It's much better if I can do it like that, much better. I really mean it .... *a god who guaranteed all conceivable security, against the fear of death, against the horror of life ....*

INGMAR'S VOICE, calmly: Take it more slowly. That's the very part you should take more slowly. It's the most terrible of the lot.

Gunnar goes on. When he is through, he asks whether Ingmar wants the whole lot at one go.

INGMAR'S VOICE: You can divide it up if you like.

GUNNAR'S VOICE: May I?

INGMAR'S VOICE: Sure.

GUNNAR'S VOICE: Thanks awfully. Actually, I haven't slept since three o'clock this morning.

INGMAR'S VOICE (absently): What?! (Then he hears what Gunnar said): No, I know.

Gunnar now rehearses the passage: *Every time I confronted god with the reality I saw, he became ugly, hideous, a spider god— a monster. So I shielded him from life and light. I clasped him to me in the dark and loneliness. The only one who was allowed to see my god was my wife. She supported me, encouraged me, helped me, filled the gaps. Our dreams. My indifference to the preaching of the gospels, my jealous hatred of Christ.*

INGMAR'S VOICE, extremely soft in the noise: .... and hatred. The sudden hatred of his wife who didn't give him the truth. It's so important how it corresponds with Ingrid. And the letter.

GUNNAR'S VOICE: .... *So I shielded him from life and light.*

INGMAR'S VOICE, softly: Don't get tense.

GUNNAR'S VOICE: *So I shielded him from life and light.*

INGMAR'S VOICE: Yes .... Supposing you say this: *That's why I shielded him ....*

(Somebody coughs repeatedly.)

GUNNAR'S VOICE, quick friendly appeal: Oh, please don't cough. *That's why I shielded him ....   — — —   My indifference to the preaching of the gospels ....*

(Someone coughs again.)

INGMAR'S VOICE, fiercely: Who's that coughing all the time?

(No answer.)

INGMAR'S VOICE, sharper: Who's that coughing?

UNIDENTIFIABLE VOICE: It's me.

INGMAR'S VOICE: Surely you realize that when we're rehearsing like this you *can't* keep coughing all the time.

MUMBLE FROM PERSON CONCERNED: I can't help it.

INGMAR'S VOICE: Well, go outside then.

GUNNAR'S VOICE, mediating: I was the one who said it, there was no need.

INGMAR'S VOICE: But it's essential for us to have quiet.

GUNNAR'S VOICE: Will you give it to me a little earlier, Katinka?

KATINKA'S VOICE: *She supported me ....*

GUNNAR'S VOICE: *She supported me, encouraged me ....*

(When the rehearsal is finished:)

183

INGMAR'S VOICE, sighing contentedly: That's swell.

Gunnar strains every nerve, under concentration and extreme tension. He gets one or two words in the wrong order; it annoys him, as it always does annoy an actor.

GUNNAR'S VOICE: It's so damned stupid, I *know* my lines. It's just these link-ups that are so frightfully difficult, because he breaks off his own train of thought.
INGMAR'S VOICE: It's only because you're rushing it. After *Our dreams* don't think what you're to say next, but instead: *Sink to rest*. Sit quiet for a moment. Let it come when it comes and have confidence. That's it, you see: as long as you have this confidence it will be *exactly* right.

About ten o'clock Gunnar's scene is shot for the second time. Ingmar's stomach is out of order and he has loud stomach pains— a dangerous sound which the microphone can pick up. He wants to move to one side, but Gunnar prefers to have Ingmar play the scene with him. "It feels better like that." "Sure?" "Yes." Ingmar: "Then you'll have to put up with the stomach rumblings."
And Åland shoves the clapper in: "270 B, take 3," and Gunnar Björnstrand makes a concentrated effort and utters the whole of the naked Bergman self-confession with his eyes turned on IB himself. In all truth, words uttered through a glass darkly.
In the afternoon the most difficult lighting of the whole film a-waits Sven Nykvist. A big long shot of the chancel, GB huddled by the altar ring— and the sun "breaking out of the snow clouds" and flinging its light through the church window.
In order to annoy director and cameraman the sun decides to go on strike, and Wednesday the 13th ends with the shot untaken.

THURSDAY 14 DECEMBER 1961
Cancelled today. IB ill.
A few are glad about the sudden time off for Christmas. Others are distressed. Some who wanted to be finished by Christmas but have mumbled "Knock on wood, we're not going to be finished by Christmas," suddenly find that their words have come true and to their surprise, taste bitter in their mouths.

WEDNESDAY 20 DECEMBER 1961
Ingmar's bad throat makes his telephone voice sound as if it were

just breaking. But he's getting better anyway.

He has had a couple of nasty days, however, when his throat was so congested that he felt he was choking. A fear of death clutched at him— until his throat finally cleared and he could get his breath again.

(When I read this note six months later, I am reminded of Ingrid Thulin's death scene in THE SILENCE.)

He admires the great, objective, visionary strength in Brigitta Trotzig's novel, *A Tale From the Coast*, which he is just now reading.

He is thinking of going up to the Siljansborg Hotel on January 15th to write THE FOLKTALE.

He is happy about Gunnar's big confession: "When Gunnar once let himself go he was awfully good."

CHRISTMAS EVE 1961

His voice still sounds a bit dull and croaky:

".... and I've just read Marianne Höök's book about me. The proofs."

Outburst and comments.

WEDNESDAY 3 JANUARY 1962

At the coffee break Lenn looks in with his practical list and consults Ingmar about tomorrow:

"Where do you want to be? In the restaurant?"

"No, down here. In my room."

"What shall we offer her?"

"Tea. Biscuits. And then we have that English marmelade. Nothing out of the way. Nothing special."

A smile and an explanation:

"Miss Gustafsson wants to meet me."

THURSDAY 4 JANUARY 1962

I catch a glimpse of her in the corridor. She is very simply dressed, her hair is straight.

Ingmar, afterwards:

"Her voice is so nice and gentle. It has a slight huskiness that makes it interesting. And her eyes! And a quiet sense of humor. She speaks slowly when she laughs, the blood is pressed out of her cheeks, pulsating softly under the rather heavy make-up she uses;

at the same time her eyes sparkle ...."

Indeed the director describing the actress's face.

"What about her as an actress? Do you think she's finished as an actress?"

Ingmar gives a broad smile that comes from within:

"Nothing done for there! She has it *all*!"

"Then why did she stop making films?"

"Because she was humiliated by Hollywood."

"Did she say so just now?"

"No, but I had a feeling that that was at the bottom of it."

"Did you talk about the film parts at all?"

"Not a word!"

Last year it happened that Marlene Dietrich took a taxi out to Djursholm and went to see him in his house (she warned him *en passant* against going to America and filming). Last autumn he met Igor Stravinsky. And now this.

His face at the moment is very gay and boyish:

"Now at any rate I've met three of the institutions of this age: Marlene Dietrich, Igor Stravinsky and Greta Garbo."

MONDAY 8 JANUARY 1962

The holidays over, IB recovered-- we continue in Jonas Persson's cottage: the parson comes in with the news of his death.

TUESDAY 9 JANUARY 1962

The sun shines out

The sun works perfectly today. Thomas sinks down at the altar ring, Märta comforts him. ("Moving," I write. "The same fine outburst as in THROUGH A GLASS DARKLY. The same boyish forlornness.") And Ingmar has one of his quiet days:

"I find this scene the climax of the film— denial, contrition, the lowest point and grace all converge. That's why I want this enormous *tenderness* between them: grace which in some way flows in over them."

He sits calm and collected in his director's chair, unconsciously twiddling his wedding ring.

WEDNESDAY 10 JANUARY 1962

Yesterday afternoon the old woman from Hol was suddenly standing in the aisle. Elsa Ebbesen had a strangely high pitch when

186

she lamentingly gave the parson the news that Jonas Persson had shot himself. I was amazed and asked IB today how much he had instructed her.

Ingmar:

"Not at all! You see, when I arrived yesterday morning I asked her how she was. 'My husband died the day before yesterday,' she replied. 'We have lived a whole life together.'"

All the same, it was a matter of course to her that she should work; and that perhaps she could make use of the experience in her job.

"Perhaps I can use it in this scene," she said.

Ingmar's tenderness when he tells me about it:

"There's an *actress* for you!"

(After today's rushes he classified his film; with a smile: "Never before has a Bergman play been so close to reportage and yet so far from it.")

THURSDAY 11 JANUARY 1962

Conversation with Ingrid in the pauses. (Retake of the intercession today, P. A. has reconstructed a bit of Skattungby church in the studio.) Ingrid speaks of her need of solitude. She retired somewhere into herself:

".... where I go, I don't know. But it takes so long for me to come back again, that often I think it isn't worthwhile."

FRIDAY 12 JANUARY 1962
54th day of shooting

Now that the big heavy job is over, Gunnar fluctuates between fatigue and satisfaction:

".... the joy of knowing that *a few* times in one's life one has been in some remarkable jobs. Whatever reassessments of IB's films that may be made in the future— *that* remains."

Then it fades away: the feeling that however hard you work, Ingmar is the only one who gets any credit (others in the team have the same feeling). Suddenly it's worth it all: the torment of work, the arguments, the conflicts.

Today, the 54th day of shooting, the vestry scene between Märta and Thomas is shot for the *third* time. (See October 10th and December 5th.) But only the beginning. (The end of the December 5th take is fine as it is.) Take 1 is stopped. Take 2 is printed.

Now the scene is ready for tomorrow's TV filming.

The team's tiredness is noticeable at today's rushes. In yesterday's take, the Rev. Thomas Ericsson walks into Frostnäs church with his hat *on*. Gunnar, Ingmar— nobody has thought of it; and Katinka, always on the alert at every take, blushes at her blackout. That was *her* miss in this film. Retake on Sunday.

IB, satisfied, hands out praise: for the lighting, for the sound; he is pleased and contented that they retook Olof Thunberg's gossip and Ingrid's intercession.

"We *sulk* our way right through this film."

SATURDAY 13 JANUARY 1962
The TV cameras steal into the studio

Tricky day in the TV series.

I am upset and dissatisfied. Disappointment in my documentary ambitions, hurt that the TV cameras manage to capture so little of the spontaneous talk that keeps cropping up. (They do succeed a few times: on the film strip one can tell exactly *when* Ingrid, Gunnar and Ingmar are conscious that the cameras are turning.) But how did I intend this program to be made? Did I really think that we could *steal* into the studio and secretly surround the film team with two 16 mm cameras? The other day I showed Ingmar exactly *what* instructions he gave when the vestry scene was shot for the first time on October 10th. Did I imagine that he would repeat just that? What a strange form of "documentarily genuine" that would be.

No, it must all be done deliberately, directly for the TV cameras. My only objection to the result: Ingmar talked too much (in reality he is afraid of "over-rehearsing"). Gunnar and Ingrid too. (Compare the original instructions on Tuesday, October 10th.) Not a serious objection: the whole idea is to give a summary of the studio work. And IB plays his director's part so well that the usual nervous tension arises in the collective: finally everyone worked as if they had forgotten the TV cameras.

After lunch I interview IB about his work as a director. In the middle of all the questions I ask him for a self-description. Have you any weaknesses as a director?

IB: My great weakness (also as a private person, it usually belongs together) is, I suppose, my "bossiness." The fact that I have an awful need of ordering people about and telling them what to do— it's of

188

course a sense of power or a need of power. I've had to keep a terrific check on that both in my private life and in my professional life. It can creep into my work with the actors, and sometimes— for those who are very sensitive to that— it can be difficult. And I have to watch out that I don't bind the actor and his inspiration and his feeling of independent creation with an awful fussing and busy-bodying with himself; I must leave him alone with his part and with his thoughts and not chip in everywhere, so that at last they feel so hemmed in that they don't know where they are.

That's why it is easy for him to portray a bossy person like Mārta Lundberg.

SUNDAY 14 JANUARY 1962
"The best scene in the whole film"
The church in the big studio is pulled down today. Thirteen men work overtime all day on Sunday until the chancel is left. (An expensive day, one of them guesses, twenty-five hundred in wages plus overtime, probably.)

But in Studio 5 a good, calm concentration prevails. It's *nice* to film on Sundays. Allan Edwall is to do Frövik's thoughts about Christ's suffering and gives a little smile: "The best scene in the whole film," he thinks. But it pains him that Ingmar has cut all the lines about Frövik's private life.

"Didn't you think they were good?" he asks.

"Oh yes. But we're at the end of the film now and must stick to essentials. If they were at the start of the film, it would be different."

IB in his gentlest mood: the same tenderness today towards the actors as when Ingrid did the letter; he whispers contentedly:

"You just put two people up against a wall. And Gunnar today! Utterly relaxed, completely Gothic."

He kept waking up all last night. He pondered on all sorts of moves for Thomas and Frövik, afraid of the simplest solution.

"Not until this morning, on the way here in the car, did it occur to me that the most natural was the most right: that they just sit straight up and down against the wall."

They sit, yes. But the *camera* moves like a searching eye over their naked faces— to and fro between them: and each time still closer!

The mere fact that Ingrid kneels down when she prays the inter-

189

cession, there's nothing about it in the script. But one evening at Siljansborg I went in to her, slightly embarrassed, and asked: "How does it feel to you to kneel down there?" Then she replied, simply and dryly as only that girl can: "I don't mind."

It's cold in the Frostnäs vestry. Frövik bends down and plugs in the electric fire. K. A. sees to the instruction and shows Allan Edwall how he himself does it when he bends down.

Ingmar tells Sven Nykvist not to bother about the logical light just now.

"Make a beautiful light, Sven. Frövik is an angel."

MONDAY 15 JANUARY 1962
Film born in dream
Just before lunch today he began to unfold a brand-new film idea:

"What about this .... "

Two women and a thirteen-year-old boy in a completely strange city. The older woman has a hemorrhage and they stop at a hotel. Ingmar explains that some of the material goes back to an old radio play THE CITY. The rest is quite fresh and is based on a dream he had during his illness in December.

Some of the things in the idea link up with Kābi's world. The action of the film takes place in a country with troop transports, in smoke and grime, somewhere behind the iron curtain. Moreover, he himself is going to invent the language that is spoken in that country— but he is thinking of using Estonian ("which is *utterly* incomprehensible to me!"). He only needs to change a few consonants in it.

"Are you going to see everything from the boy's point of view?"

"No, that would be too narrow. I want to see it from the younger woman's."

For a time he thought of masking the older woman in some way; he was afraid that the part was too close to himself.

It always makes you anxious telling about fresh ideas; everything is untried, fragile in them:

"Do you think I can make something of it? But those of my films that have sprung out of dreams are usually good."

TUESDAY 16 JANUARY 1962
Chance, not the director, has seen to it that the film has moved

190

from *male* to *female* even in the religious symbols. IB did decide that he wanted to have a "throne of grace" (Christ between God's knees) in the first church. But chance supplemented this: Skattungby church happened to have a madonna.

(Sylvia Edmond, Cordelia Edvardsson, Tore Zetterholm are three of many critics who have attached importance to the madonna in the church.)

WEDNESDAY 17 JANUARY 1962

"Hallo, old cock," Blom splutters to Frövik. *"Well, what's it to be, are we going to hold the service or not?"*

And the camera turns for the last time in this film, a Wednesday morning between 8:30 and 9:30. (Allan Edwall has to be at the Royal Dramatic Theater at ten for a dress rehearsal of Max Frisch's ANDORRA, he is playing the lead.) Ingmar gathers in the entire production with a gesture:

"Listen, everyone .... It's been a long, trying production, and maybe not always such fun. But you've all been splendid, absolutely splendid."

He is tired, smiling, restless; impatient for new tasks.

In the big studio, only the chancel is left of the church, standing in reserve for possible retakes. It gapes like a shell broken open, dusty, dirty, ragged; while new sets are being built beside it, for new films.

THURSDAY 18 JANUARY 1962

Ingmar and Sven entered the screening room known as "the Opera" yesterday afternoon to see the *whole* film. Today they will see the rest. It takes nearly five hours to see all the material. (As it is, many duplicates have already been eliminated.) Out of this five-hour dough a cake in the form of a presentable film is to be baked!

They come out of "the Opera," looking secretly satisfied. Sven hardly dares to show that he is pleased; but his eyes are screwed up into happy slits:

"It feels rather like Christmas Eve."

SATURDAY 20 JANUARY 1962

That Which is Willed

I must have patience. I must quiet down and have patience. The

191

vital condition is patience, IB wrote to himself in the working script of THROUGH A GLASS DARKLY. And during rehearsals he often appealed to Gunnar Björnstrand and Ingrid Thulin: Do have confidence in the creative forces! Sink to rest! Sit quietly for a while! For this is his problem at the writing desk, he says today:

"Not to force my own will on the characters. In general I must learn *not to will*. Formerly I wanted everything, quickly, rapidly! Käbi often says to me that I must have confidence in the creative forces within me."

The car is driving up to Rättvik and the Hotel Siljansborg: towards relaxation in new work.

Käbi's piano teacher, Maria-Louisa (who is a "fantastic woman") often mocks *Das Gewollte* in all artistry. The shaft goes home to Ingmar. Not even in THROUGH A GLASS DARKLY did he manage to avoid That Which is Willed, he says. But he did in WINTER LIGHT. He describes his present working method:

"First I write down all I know about the story, at length and in detail. Then I sink the iceberg and let some of it float up. Just a little."

First the old kind of script writing, that is, in clear acting scenes. Then he gets to work and cuts drastically, bridging the gaps. He sulks slightly over this fussiness in himself.

Lately he has been like a hen about to lay. What is he going to write now that he is going up to Rättvik?

"Will it be THE FOLKTALE?"

No. It will be that thing about the woman and the boy. Käbi has helped him with the decision: "She made me realize that I can't avoid this material." He is toying with the idea of a new technique:

"There won't be any acting scenes. And not a word will be said about 'dream' in the whole film, but the film itself will *be* a dream. I'll call it THE DREAM, I think."

The afternoon light is fading and the ridges of Bergslagen rise outside the car windows. Sten Lindén is driving SF's Opel and Ingmar sleeps between Sala and Krylbo, like a little old woman with hands clasped and helplessly hanging head. "The director's position" he calls it when he wakes up:

"It's a matter of habit. When you sit at the direction desk down in the stalls in the dark, watching the actors .... it would look very bad to sleep with your head tilted backwards. If you have your

192

head down, on the other hand, they think you're reading the script."

SUNDAY 21 JANUARY 1962

In the middle of the after dinner coffee chat:

"If I hadn't been so tied up with woolly jackets and females when I was little .... I could cope better with loneliness."

He paints a picture of his dependence on his mother. Then he has a hypothesis about the theater world:

"No one can be a great actor who hasn't a sensual magnetism and talent. Who doesn't experience everything with his senses. You can imagine the sort of atmosphere it is when a flock of such people gets together. I had the idea of teaching a friend about this, but when I saw how alarmed he got, I was turned off. This physical and mental intercourse in which everything overlaps, quite amorally— I couldn't initiate him into all that."

Formerly he felt a desperate need of *liking* both his men and women actors. He wanted to feel that they were under his influence, he says, and he guarded them jealously.

(Compare Märta in the classroom: *"I know I'm an awfully bossy person."* Thomas makes a deprecating gesture and Märta reacts in a wonderfully logical way: *"No, no! don't contradict me!"*)

MONDAY 22 JANUARY 1962

Ingrid Thulin is interviewed on the radio. What is she like, this Märta Lundberg in WINTER LIGHT?

"Like a stone in a northern Swedish river that the water just keeps running over."

During one period, IB says afterwards, Ingrid had such trouble with her voice that he placed her in parts (WILD STRAWBERRIES) where she could make her effect with eyes and silence. (Compare October 30th, 1961.)

TUESDAY 23 JANUARY 1962

He doesn't make it easy for anyone wanting to write about the course of the work: *today* came a vital piece of information about last summer's manuscript job.

"You see, that goddam letter in WINTER LIGHT .... Lenn was going to the station, the whole script was ready. I just sat down and the whole letter just *came*. So there I was with it in my hand, and

I thought: Here I am landed with a letter! What am I to do with it?"

Märta, pushing in and competing with Thomas's self-confession! Out of *that* yeast in the oven arose this film's great technical experiment: Ingrid Thulin's 8-minute-long reading straight into the camera.

THURSDAY 25 JANUARY 1962

The bulldozers are at work on the new highroad outside the hotel. Ingmar is still vacillating between THE FOLKTALE and THE DREAM. THE FOLKTALE could give a nice summer's shooting in Dalarna; THE DREAM would involve trips abroad: Hannover or Grenoble.

"Grenoble?"

"Mmm. I recall it as grimy and awful and lacking in culture: no concert hall, no theater, only striptease."

He is considering Gunnel Lindblom as the younger woman. And the elder? He gives a laugh:

"It would be something for Garbo."

"Can you get her?"

"Never."

FRIDAY 26 JANUARY 1962

The crisis over

After "Sunday at the bottom of the vale of tears" Björnstrand and Bergman have emerged into the warmth of the sun again: together they create a fantastic atmosphere around the dinner table. GB has come up here to Siljansborg for a short relaxation; he comes with a fresh report of an interview he has done for the Italian TV:

" 'How does Signor Bergman direct? Does he say much?' asked the Italian. 'No, no,' I said, 'he transforms the actors into animals of intuition.' "

Ingmar laughs loudly.

"Not far out, actually."

The state of crisis in the schoolroom seems unreal now that one is drawn into their cozy ring of well-being.

Ingmar:

"Did you see the picture of us in *Women's World*? Two old draught horses under the yoke. Who have toiled and plodded along

194

together, have sulked and jostled and buffeted each other for eleven years .... "

Two sensualists, let out of the working establishment, freed from the compulsion of achievement— gaiety reverberates through the dining room.

P. S.

It's a slow business writing about those two women, he says. But he has promised himself *not* to force it.

PART III

**EDITING,
MIXING,
PREMIÈRE**

WEDNESDAY 21 FEBRUARY 1962

Discover afterwards that Ingmar has started to edit WINTER LIGHT with Ulla Ryghe today.

THURSDAY 1 MARCH 1962

They went on working on Monday, Tuesday, Wednesday, and to-day. If luck is against me his editing collides with my own film production; I had my life's first, nerve-tingling, unreal studio day last Tuesday when I took the first shots of THE MISTRESS. If he is going to edit WINTER LIGHT during March and April it will slip out of the way of my diary.

FRIDAY 4 MAY 1962

Luckily not. He has used March and April for writing the new film at home at Djursholm and doesn't start editing until today, in earnest. (I am ill in bed and can't be in on it yet.)

The new film will not be called THE CITY and not THE DREAM, but TIMOKA.

Timoka is the name of the town the women arrive at. He invented it on his own and discovered afterwards that in Estonian it meant "belonging to the hangman."

SATURDAY 12 MAY 1962

Dagens Nyheter today tells of Buñuel's love of Bergman:

Ingmar Bergman— a tragic case

thinks the Mexican director Luis Buñuel, who in the latest issue of ABF's magazine *The Window* is interviewed by Björn Kumm. According to Buñuel, Bergman is "a man who squanders his talent on rubbish. He is a very good director, but he is taken up with questions that are not interesting. What is it he asks about in every film? God, evil, good, whether God exists— you can't keep on with that sort of thing! I can hardly sit his films out. He can keep on selling this superficial quasi-philosophy to a decadent public. It's typical that he has gained such success in America. The Americans, these gringos, are interested in that sort of thing.

Love passionately requited. This was noticeable when a TV program on films ran the communion parody from VIRIDIANA last winter; IB's disgusted mutter:

" .... how utterly tasteless and puerile."

MONDAY 14 MAY 1962

"The editing school" starts today. Working schedule: morning lesson in with Ingmar and Ulla Ryghe (I look on). Application exercises in the afternoon (I go in to the experienced editor Lennart Wallén and start cutting THE MISTRESS).

Ingmar has been at it regularly since May 4th. During that time he has edited the entire introduction. But he's afraid that the communion service will make the film lopsided at the start:

"I'm thinking of cutting the beginning of the service and starting with the sacramental words: "Our Lord Jesus Christ in the night when he was betrayed."

Cut the service?! After all the work he put into it during shooting?

"Do you think *that* is an obstacle? Never. If it's wrong, it's wrong; and it must come out. However hard you worked at it."

How can the actual editing work be described? When one was a child and got hold of a big jigsaw puzzle— does it resemble that feeling? This mixture of boredom and exaltation. Hour after hour, week after week they sit at the cutting table, the director and the editor. They groan, suffer agonies, plow their way through the pile of pictures; the whole time feeling a kind of excitement. This expectation of the final result. At long last every piece of the puzzle fits into place.

Even the technical part of it is hard to describe. The cutting table has a very small picture window. There are two turntables for the film strip, two turntables for the sound track. A system of buttons that make it possible to spool forwards, to back, to stop, to spool forwards at double speed, to back at double speed (when the voices sound like Donald Duck), or to run at extreme slow motion ("frame by frame").

Lift out a film strip, hang it up, put another in its place— the tedious, endless work of the editor, demanding infinite patience.

The same scene has been shot in two positions: medium shot and close-up. Which one shall we choose, which is best? Supposing we use both? Then we'll start with the medium shot, cut to the other player and finish with the close-up— how's that?

Ulla Ryghe cuts, sticks together and runs the strip, then looks at Ingmar questioningly. He scratches his head.

"No-o, it's not good like that."

Long pause for thought, Ulla waits. Together with others she

200

would start talking until a suggestion emerged; with Ingmar she has learned to wait. For his solution.

"Let's do this instead!"

She takes the strip, looks for the bits she has just glued and rips open the joins.

Ingmar hums a Stravinsky theme from THE RAKE'S PROGRESS. He takes pleasure in the neatness and cleanliness of Ulla's room. Other editors may surround themselves with a nice, homely mess in poky, smokey rooms; Ulla's is as tidy as the operating theater in a provincial hospital. The film is kept in boxes, the boxes in stacks; the stacks are meticulously numbered— it is a point of honor with her to be able to put her hand instantly on any bit of the finished film, if it is only two frames that are missing from a join. Just now the room is freshly painted— it gives it an extra neat, clean touch. When I want to tease Ulla, I call her "the china doll." IB doesn't. He and Ulla have the same need of order, pedantry, freedom from dust.

Ulla always works in a white coat and with small, soft, white gloves so as to protect the film from scratches. The white gloves get slightly soiled from her work, a little fluffy.

Some editors let others do the joining work for them: this means that the director has to wait a day for the result. Ulla Ryghe, who has always had a technical interest, does the joining herself, by hand, so that Ingmar can immediately see what the cut looks like.

Ulla Ryghe (university studies at Lund, later journalist) is editing her second feature film. She got her basic training in THROUGH A GLASS DARKLY. She works perseveringly and puts in an enormous amount of overtime in order to maintain the editing pace that Ingmar needs.

Two hours' séance this morning: Ingmar goes through the series of pictures, marking all the cuts he wants done. Then he leaves Ulla to carry them out— she works overtime, it is late at night before she starts her Karmann Ghia and drives home.

TUESDAY 15 MAY 1962

The morning's séance starts in screening room 2. We see the short bit that is the result of yesterday's toil.

"Aha. So that was that."

The bit is laid on one side, and IB goes on.

I am astonished at the character of what we have seen. It feels heavy, drawn out. A lot of lines come twice. The pauses make the scene sag, the shots seem too long. Why does he do it this way? Why doesn't he try to find the right rhythm straight away? (And surely it would agree better with Ingmar's quick temperament?)

"You're crazy .... that comes later, when one has gone through the material over and over again! Only then does one begin to feel the rhythm, in the fingertips .... Don't forget that, for God's sake: It's far better to take too much at the start of every cut, and then slowly, slowly bake the whole cake together until you get the feel of the rhythm .... "

Quite by chance he and Käbi went out to Drottningholm last evening and found themselves in the middle of the visiting English theater company's dress rehearsal of Purcell's opera "Dido and Aeneas." The feeling of happiness remains with him all day today: "To think that in this age, in this country, we can at last see something so thoroughly prepared and so perfect .... it happens all too seldom."

THURSDAY 17 MAY 1962
"My mania for close-ups"
In this first time around with the editing Ingmar today has reached the moment when the old woman from Hol, Elsa Ebbesen, stands down in the church with the news that Jonas Persson has shot himself with the gun. Ingmar runs the long shot, with the old woman standing, small and alone, far down in the church— like the lamenting chorus in an ancient drama.

Then he runs the close-up of her as she peers to see the parson's reaction. Ingmar's forefinger flies out at the tiny projection window of the cutting table.

"Just *look* at the change. Just now she was the tragic chorus, and *now*, and now the old village gossip is peeping out of her!"

"Did you want the village gossip out of her? Did you *direct* it out of her?"

"Not at all. I just stood her in front of the camera, and she did everything herself."

Soon afterwards we have reached the two long shots at the scene of the suicide. He is cocky about them. (I make a mental note of his pride and take it out when we do the TV interview about the editing, June 25th, 1962. Why long shots in particular?)

202

IB: I suppose it's because I want to counteract my mania for close-ups. I
       love close-ups, but I think that this is one of those really horrible mo-
       ments with this dead man lying there, who has shot himself. And the
       parson who comes and looks at his victim. And I've a feeling that the
       very snowstorm is taking part in the scene.   And the surrounding sce-
       nery and the rapids. And that darkening Sunday afternoon. It's just as
       important, in fact more important than suddenly showing close-ups,
       because I've a feeling that just there we should stand silent and objec-
       tive, at a distance, like a frightened observer of what is happening.
       Just register it, that is. It's so awful that every close-up of the parson or
       every close-up of the dead man's face or of those around about, it
       would be like making something fancy of what is so intolerably diffi-
       cult— a suffering which is so terrible that any close-up would be just so
       much acting and a profanation.
INT: Do you really want to call close-ups a *mania*, as you said just now?
IB: Yes, it's a passion: to be right in close to people. To look them
       straight in the eyes and to try and get their mental movements to re-
       flect in their faces. And to convey this to the audience in as direct and
       as naked a way as possible. That's the technique I've learned over the
       years. And it's good sometimes to jump back with the camera and just
       stand far away and register.

Compare the axiom in the essay "Every Film Is My Last Film":

We should also bear in mind that the actor's finest means of expression
is his *eyes*. The objectively composed, perfectly directed and acted
close-up is the director's strongest means of influencing the audience
but at the same time is the most flagrant proof of his skill or his ignorance. The scarcity or plenitude of close-ups characterizes in a merciless
way the film-maker's temperament and degree of human interest.

That is why his pride is so striking: he feels that just here, at the
scene of the suicide, he has managed to resist a temptation. And a
shameless curiosity.

We arrive at the moment when the parson tries to console the
fisherman's wife. Ingmar:

"Someone is going to say here that the parson has no responsibility, Jonas Persson would have taken his life anyway."

"According to a naturalistic view, yes. Not according to a Christian one."

Ingmar, mumbling laconically:
"Not according to mine either."
The scene has been shot in several camera positions. In one of them the parson and the fisherman's wife are seen in a long shot. In another the camera goes into a close-up of the fisherman's wife. Ingmar decides on the close-up.
(Next time he goes through the film he tries out another solution. Should he not, on the contrary, save the close-up? Wouldn't it be better to let the parson and the fisherman's wife remain two figures away in the gloom of the hall? Two people whose faces we do not see until the parson has finished speaking?

THOMAS: Your husband is dead, Mrs. Persson. They have taken him to the cottage hospital but there's nothing to be done. He has shot himself.

Only then, at the words *He has shot himself*, do we move in on a close-up of the fisherman's wife!
"Get out the long shot, Ulla, and we'll see .... "
Yes, of course. Much more effective like that.)

FRIDAY 18 MAY 1962
Jörn Donner's book about IB, *The Devil's Face*, appeared at the end of April. The reviews are still rankling with Ingmar. The theme: He had thought that the contempt of the Swedish intellectuals for him had been moderated of late. What a mistake. Their manner of writing about Jörn Donner's book showed that everything was as it always had been: hatred and rancor. The desire to humiliate and discredit.
Åke Runnquist, publishing manager at Bonniers, has written to him that now would be the right time to publish his film scripts in book form for the Swedish market. Head-shaking: This business of Jörn's book has shown that it could not be a worse time.

UNDATED, 1962
Erland Josephson has paraphrased an English nursery rhyme:

Ingmar, Pingmar, pudding and pie
kissed the girls and made them cry.
When little boys came out to play
little Pingmar ran away.

Some truths about ourselves we accept, others not. Ingmar quotes this verse delightedly.

SATURDAY 19 MAY 1962

SF is deserted today: free Saturday; but Ingmar is already at work at 8:30, he wants to get a lot done today. They are in the final scenes of the film.

By the time they go home today the rough editing is finished. On Monday the first stage of the polishing starts.

UNDATED, MAY 1962

He has ordered a copy from the sound department of the Bach thing he used in THROUGH A GLASS DARKLY: the beginning of a slow movement from suite no. 2 for solo cello, D-minor. He wants exactly the same motif in this film too.

He will put it in during Märta's and Thomas's car drive (when we see their profiles through death's floating tree shadows).

He is thinking of having the same Bach motif in THE SILENCE too— as a linking musical element in these three films.*

TUESDAY 29 MAY 1962

"Anti-church" but not "anti-religious"

The recurring cogitation while Ulla Ryghe cuts and joins: shall he shorten the communion service?

"In some way I think the entire inexorability disappears if I start snipping at it."

But there's a public reason to shorten it.

"Public?!"

"Yes, don't sound so contemptuous! This is what I mean: People can get so exhausted by it that they are not receptive to the rest of the film. If they are bored at the beginning, they won't listen to the rest."

While waiting for a join:

—

*He gave up the idea of this later because it "felt like a gimmick," like "something irrelevant, something contrived," he says in a TV interview on 7.2.63.

"Besides, wasn't the effect rather sentimental?"

"Yes, a romanticization. Oddly enough, as that sonata is very far from being sentimental. But above all it felt like a gimmick. So there was nothing to do but remove it."

"I've a feeling that only now, with THE SILENCE, am I starting to be myself. Frightening and fascinating all the possibilities that are opening up now."

While waiting for another join.

"All day today I've been wondering whether I'll put all the natural scenery shots *in the middle of* Our Father. I rather think that might be (with a typical IB word:) *exact.*"

We walk across the SF yard towards the office.

"The more I edit this film, the more I find how *anti* it is."

Anti the Christian form in which he was brought up?

"Anti-Christian, yes," he emphasizes, *"not* anti-religious."

Adding:

"I'll stress that as I edit."

How? The material is what it is: I haven't yet been able to discover any radical reshuffling. But I'll remember the problem for the TV series.

(The result in front of the TV cameras a month later was this:)

INT: You once said as we came out of the cutting room here that you had found that this film was more and more *anti.* Not anti-religious but anti-Christian. You said you stressed it during the editing. I suppose you can't say just what you did on that point during the editing?

IB: I can't remember. I've said so many extraordinary things about this film. You see, it's this way: during such a long time as a production like this takes, one's mood keeps changing— that's only reasonable— both as regards the film itself, the material, that is, and the technical side of the production. And sometimes you say one thing and sometimes another. I've forgotten what I said on that occasion. If I said that the film is anti-Christian, then I must qualify that statement. I'll certainly stand by what I said that the film is anti-church in one way, that is, as the Swedish church is run today in many parts of Sweden. But a character like Algot Frövik, for example, can never be anti-Christian, I mean can never be created with an anti-Christian way of thinking, can he?

INT: Well, it's one thing for one's mood to keep changing. But do you also mean that the aim changes too, while one is working on something? One's approach to the material ....

IB: One's approach to the material can have the most peculiar changes. But at the same time one must be awfully careful to keep in mind the original vision and lead oneself back by the ear to the original vision. To begin in one way and finish in another is disastrous. The whole film becomes terribly unclear. And sometimes of course one can get furious with the whole thing and call it anything at all. But that's just a fit of temper.

INT: Well, I thought it was interesting because all the time I'm conscious of a doubleness with this film on the part of the one who has made it, in regard to the things he depicts, for example the church and the service and ....

IB: Yes, churchiness, what Pär Lagerkvist calls "the holy rubbish," isn't that the expression he uses? I think that's terribly correct and expressive: how "the holy rubbish" hides what is holy. And I suppose that's one of the things that, although I wasn't really aware of it when I started, has been stored up during the years ever since my childhood— a deep dislike of all that external bizarre rubbish which clutters up and hides the essentials.

FRIDAY 1 JUNE 1962

Editing jargon

Gunnar Björnstrand was called this morning; Sven Nykvist is to take an additional shot of Gunnar's hands holding the wafer on a silver dish as he waits for the congregation to come forward.

More supplementary shots: Sven is to take a series of pictures of the crucified Christ hanging in the film's vestry. (The same Christ image that was used in the flagellants' procession in THE SEVENTH SEAL, carved by P. A. Lundgren.)

"It suddenly occurred to me that the main character must of course come in during the singing of the hymn."

The main character, Christ. Sven photographs the head with the crown of thorns, the feet with the nails in them, the pierced hands (on one hand Ingmar has twisted off a finger). Ingmar sighs with gratitude when he sees the result.

"That Sven has some sort of magic, I don't know what it is. He has only to turn two lamps on to an object, and .... "

The shot of Christ's pierced feet is called in the cutting room "the tootsies."

It's a typical example of editing jargon— it flourishes in every cutting room and fulfils a necessary function. Character A. takes a slight breath in one shot— and that shot is then called "the snuffle" so as to distinguish it from corresponding shots in which the breathing-in does not occur.

SATURDAY 2 JUNE 1962

IB, the technically handicapped

Sudden self-description this morning during a pause while sunning ourselves on the steps of the editing pavilion. In the ground swell of the morning's stomach pains he gave a sample card of his technical difficulties, with a wan smile.

" .... I can't sing a note in tune. Käbi has helped me with that, there must be a deep inhibition somewhere, because I can't be altogether unmusical. And I can't *draw* either. I can never draw a stage set, never sketch a picture composition! You can guess how it feels for a director. During all the years that Lars-Eric Kjellgren directed out here— if you only knew how envious I was of his technical skill. Anything technical came so goddam easy to him, and there I sat with all my problems .... To say nothing of how hard it is for me (big laugh) to mix *with people*. To have to talk to them, to be forced to make contact with them. You should have seen me in the old days, when I was so scared of them that I rushed up to them with a heartiness that completely crushed them .... "

Is *that* what it looks like, the inside?!

The outside is more familiar to me: his reputation out here as a thoroughly competent technician.

WEDNESDAY 6 JUNE 1962

The polishing work is progressing. But the more discernible the whole becomes, the more IB speaks of how unpleasant it is with the first screening: *that* is when you feel for the first time whether or not the material hangs together— or whether you have made some disastrous mistakes.

UNDATED, JUNE 1962

The train, belching smoke, comes through the winter dusk towards Frostnäs station. Ingmar loves every foot of the train shots, with all the train romanticism of his childhood— and the nicest moment of all is when the steam locomotive starts snorting smoke out of its nostrils. That is the very shot he cuts out:

"Kill your darlings."

The beginner loves every shot he has created; only experience teaches him hardness of heart, discrimination.

Be suspicious of what you have fallen in love with— the soundest of all working axioms.

Kill your darlings!

FRIDAY 8 JUNE 1962

Ingmar runs his film for the first time this evening in "the Opera's" screening room.

The first testing.

Present: himself, Allan Ekelund, Ulla Ryghe.

SATURDAY 9 JUNE 1962

The morning of Whitsun Eve in Ulla Ryghe's cutting room.

"You were not hurt because I didn't ask you to join us yesterday?"

"Yes," I reply.

"Sulking?"

"Of course I am. Here I have been noting down every little trivial detail that has happened in connection with this film since you got the first idea for it. But when you've reached such a goddam important moment as the first screening, *then* you push me out. I very nearly chucked the diary to hell."

What reply will he think up now? He justifies himself with:

"I didn't want to sit there feeling your reactions, I wanted to have absolute objectivity."

I swallow my disappointment and ask how the screening turned out.

"One thing is certain: the communion service is too long. And besides, it feels contrived."

The decision made: the beginning of the service must go. The film will begin with the sacramental words. He again orders the shot when Gunnar Björnstrand reads the sacramental words, it has been cut too much. Ulla Ryghe is told to rearrange the shots according to the following plan:*

a) Gunnar Björnstrand from in front

b) Gunnar Björnstrand from behind

c) "Our Father"

d) the natural scenery shots

e) Ingrid Thulin's close-up while the hymn is being sung

f) Karin Persson's, ditto

g) Jonas Persson's, ditto

---

* Thanks to this recutting a greater symmetry was attained than before. The film begins and ends in exactly the same way— with a close-up from in front of the parson. (In the first shot he has his back to the congregation; in the last shot he turns his face towards it.) In the first edited version the film began with the parson's profile against the rainy window.

h) Algot Frövik's, ditto

The plan makes IB hopeful:

"There will be a terrific firmness and order now, the beginning will have a hell of a stringency and will lose that slight 'flappiness' it has had up to now."

Ulla picks out the picture of the child fidgeting with boredom in the pew, the girl Helena Palmgren.

"We must save that little child. Her sigh is precious, it expresses the whole of that infinite dreariness."

I note that the new plan is the exact opposite of the original thought. *Then* he began by presenting each individual in a series of close-ups— not until afterwards did he show the empty church in a desolate long shot. Now he saves the individuals until the hymn singing.

(Why did he shoot the whole communion service in the first place? Didn't he feel even then that it was too long? Yes, but he was "arrogant," he replies in a TV talk on June 25th:)

IB: First it was my intention, when I was working on the script, to begin with the sacramental words. But when I started writing the script in earnest, I thought one couldn't very well divide up the communion service. To do that would be faking it in some way— it must be shot in its entirety. So I wrote it out at length in the script. Of course a little imp of arrogance had crept in somewhere. I thought, now this idea of a communion service is something that is frightfully difficult to bring to life in a film.

INT: Everyone will say that it's impossible?

IB: Yes. And I felt myself that it *was* practically impossible, and of course that brought out my purely professional arrogance. I'd soon show them that there's nothing easier than to make the whole of the communion service interesting. And so I filmed it all in accordance with the plan I had. But then I found it was wrong when I ran the film in its entirety. And that my very first thought had been right. Then I acted according to Faulkner's principle: "Kill your darlings!" So I cut out 125 meters and started now with the sacramental words.

On this Whitsun Eve we run through the first three reels. The beginning of the vestry scene between Ingrid and Gunnar he is dissatisfied with as usual. When Ingrid sighs *A Sunday at the bottom of the vale of tears*:

"She could never say that line."

Ingmar's spirits always rise towards the end of that scene. He

210

thinks the acting is just as strong at the end as it is weak at the beginning.

"But the end is much better written," I reply.

Yes, of course. Of course it is, he agrees with me there. Actors always act better when they have something to get their teeth into. No doubt about that.

MÄRTA: Oh, Thomas, what a lot you have to learn.
THOMAS (ironically): You don't say, teacher.
MÄRTA (same tone): You must learn to love.
THOMAS (same tone): And *you* would teach me that?
MÄRTA: I can't do everything. I don't have the strength for that.

And she leaves. The writer's satisfaction:

"What an exit line, eh?"*

The next moment I find a dissolve that I have never seen before. Märta disappears down through the church, stops, leans her head against a wooden pillar with a soft moan— *there* he fades back to a close-up of Thomas who mumbles in the vestry:

He (Jonas Persson) *must come.***

On this morning he decides on another dissolve: Thomas looks anxiously around the church, the picture stops on the skull of an epitaph— *there* he dissolves to the profile picture of Thomas in the vestry door.

Another important dissolve: From Thomas in the vestry to the picture of the altar's "throne of grace" and Thomas's whisper:

"What an absurd picture."

Dissolves are often put in as a technical necessity in order to denote that 1) time has passed, 2) the characters have moved from one place to another. For *these* dissolves there is no technical necessity: in all these three cases IB could very well make ordinary direct cuts. But he wants to give the feeling of a dream to what is happening in the church. He wants to create the atmosphere of a long, unbroken waiting— with no definite time limits. (During the —

* The end of this scene was good even at the second retake (Dec. 5th, 1961) and was not shot any more. The beginning of the scene was shot for the third time on January 12th, 1962.
** One day, late in the mixing, he went into Ulla Ryghe and cut out this dissolve plus a bit of Thomas's waiting in the vestry. Reason: He was afraid there would be one hell of a dull patch just here.

TV program on June 25th I referred to both dissolves and the impudent abbreviation of time. Answer:)

IB: .... I found out at a very early stage that time doesn't exist in films. That is: the logical time ceases to exist for the spectator. In fact one can play about with time more or less as one likes. This isn't *my* idea; it was shown ages ago by a brilliant amateur like Cocteau, who lets the whole of A POET'S BLOOD take place while a factory chimney is falling. − − − It starts with a chimney beginning to fall and ends with its falling. So that during that moment of fall— which is perhaps a second long— the whole drama is enacted. − − − That's what is so wonderful; it's part of the magic of films, that one's awareness of time vanishes completely. − − − .... discovered by degrees, to my great delight, that you can juggle as much as you like with things. Even in the days of silent films they had dissolves, so-called *visions*, between close-up and long shot or long shot and close-up, in order to make that jump (as we call it) softer, which often gives a fantastic effect. So that those are conventions and fads that one plays about with in different ways and at different times.

About the dissolves in the church:

These dissolves— duplications as it were of the pictures— are always between Thomas and Märta. From a close-up of Thomas's face over to a close-up of Märta's face. Or from Märta's face back to Thomas.

"Duplications" of the pictures— Ingmar's favorite dissolve (just now) is 30-30-30. Thirty frames are needed to fade the new picture into the old. For 30 frames *both* pictures lie double *in each other* (that's the moment he loves; there lies the dream feeling). Finally 30 frames in which to fade out the old picture and change over to the new.

TUESDAY 12 JUNE 1962
The abbreviation devil
The golden variations
Memory of Niels Ebbesen
Whitsun is over.
Now the abbreviation devil has grabbed hold of the director. Even a week ago he dealt roughly with Thomas's monologue to the fisherman. At the screening on Friday it was still more apparent, he thinks, that Ingrid's letter and Gunnar's monologue lay

like two great competing chunks next to each other. The letter he can't cut. There is nothing left but to nibble at the monologue.

"Too much chat. The most important thing with the monologue is to arrive at the parson's denial."

Even the words about "the spider god" have been cut out: *Every time I confronted god with the reality I saw, he became ugly, hideous, a spider god— a monster.* That cut smarts. I think of Karin's conception of "the spider god" in THROUGH A GLASS DARKLY. I want to keep everything that links up with THROUGH A GLASS DARKLY.

Ingmar has also made drastic cuts in the organist Blom's jeering remarks to Märta. He is even about to cut away the whole of the ironical quotation from THROUGH A GLASS DARKLY: *"God is love and love is god. Love is the proof of god's existence."* Yet that is the very heart of the Blom scene.

In that way he will ruin the whole dialogue between the two films!

Ingmar waves my objections away. It's too special. The specialist may perhaps take pleasure in such things— not the public at large. The important thing is to make *this* film as buoyant and alive as possible. If WINTER LIGHT is better for cutting such things out— then out they must go!

He's also busy chipping away a little at Allan Edwall's last lines today. He's taken it into his head to cut out the final phase, when Algot Frövik stands smiling behind the Rev. Ericsson and says: *"So we are going to hold the service then?" "Yes."* But it is a key moment. In Allan Edwall's smile I seem to feel the secrecy of all mysticism. From a Christian point of view, this is the "happy ending." If he cuts this, he will upset the very basic structure of the film.

"Is it wise?"

He admits being at the stage when he's prepared to cut out anything at all.

"That's the danger of handling your own text. You sit there looking at it over and over again, and suddenly you think, I can do without that. That's not at all good. That is shockingly bad; how could I have written anything so silly? And then all sorts of things get thrown out."

The director puts in. He takes out. He puts in again.

It's the stage that he himself calls "the neurotic pruning."

213

The spider god, the "God is love" quotation, "So we are going to hold the service then?"— they are all there in the completed film however. He took bits out of the scenes but decided in the end to keep those lines.

Tomorrow Ingmar and Ulla will get down to the service. They have recorded the material that has to be reordered. Time to work their way through the new version.

His tiredness is hardly noticeable. Yet he and Käbi have had to stay awake a great deal of the night. He calls it a "promenade concert." The program kept mainly to Bach's Goldberg variations.

"I tried to give a short lecture on 'The Magic Flute' too, but it wasn't very popular."

It's a discovery one makes, he says: that one can in fact manage with a few hours of sleep.

"Especially just now. At this time of year. The summer night was so fantastically beautiful with all the fruit trees."

(Whether or not the Goldberg variations are a new or an old love, I don't know; but he came to use one of the last variations when he was selecting Bach music for THE SILENCE: a harpsichord disc, played by Kirkpatrick. Also a Bach development: from the heavily vibrating cello in THROUGH A GLASS DARKLY to the delicate, spiritualized harpsichord playing in THE SILENCE.)

It occurred to me today how protestant WINTER LIGHT is. And up out of memory floats an episode from the Polytechnic School in 1943 when I was a senior schoolboy and had a walk-on in IB's production of Kaj Munk's NIELS EBBESEN. The play contains two kinds of divine service plots. Ingmar took a childlike delight in depicting the catholic morning service as something extra superficial and noisy. But every time the rehearsal reached the moment when the drunken protestant parson (Sture Ericsson) gave communion to Niels Ebbesen (Anders Ek) the same tense atmosphere automatically arose. Everything grew still, bleak, harsh and pure.

WEDNESDAY 13 JUNE 1962
Mock the critics with a farce
Married to the camera

Violent outburst this morning. He entered the cutting room in a feeling of "now he could get the better of the communion service." He knew exactly how he would have all these pictures— and the long, important opening shot of Gunnar Björnstrand was miss-

214

ing. Everything else was there, but not that one. Yet it had been reordered and should have been there today. This afternoon at 3 o'clock the sound department is to see the whole film. It must be ready by then.

The bitter disappointment: to arrive keyed-up, vital, with all the artist's feeling of *now* I'll fix this!— and there's a hitch in the machinery. The technical material is not there.

He calms down and apologizes to Ulla for his outburst. He was tired too, hadn't slept enough. And another assistant had slipped up in the morning. Etc. The explanations don't take the disappointment out of his voice. His happy anticipation of work is gone.

They try to find an extra time later in the day: then the opening shot should be there and the film be ready by 3 o'clock after all.

Slowly they make their way through the pictures of the service. Ulla tapes the bits together, Ingmar tells of a farce he is writing together with Erland Josephson. It is about a critic who is to write a biography of a world-famous artist (a cellist called Felix). It will be called "The Moral Lecture" or "A Hole in the Middle" (the leading character is never seen). All his hatred of critics flares up as he describes the idea, the humiliations he suffered in connection with the reviews of Jörn Donner's book. Oh, to get his own back! To be able to show the pettiness of the critics! Their lack of productivity, their sponging off the artist!

Chat about actors and the film camera. He quotes:

" 'The really great film actors are married to the camera.' It's true. The camera is their real fellow-actor."

Ingrid, moreover, found herself in the unique situation that she had to read her monologue straight into the camera.

"But I moved the camera forward, so that it came closer to her."

"I never noticed that."

"She thought it was too far away. From a practical point of view it didn't matter where the camera stood. And it was terribly important that *she* felt the intimacy and nearness when she was going to do that difficult scene."

Time to move the ready-edited film over to the sound department.

Tomorrow morning he's to go up there and have "a run-through at the table" (the first procedure in the sound department before there can be any talk of putting in the sound and of mixing).

THURSDAY 14 JUNE 1962

So this is the "run-through at the table":

At ten o'clock they meet at Erik Nordgren's, the musical director's, cutting table up in the sound department. Evald Andersson writes down all the extra sounds that have to be put on. You can't mix the sounds if you haven't first put on all the sounds that are missing. Stig Flodin, chief sound engineer, makes a note of any post-synchronizations and adjustments of the sound already recorded. The whole film is run, reel by reel. Braking at every problematic sound spot: suggestions are called for, there is a discussion. IB is particular about taking a pause between every reel: the black-out blind is pulled up, the window is opened, a breath of fresh air is let into the stuffy little room. Erik Nordgren has time to smoke a quarter of a cigarette each time a reel is changed.

At the pictures of the churchwarden Aronsson during the service (where Kolbjörn Knudsen himself only makes the lip movements):

"This first bit is a hymn that the churchwarden has never been able to learn," IB says, "so he doesn't join in the singing. But here, next time, he does sing. Here we must get hold of a bass and put in new sound, Erik!"

At the close-up of Allan Edwall, Elsa Ebbesen, etc.:

"Let the voices in the various close-ups dissolve into each other, so that they don't stop abruptly right at the end of the close-up."

At the actual communion:

"It says in the manual that during the celebration of the communion the organist shall play a prelude. I myself think that silence is much more effective, don't you? But Erik! Have something with the organ in any case, I want to try it out. Only it mustn't be mood music, remember. The organ must miss a note here and there, well, you know ...."

A lengthy discussion with Erik Nordgren, who recommends silence and no organ at all.

During the delivering of the communion wine:

"The blood of our Lord Jesus Christ, which was shed for thee .... we'll let Gunnar post-synch it, because there's a great unevenness in the atmosphere here, isn't there?"

Stig Flodin nods.

At the tracking-in on a close-up of the anguished Thomas:

"Put in the footsteps of the communicants as they go away from the altar, down into the church. Thomas stands as it were listening to the footsteps before he says anything."

(It is part of Evald Andersson's duties to produce such footsteps and lay them on the sound track.)

When the congregation joins in the "amen," the parson's son IB laughs at a childhood memory:

"What a relief to my young mind when they started to sing the first 'amen'. Then I knew there was only the blessing and the last hymn left."

The sound technicians make very few comments on the film. I sense that IB has an empty feeling. After all, this is the first time the edited film encounters an audience— hence the sound department's special position in the chain of production.

"Just look, isn't that typical of organists .... Look, the way women carry on. And nobody stops them ...."

He eggs them on with small exclamations of this kind. Sometimes he repeats, unconsciously, exactly the same things as he said to Ulla Ryghe in the cutting room, trying them out on a new public. He seeks support, agreement, contact. And he is relieved and grateful when someone says something.

"That's very kind of you, Erik."

Fredrik Blom, the organist, looks at his pocket watch during the singing:

"This is where the clock in the tower starts striking twelve. Get hold of a good country church, a rather sharp tone. Not a city church!"

When the film pokes fun at the organist's utter indifference to his work:

"I'll get a letter of protest from the organist's union, don't you think?"

This leads to a discussion about organists in general and their possible alcoholic problems. IB has a theory: There's something in the dust of organ galleries that induces a thirst in organists.

The film reaches the vestry:

"Here, boys, we must find a genuine old grandfather clock. With a good, substantial, live tick."

"There's a Mora clock in shot," Evald Andersson says.

"Like hell there is! It's a Stjärnsund clock."

Now the camera tracks in to a close-up of Gunnar Björnstrand, it's just before the entrance of the fisherman and his wife.

"Here, here the ticking of the clock gets louder and louder so that we feel that the guy has a temperature .... Back a bit, please, Erik!"

The film is backed until the grandfather clock is visible at the edge of the picture (beside Allan Edwall).

"Here! When the clock is seen in shot, then we start to hear it for the first time. And then, when we track in on Gunnar, it doubles in intensity. It must get so loud that it goddam sounds like blows of a hammer!"

IB tries to describe how he means this doubling to be done, from a purely technical point of view. Stig tries to understand the description. There's no real understanding on either side. To Evald:

"When they start to say their lines, the clock is normal again. Write it down, please."

(This part was later called during the mixing "the temperature clock.")

When Thomas says to Märta that he is suffering from God's silence, IB gives a laugh and does a parody:

"Bong! Here we should really have a huge symphony orchestra .... as in American films for instance."

Gunnar Björnstrand walks about in the vestry cell:

"The grandfather clock is heard incessantly. And there, there the clock strikes one."

Gunnar's steps echo in the empty church:

"I love this sound. Gosh, I'm glad we laid the floor with stone slabs. What fantastic acoustics we got, eh, even if it was only a studio church."

We come to Ingrid's letter reading:

"If you look hard .... the odd thing is that it gets dark under her eyes as the minutes pass and she reads the letter."

(I examine Ingrid's eyes time and again after this; but give up. *I* can never notice the change.)

"Now the clock ticks again, during the whole scene between Max and Gunnar .... But now! when Max goes out, that's the end of the clock. Fade it out."

The parson has carried out his denial, the fisherman has gone away to die— as regards sound this is one of the most important passages:

"It's just as if there were no sound left in the world. Here there must damn well be a silence that is so horrible that .... no atmosphere, nothing! And the silence must continue on Ingrid's shot out in the church. No atmosphere there either! Take out Gunnar's footsteps when he goes out into the chruch! It must be silent right up to the moment when he starts coughing at the altar ring .... The coughing attack must come almost as a relief from the silence.

"God's silence"— on the technical plane.

When Gunnar Björnstrand's head is hanging right down at the altar ring:

"That's where the clock in the tower must start striking! Two strokes! Two goddam short strokes!"

Evald Andersson:

"I just thought of something. Just now, when you wanted the Stjärnsund clock to strike one stroke— what about having the tower clock there too?"

"Yes, of course. Quite right. Why didn't I think of it."

Now we're at the scene of the suicide. Now Gunnar Björnstrand is walking back alone to the car:

".... and there, *there* Bach must come!"

(I didn't know that: that he was going to have Bach in this of all scenes.)

Now Ingrid Thulin walks into the schoolroom. ("Put in footsteps so that we hear it's a wooden floor she's walking on." During shooting she walked on a carpet so as not to disturb the dialogue.) Gunnar Björnstrand leaves the window and goes and sits down. ("We'll prolong Ingrid's weeping until Gunnar has sat down. There is quite enough weeping, we recorded a whole lot.") Now the car is driving up towards the fisherman's house.

"The goddam silence of death prevails here. (Pause.) Christ, no! *The dog* must bark. And none of your dachshunds, it must be a Lapland spitz."

The parson talks to Mrs. Persson and steps out to the porch.

"I have an idea here. I'd like that steam locomotive to be heard now, the one we hear later. But we hear it now, far, far away .... very faintly. Then comes Bach for the second time, when Gunnar steps down in front of the house. And Bach takes away all the other sounds .... until the train comes again, here, at the railroad crossing."

After the railroad crossing Thomas and Märta reach Frostnäs church. Real church bells started ringing inside Skattungby church when that scene was shot.

219

"You know, the original sounds can never be copied. There's something indescribable about what is recorded direct."

Allan Edwall talks to the parson about Christ's suffering. Ingrid Thulin, alone in the pew, throws up her head:

"There, when Ingrid throws up her head, that's where the church bells must come. Look, boys, will you please do a pre-mix here, so that I can try it out and see where to have the church bells during the prayer. I'll recut her prayer and feel my way here ...."

The time is two o'clock. The run-through for sound is over.

"As you see, boys, there's not an awful lot. But some of the sounds are a bit tricky, aren't they?"

It takes time to procure and put in all the extra sounds. The ideal thing is for the sound department to have three weeks for all the sound laying.

Only then can the mixing start.

Meanwhile Ingmar goes up to Rättvik and the Hotel Siljansborg with the technical crew to plan the new production, THE SILENCE.

They leave tomorrow.

SATURDAY 16 JUNE 1962

They have been sitting in the bridge room all day with THE SILENCE, discussing every practical problem in it.

Evening, TV show by Åke Falck. Monika Zetterlund the main attraction.

After TV the whole team drives up to Finnbacka. What a contrast. Then, it was misty November; now it is light all night long. And in Märta Lundberg's schoolroom they're dancing and singing to an accordion! It's the local village hall again, Saturday evening dance, the young people whisper together in the cars in front of the house.

All the magic of the Swedish summer night.

On the way to Finnbacka Ingmar and Sven talk of how very helpful it has been today to go right through the script. They made a start with WINTER LIGHT — but had no time to discuss every problem.

"You could see that when we got to the letter," Ingmar says.

"Why just at the letter?"

"Ingmar means that cut-in shot in the letter," Sven explains. "When Ingrid stands with the summer flowers in her hands and kneels down at the altar ring and prays. We had never talked and agreed about how we would have the light there."

And that's why there was friction between Ingmar and Sven on that particular day in the studio.

But in the car on the way to Finnbacka it suddenly occurs to IB what he has missed in WINTER LIGHT.

"One thing I didn't bring out, do you know what it is? Thomas's feeling that when his wife died God *afflicted* him. That was one thing he felt deeply— and I haven't managed to make that clear."

"But whereabouts in the film *could* you have brought it out?"

"When Thomas looks at his wife's photographs in his wallet. I did think of writing it in afterwards. Or even better of having it in the service at the beginning. During the hymn. But it would break this strict character the film has."

Sigh.

"So I don't see how I can."

What is done cannot be undone; and all there is of *that* theme is to be found only in the left-hand column of the script: *His wife is dead but Thomas is in God's hands, all doubt is silenced and uncertainty is dissolved in a triumphant shout: "God has struck me!"*

SUNDAY 17 JUNE 1962
The summer consists of six sound tracks

I sit writing in an easy chair on the Siljansborg terrace. A breeze is stirring. When I close my eyes I notice how new experiences impress one: I begin to count the sounds I hear.

1. The faint slapping of the cord on the flagpole.
2. The clatter of the lawnmower.
3. Voices of the guests (distance character).
4. The noise of traffic from down on the road.
5. A few bird calls.
6. I even hear the distant lapping of Siljan on the stones by the shore.

The most distinct sound is the slapping of the flag cord— I am sitting near it.

It would take six sound tracks to recreate the sounds constituting this fine summer's day. (But it would no doubt be most effective with one or two sound effects.)

MONDAY 18 JUNE 1962

221

How does THE SILENCE fit into the trilogy?

Summer evening in the Rättvik churchyard. The inscriptions on the tombstones, the crunch of our footsteps on the gravel. Sven and Ingmar go into the church for a moment.

"What a lot of running in and out of churches we did last year when we were going to make WINTER LIGHT. Then no more when the film was finished. As when I had done THE SEVENTH SEAL. I lost all my fear of death and all that religious brooding faded away."

"One thing I don't quite understand: the connection between WINTER LIGHT and the new film. How can a film like THE SILENCE form the last stage of a trilogy?"

"Why, don't you see? In THE GLASS the predominant thing is God and love. Then comes WINTER LIGHT, criticizing this and ending in a bare-scraped lowest level with a prayer to an unnamed god. A god beyond the formulas, the living religion represented by Frövik. And then THE SILENCE— everything is still more bare-scraped, a world utterly without god. In which only the hand— fellowship— is left. And the music."

Hand is "kasi" in the foreign language that is spoken in the city of Timoka. And "Bach means Bach of course."

"Squarely expressed: Anna is the body; Ester is the soul."

He laughs at how flat everything becomes when it has to be explained and reluctantly mumbles something about the battlefield in THE SILENCE: the tumult arising between body and soul when God is no longer there.

FRIDAY 29 JUNE 1962

Reel by reel in the mixing room

Preparations for the mixing.

The film is projected onto a relatively large screen in a relatively small, soundproof room. A strikingly large clock stands on the right of the screen. A peculiar clock— the hour hand marks the course of the minutes; the minute hand, that of the seconds.

The clock is important. With its help the mixer, Olle Jacobsson, spots the sound effects to the very second. Evald Andersson, who puts in the sounds, has added a train whistle at "3:42"; it has been carefully noted on the list he has given Olle. The clock shows "3:39," "3:40," "3:41" .... *now* comes the train whistle. A dividing up of the work: Evald sees to it that the train whistle is in the

222

right position; Olle's job is to make sure that the train whistle sounds as loud or as faint as it should. He regulates the volume from his long instrument panel. A door that has let in some fresh air is closed. It shuts out the summer rain in the yard of the film town, the summer voices, the summer smells. Ingmar sinks down in his chair, the chief sound engineer Lennart Unnerstad in his; Erik Nordgren in his. Quite an ordinary film showing, that is, in quite an ordinary darkroom— only with the dimly lit instrument panel at the very back of the room. There sit Olle Jacobsson and Evald Andersson.

An ordinary screening— but with frequent discussions. Sometimes while the film keeps running on the screen.

"Olle, I'd like to have the clock darker in tone. And a *shade* slower. Sort of more weird, eh?"

Up on the screen Gunnar Björnstrand makes his way in anguish around the church. Olle puts a slight echo in his footsteps.

"And keep the footsteps in when you go from the skull to the close-up in the vestry. And keep the echo in for a little while in the vestry. He is pursued in there by his own footsteps, as it were .... Try it and you'll see what I mean."

Olle Jacobsson gives an order to Edvin Rydh in the projection room to stop. Olle's voice in the microphone:

"Back to 4:52."

To back at a cutting table is easy— you are working only with two tracks, the picture track and the sound track. To back in the mixer is a slow and tedious business. You have to back not only the pictures but a whole series of sound tracks:

"The dialogue track" contains the dialogue that is recorded in the studio. *The blood of our Lord Jesus Christ, which was shed for thee* .... on the other hand, is post-synchronized sound and is on a track of its own. The train whistle is on yet another track. And so on. At particularly complicated passages Olle and Evald are working with all the sound tracks at their disposal: eight of them.

Now the film is backed. The clock over by the screen is synchronized with the projector and goes backwards to 4:52.

New start.

Olle holds the footsteps over, very cautiously. With echo.

"Just like that, Olle. That's exactly right."

Now Ingrid begins reading the letter up on the screen. Ingmar: "I think all those small sounds give such a good atmosphere. The throat sounds. When she swallows .... just listen! Bring them out properly!"

It suddenly occurs to him that abroad there will be a subtitle at the bottom of the picture.

"The entire letter will be ruined in the international market, because the spectator's eyes will move up and down between the subtitle and Ingrid's eyes. Pity. It will spoil the whole fascination with her eyes. This is indeed a specifically Swedish film."

And then he recalls how hard it was to find the right position for the microphone during the letter reading. A position where the mike picked up as little camera hum as possible.

"In this scene we have tried the technical resources to the utmost. Though no one will believe it of course. They think all you have to do is to stick a camera straight in front and that's it."

When Thomas has read Märta's letter he tries to put it back into the envelope; but gives up— there are too many sheets. Olle Jacobsson automatically tones down the terrific crackling of the paper.

"No, keep it right up! He's trying to put away all his guilty conscience."

The moods keep changing. I remember the affecting scene Ingmar created during shooting when Märta is to console the huddled Thomas in front of the altar. (See Tuesday, January 9th, 1962.) Up here in the mixing room he doesn't show he's affected in the very slightest:

"Keep the dialogue down, boys, so we get all these nasty, messy kisses— it must be so that we want to spew on the woman .... "

There's mixing room jargon as well as editing jargon.

And the sound department is an utterly male world.

TUESDAY 3 JULY 1962
To create an acoustic climax

This is the sound department: *here* surely there will be no difficulty in recording all the "shop talk." Oh no. A mike is installed in the mixing room; I start a tape recorder and get all the atmosphere in the room: laughter, chat, discussions. I was in luck today moreover: suddenly the talk extended into a short lecture.

It was when Gunnar Björnstrand left the fisherman's wife. He glances through the kitchen window: she can be seen inside at the meal table with her children. The parson walks heavily over the dark yard. In the next shot Thomas and Märta are sitting in dead silence in the car. Then Märta pulls up by the level crossing.

INGMAR: Then they come to the level crossing booms. We'll have the sound of the car goddam soft there, it was too loud just now. Because the main thing is the "pling" from the booms and the sound of the train, isn't it?
EVALD: The car was too loud there.
INGMAR: Yes, we must almost fade the car right out there. And then comes the train. And after Gunnar has said his line (Father and Mother wanted me to be a parson) turn it up like hell! You can do it this way— as soon as the wagons are out of sight, do a loud scream, for there's a station close by, that's the idea we get, eh? You see? So that there's a hell of a noise there from the train when the car drives off again. Because later, when the car has come up there and stopped (in front of the last church), it must be dead silent for a while. See? The line of thought is purely acoustic: first this slow bit with the train, then the train goes away and then comes the music, loud, and then come all these unbearable sounds, and this hard .... And there we'll have that sound you hear with trains, you know: Clank! Clank! Clank-clank! when the buffers and things knock together, you know?
EVALD: Oh, so you want a sort of slowing down there ....
INGMAR: Exactly! And you see there's a clinking and clanking in those chains and couplings, so that we get all those hard, metallic sounds in one long series, eh? So that we get a sort of *acoustic climax* in the film here. And then it dies down a bit with the car going up the hill. And then suddenly silence. Dead silence. They open the door (the car door) and hear the sound faintly— and then comes the ringing of the bells. It must come as a *relief* out of that series of sounds. You see? That's the idea. See what I mean, Olle?

Afterwards I noticed that IB gave a lecture on a Bergman speciality. For if you examine the sound effects in the film trilogy that ends with THE SILENCE you'll find an "acoustic climax" in each one of them.

In THROUGH A GLASS DARKLY it consists of the terrible roar from the helicopter that comes to fetch Karin— followed by the silence afterwards. In WINTER LIGHT it is in the clatter of the train— followed by silence and the ringing of bells. In THE SILENCE it is made by the horrifying, persistent alarm signals that pierce the city of Timoka— in the midst of Ester's fear of death.

The inventiveness is great, but the basic pattern is the same.

WEDNESDAY 4 JULY 1962
Gloomy calculations for WINTER LIGHT
Yesterday, just as the second tape gave out during the recording,

Ingmar started talking to the sound boys about how badly WINTER LIGHT will go.

"Kenne and I calculate quite coldy: WINTER LIGHT will bring in 400 000 in Sweden. It's the lowest takings for any of my films during the last few years. Then I suppose we can count on one of the state "quality grants," say 200 000. That brings us up to 600 000. Then WINTER LIGHT has been sold in a packet to other countries— poor bastards, they don't know what they have bought. For half a million! So it will pay its way. But no more."

Why make a film like that? No one said anything, but the question hung in the air; he met it with an explanation about how necessary it is to make experiments. This film is one of those that must be made, even if it's not a success.

"Well, nobody ever thought THE VIRGIN SPRING would go."

This evening over dinner, before we drove out to the film town and screened the edited copy of THE MISTRESS:

"Just think, in the old days: how *boring* I thought Tchekhov was. And what a lot I've learned from him now!"

A good subject for a student's essay: how Tchekhov's patterns of style criss-cross the Strindberg pattern in WINTER LIGHT.

THURSDAY 5 JULY 1962

The preparations for mixing continue. Reel after reel is tried.

One sound effect is moved thirteen seconds backwards (better so). Another is taken right out (what a relief). Some reels are remarkably easy, mature quickly. Others prove obstinate and difficult and cause constant headaches. Before the sound department gets hold of acceptable bells from a country church, IB has lost his temper four times. The dog that barks in the dusk outside the fisherman Persson's house ("and none of your dachshunds, it must be a Lapland spitz") is just as hard to find. Time and again his voice growls:

"That's a dog from the sound effects department. We can't have that!"

Evald hunts about in the dog-bark department and finds a new dog which is a little better.

"*Another* recorded dog .... Now look here, boys, you'll damn well have to get a real dog. We can't go on like this."

Olle Jacobsson runs every reel through together with Evald and Stickan until he has every single effect at his fingertips.

"Today we can get Ingmar up, and he can see reels 5 and 7." Ingmar comes. Reel 7 seems complete: no fault to find. Approved. But reel 5 has one or two small things that need polishing. He wants to see that once more.

The mixer practices an artistic handicraft and Olle Jacobsson is an artist. He practices each reel in the same way as a pianist practices a piece of music; then he plays it from the keyboard of the instrument panel. Sometimes he swears at his own poor performance: he got off to a false start. Sometimes he feels in good form: no obstacles anywhere, everything went smoothly— "Ingmar should have been here now." When Ingmar does come perhaps the performance doesn't go so well.

All this work is not mixing in the strict sense; it is only preparation for mixing. This starts when Ingmar has approved Olle's interpretation of the sound score. Only then does Olle transfer the sound effects from magnetic sound tracks to one optical sound track (the one that later runs along the film strip in the completed film reel).

SATURDAY 7 JULY 1962

"Just look what very few in-between positions Ingmar has! If you go through WINTER LIGHT, you'll see that he either has great big long shots or else intimate close-ups," Ulla Ryghe pointed out yesterday. An observation that one could verify with statistical measurements: close-ups, long shots, track-ins (and compare with IB's other films).

MONDAY 9 JULY 1962

The shooting of THE SILENCE started today.

FRIDAY 13 JULY 1962

The last check screening before the sound is transferred from magnetic to optical sound track. Olle Jacobsson is therefore the technical leading figure this evening: Ingmar and Olle sit right at the back of "the Opera's" darkness, whispering. The electric heater is on. It is a rainy summer this year and damp in here.

Ingrid Thulin is present.

Today I saw her lying white as chalk in the big bed in the hotel room of THE SILENCE, while Gunnel Lindblom put on some lipstick. This evening Ingrid has bronze-colored slacks and a white jacket of some towelling material. Just now she demonstrated some dance steps out on the asphalt in the dusk, she is going on with her dancing lessons, now with Walter Nicks.

It is fascinating to let one's eyes wander from Ingrid on the screen down to Ingrid in the cinema seat. Slumped down, with her legs stretched right out, she looks at herself: the actress inspecting her work.

It's the first time she watches Märta Lundberg. She has never before seen one foot of the film.

To me they are two completely different persons: the schoolteacher on the screen and the actress in the auditorium.

The lights go up. The film is over.

The self-examination she then makes is no less fascinating.

"I didn't get into the part until in the schoolroom, that's plain enough. That was the scene that moved me most, too. I started to weep when I got to it in the script. It never fails: whatever goes home to you straight away, is there for good .... " She gives a little surprised laugh: "I'd forgotten that the scene in the schoolroom was so *long*."

She thinks that she is rather superficial in the beginning, in the vestry with Gunnar. There's still "a bit of Hollywood" in her. "In what way?"

"Oh, in the way I moved around him. In the way I act .... "

Even when she kisses the parson in front of the altar: "a little Minelli" there too, she thinks. What does she think of the big letter reading? "My eyes are so *dead*. Not a blink .... I had Basedow's disease when I was little."*

—

*Playing with explanations, playing with statements— it gives Ingrid pleasure. Especially when she notices that people are astonishingly inclined to believe in even the oddest remarks. She did have Basedow's disease when she was a child— but of course *that* is not the reason why she doesn't blink during the long letter reading in the film, she points out a year later, in July 1963, after having read the proofs of this book.

"It's the sort of thing one says on an evening like that on seeing the film for the first time, so as to safeguard oneself. One adopts a defensive attitude towards that which one has done in the film— a safeguard in case anyone thinks it's not a success. I sat there, afraid it would seem too staring, the way I didn't blink during the whole of the letter reading."

"Had you agreed with Ingmar not to blink?"

"No, I just decided to do it that way. I thought it was the only way to hold the audience's attention during such a long close-up."

228

"The letter reading," Ingmar says. "Actually you should have it printed on to substandard film and run it for yourself— there you can study *exactly* where your tensions are, Ingrid. (The gentleness, the consideration:) There you can see exactly *when* you are quite at ease in your speech and when you're not."

Ingrid puts her finger to her lips:

"And then that bit on the lip .... when I hold my lip like *this*."

I myself think that this evening one is really made aware for the first time of the stature of Gunnar Björnstrand's performance. His eyes alone— their fantastic expressiveness. Towards the end his role gets more and more taciturn as the suffering within him gets heavier. It is then left to his eyes to express the whole climax of his part.

The schoolroom is the great moment of human portrayal in the film. How they slice their way through layer after layer of lies, truths, loneliness, exposure— all three together, Ingrid, Gunnar, Ingmar. What a result of the ordeal during the days of shooting!

And so on, on the credit side.

What have I in the way of criticism?

This:

Isn't it possible to create *drama* without interweaving so much *anguish*?

I have felt this with many of IB's films, but never so strongly as with THE VIRGIN SPRING. I thought then that IB bought the whole of his intensity by forcing the spectator into a vice of anguish. One sat in a tight grip right through the film and was not released until the final moment (when the spring welled up).

In THROUGH A GLASS DARKLY it didn't feel like that; one could breathe much more freely. But in WINTER LIGHT the grip of anguish is back again— though not as in THE VIRGIN SPRING. Here the vice-like grip is released a good bit before the end.

When?

After the "hate orgasm," I think. Märta and Thomas go out of the schoolroom— after that one breathes more easily. One doesn't relax completely, but there is a current of air, a softening down. The spectator rests on the emotional plane that the outbursts have created.

These recurrent technical lessons in IB's films. Question: What is the condition for a restful moment in a film? Answer: That it is surrounded by outbursts.

No adagio without a forte. Simple lesson. Hard to learn.

That is why we can stand two such long, explanatory scenes (the churchwarden's and the organist's) so late in the film. The suicide and the hate orgasm have raised the emotional level so much that a more restful scene comes as a relief.

I ask Ingmar whether he remembers how skeptical I was about those analytical final scenes when I read the script for the first time.

He gives a laugh.

"Sure. And I'd never have passed them in anyone else's script!"

What does he think otherwise?

"Well, I'd like to make another fifty cuts or so. But one has to stop sometime."

UNDATED, JULY 1962

Lunch. Ingmar is thinking hard about the credits. He has a dream: he'd like to dedicate the film to Stravinsky.

He is shy about saying this. He's afraid of sounding pretentious. Excusing himself quickly:

"But I got the idea for the film when I heard a work of his!"

"Was it when you were doing THE RAKE'S PROGRESS?"

"Yes. I used to play masses of Stravinsky at home for myself."

"Which Stravinsky work was it?"

"The Symphony of Psalms."

(Well I'm damned. How many origins of this film have I gotten hold of now?)

WEDNESDAY 19 SEPTEMBER 1962

The shooting of THE SILENCE completed today.

THURSDAY 7 FEBRUARY 1963

"See your film with an audience!"
Prediction about the reception of WINTER LIGHT
State at première: panic, a feeling of inferiority, humiliation

Over six months have passed since I last noted down anything about WINTER LIGHT: now the première is approaching.

The TV series has started: programs 1 and 2 have been put out the last two Sundays. A whole lot of recorded interview material had to be cut out, of course, before two manageable programs resulted.

But the situation at TV is so hectic that program 3 is not edited and ready until five days before transmission. A nice time *then* to discover that it sags. Nothing to be done except cut half of it and chase up people for a new recording.

INT: You often preach to younger directors: "See your film together with an audience!" Do you see *your* films with an audience? Are you going to the première of WINTER LIGHT?

IB: No, not to the première, but I'll probably go some Saturday night when there's a really mixed and difficult audience. It's awfully instructive.

INT: How do you mean, "instructive"?

IB: Well, that's when you feel if the film is properly made or not. You know then down to the smallest detail. Because, once you've gotten used to it, you can follow the audience's reaction exactly and interpret it. It's as if you had a seismograph inside you. It's like that curve being drawn on a revolving strip inside you. You learn an awful lot from it.

INT: What do you mean by "properly made"?

IB: Above all: that people can go along with it. That they have a chance emotionally— I don't mean intellectually, but emotionally— to respond to the film. And that you don't get those awful dull patches when the film sags, and people sit there fidgeting and coughing and rustling. Or that soggy silence, which is also so horrible, when it's just as if everyone had fallen asleep. I've been through it all.

INT: When you see the film with an audience— do you look at it quite dispassionately?

IB: I shan't be able to look at this film dispassionately for about a year. I have a substandard film projector at home, you know, and I usually have my films printed down to 16 mm so that I can run them at home. When I'm alone at home some evenings and there isn't a soul in the house, I sometimes put a film in this projector and run it for myself. Then I know exactly where I am with it. For then I can sit there, with no outside influence, and say that's good and that's bad and that's good. Then I can award the film its final marks and it's gone for good.

INT: During these days before the première— do you think a lot about it?

IB: It's always so that when the first première advertisements begin to appear in the papers I feel slightly sick. There's no doubt about it. Then the nasty feeling gets gradually worse. Then comes the press show. Then comes all the preview chat. And then comes the big show itself— next Saturday. Then comes the première. It's always so that you go about feeling pretty wretched.

INT: Do you ever have a hunch as to what people will think of the film?

IB: Well, one is always negative oneself. You're always prepared for people not to like what you do. I suppose it's some kind of insurance you take out so as not to be upset when it perhaps turns out that people don't like what you've done.

231

INT: Can you sort out later what people think and what the critics and others think and what you yourself think about what you've done?

IB: Yes, I can do that all the time. No problem there. I know exactly what I think. It's just that you're so terribly naked and vulnerable during the days before and after a première, and it's the same in the theater when the great moment comes when the film or the play is brought to life, when the meeting takes place between the audience and what you have done. To my mind, until a play or a film has encountered the audience's consciousness it's neither a play nor a film, but is still a semi-finished product. It's not until that peculiar, awful meeting that the work comes to life. I've thought an awful lot about the reason for this fear and horror that you have, and this feeling of nakedness and impotence. I think it's because you regard your work as only half-finished and terribly defenseless *until* it is enclosed in the audience's consciousness.

INT: Have you succeeded in doing what you wanted to in this film? Is it the work you had in mind?

IB: The situation for me today is that I know almost for certain when I've done something I think is good and when I've done something I think is not so good. Of WINTER LIGHT I can say that I think it's a good film. It stands on its own feet, no matter what people think. So I think it's a work I can be both satisfied with and proud of.

INT: What is it that is good in it?

IB: It hangs together. It's a complete unit. It's an adequate expression of something I have felt and experienced. It's an adequate expression of a vision.

INT: Supposing you were to forecast its reception? Then we can compare later with the reviews!

IB: Officially of course I can only answer as Ingmar Johansson would do in a similar context: I'm counting on a knock-out in the fifth round. But if I really say what I think, then perhaps I'd say that I think this film will be judged in very different and very peculiar ways in certain quarters. I think it will give rise to arguments. The central thing in this film— and we mustn't lose sight of this— is that it has two themes. One is the religious theme and the other is the love drama. Both meet as it were in the character of Ingrid, don't they? She is the scene of the actual passion drama. So what I mean is that some people will pick on the one theme and some people on the other. And some people will get worked up over one thing and some people over another.

INT: Does it feel rough?

IB: I think this film will be pretty harshly treated, because I thought— and it's often the way— I thought that THROUGH A GLASS DARKLY was overwhelmingly well treated. Almost too much so. And maybe the critics too think so by now. And it's usually so that the next film has to pay for the praise the critics wasted on the previous film, and it leaves a pretty sour taste in the mouth too.

INT: I think they might perhaps be irritated by the end. They want to

232

know definitely one way or the other, for instance in the religious questions.

IB: Oh yes, they always want a cut and dried answer.

INT: You haven't felt the need yourself of being more explicit than this? Or you haven't *been able* to be more explicit?

IB: No. The film involves all my doubts and my anguish in regard to these problems. And in some way I think it has been enough. It has been essential for me to express them. The entire tension is *unexplained* but not *unclear*. And I think that is quite enough. I mean, if we were to start offering definite statements and that sort of thing every time, where would that land us?

INT: Is there anything you have wanted to bring out in it which has not appeared, something you thought you would have to leave out even at the manuscript stage?

IB: Yes, of course. When I was writing the script I found that the film, and the form the film has, was inadequate for everything I wanted to say. But that will come in the next film, by itself. The feeling that something remained was strong even when I was working on the script, and still more so during shooting. And it later became THE SILENCE.

INT: Is it always like that— you feel you've left something unsaid, and so it gives rise to the next film?

IB: No-o .... But it's often the way when I'm working on a film— and especially during the actual shooting, which is a kind of feverish state, an awfully hectic and awkward state— the whole machinery as it were is turning at full speed, the whole office staff is called in, if you like, and all those creative forces are operating and then, during this high pressure, a whole host of film ideas crops up, hundreds of them, and all kinds of pressures come to light, pushing in different directions, and it's an awful nuisance.

IB: Does it get better with premières as time goes on? Can you cope with them better?

IB: Yes, I think so. In the old days I was scared stiff, and in a state of inferiority that I feel to be terribly humiliating. I used to suffer agonies, I thought this will be the death of me and I'll never get over it. I remember the première of SMILES OF A SUMMER NIGHT. I went to it and sat there thinking this is the worst fiasco I've ever known. Not a soul seemed to laugh, nobody was enjoying it, they all sat grim and silent. And it was a complete mystery to me— after that première— that people wanted to see the film at all.

INT: What is it that is *humiliating* in this situation?

IB: I think it's a feeling that you are going to be judged and awarded marks. The fact that what you've dreamed about in secret and created with the idea that it's necessary and can also be necessary for other people— and then along they come and tell you it wasn't necessary at all. That it was stupid or silly or that it shouldn't have been done that way at all, you know, that sort of thing. I think there's a sort of deep essential feeling of humiliation there.

MONDAY 11 FEBRUARY 1963
The first review
WINTER LIGHT has its première this evening at the Röda Kvarn at seven o'clock.

But Jurgen Schildt reviews it even *before* the première— the pretext being that the film "was launched yesterday in Falun." (It was a special showing there yesterday, a benefit performance for Skattunge church.) In this afternoon's *Aftonbladet* Schildt gives this account of the faith theme:

> "The parson is to help, but finds no help to give. The words dry up in his mouth, the system doesn't function. To the simple question about the meaning of life he replies (this is the key scene) by lowering his eyes. Thomas Ericsson has suddenly become Doubting Thomas.
> "And that, from a more or less normal outlook, is strange. It is strange that a parson who has spent a life of toil in the pulpit has only to be asked about the meaning of existence to see the entire edifice of faith come tumbling down around his ears. How did he manage to date? Our Lord may fall silent now and then, but as far as one knows it is one of the privileges of the clergy to have him recorded on tape so that they can get along until he gets in touch with them in person. In other words, to have access to suitable reserves.
> "Be that as it may. At any rate the origin of this clerical faith crisis is not particularly convincing. − − − All this may be of interest in establishing Bergman's positions, his temporary attitude in matters of faith and doubt.
> On the other hand, it is not of much interest as cinematic art; if by cinematic art one means such Bergman virtues as creation of atmosphere, self-contradiction, dramatic luster. With its half-heartedness and temporary moments of genuineness WINTER LIGHT is a dreary film. It moves at a snail's pace and barely gets there in the end. It discusses a problem, but from prepared viewpoints. It is simple, but the simplicity is seldom fascinating and almost never evocative. − − −
> "All in all, it is probably only habitual thinkers who can regard WINTER LIGHT as a successful film, a film worthy of one of the world's leading film makers. And possibly its formal asceticism can be considered as Bergman's snook cocked at the public, i. e. at his own fame. It is a bold move, and an understandable one. But for the present he has had to pay the price."

TUESDAY 12 FEBRUARY 1963
Secularized press reactions (the Stockholm press)
The four remaining Stockholm reviews came today.

Svenska Dagbladet's Ellen Lilliedahl, pseudonym "Lill," is very

234

much in favor of it. She is fascinated by the "incorruptible," the "supremely ascetic" side of the film; she was "as always a helpless victim of Bergman's power of suggestion." And she shows a great ambition in trying to reproduce the religious problems.

Lasse Bergström in *Expressen* dodges the religious problem by savoring the film esthetically: "First and foremost I find Ingmar Bergman's new film a report on Swedish desolation, inward and outward. The people in it ask, and get silence for an answer. With difficulty they open new doors and go into more empty rooms. Outside the dark windows the mist creeps over the countryside." He gets a lot out of the film by responding to it in *this* way. The portrayal of Swedishness in WINTER LIGHT, moreover, he regards as a "new sign" in Bergman. And he is impressed by the character drawing.

Bengt Idestam-Almquist, pseudonym "Robin Hood," wants nothing to do with the film in *Stockholms-Tidningen*. He speaks of "artistic destitution," just like Jurgen Schildt. He doesn't like the ascetic picture language. He doesn't like the approach to the whole problem.

"Cinema-goers, that is, the friends of cinematic art, can quite rightly say: 'What do I care about the individual Ingmar Bergman's religious self-reflections this way and that? A person's dealings with God should take place privately in his own chamber, not for an admission fee with entertainment tax at the cinema.' "

Mauritz Edström in *Dagens Nyheter* comes up with the most composite review. I guess that he has rewritten it many times in an attempt to come to terms with his ambivalent reaction to the film. Edström declares that "WINTER LIGHT is the Bergman film that has held me most since SAWDUST AND TINSEL," and also that he "feels an utter stranger to the film." "I myself by upbringing have a religious ballast which makes WINTER LIGHT concern me." But he dislikes Bergman's way of posing the religious questions and so his criticism gets the better of his involvement the more the article proceeds. He ends with a kind of hope: that Bergman's next film, THE SILENCE, will mean that he accepts 'God's silence,' leaves the barren and idle questions behind him and turns towards his fellow human beings."

And the end of the film?

This end, whose significance I had seen Ingmar sketch out, write down, give final shape to— what happened to it when it reached

235

"The walls that Ingmar Bergman has to battle his way through are evidently prodigious. With the picture of Mărta, who finally kneels down and proves her love, he finds an escape again. The film ends in a paradoxical sudden change— the parson decides to hold the service even though the church is empty. A faith in spite of everything or a continued battle? But then why doesn't Bergman go right to the bottom of his doubt; is he flirting with it, though he does believe?" (Mauritz Edström, *Dagens Nyheter*.)

"In the empty, desolate church she kneels down— she, the non-believer, the inadequate one— and mumbles a prayer for strength to save her parson and lover from going under in the quagmire of self-contempt and impotence. Here we see the only positive element, the only glimpse of light over this darkened drama of faith, this ruthlessly stripped winter saga." (Ellen Lilliedahl, *Svenska Dagbladet*.)

"The film ends abruptly. Almost blasphemously. After all we have been told about the parson it comes as a shock that he, ill, unhinged, stands in front of the altar and conducts the service: 'Holy, holy, holy is the Lord, the whole earth is full of his glory'— although on behalf of his office there was no need to hold the service at all. This ends, artistically, in a still more unsatisfying way than the tacked-on end to .... THROUGH A GLASS DARKLY. No 'peripeteia', turning point, purification. After the development through THE SEVENTH SEAL, WILD STRAWBERRIES, THROUGH A GLASS DARKLY, one thought that things had eased up for Bergman. The latter film does end with a beautiful God image: 'God is love, in love God reveals himself.' In pre-interviews Bergman hinted that in WINTER LIGHT he wanted to shatter this God image in order to present another more durable one. But this is not to be found. The abrupt end seems to have no explanation other than that WINTER LIGHT in more than one respect is an intermediate film, No. 2 in the trilogy that began with THROUGH A GLASS DARKLY. He ends abruptly like the serial writers in order to whet the reader's curiosity: 'To be continued in our next installment.' (Bengt Idestam-Almquist, *Stockholms-Tidningen*.)

Lasse Bergström takes it for granted that the parson is a self-portrait of the *film man* Ingmar who in the cinema has wanted to preach spiritual truths but failed— one should know this in order to understand his interpretation:

"In the final scenes he (Ingmar Bergman), desperate and proud, sees the horrifying image of his own predicament. The pastor conducts evensong

236

in an empty church. He is the preacher without a congregation, alone with God's silence and his own problems."

Jurgen Schildt thinks that the film "illustrates a man's disintegration":

"At the end he (Pastor Thomas Ericsson) mounts the pulpit again and announces the text notwithstanding. Divine service has been declassed to a grimace and a circus act, the clergyman's concession to his dwindling congregation."

All five critics, therefore, have felt negations in the final sequence: the empty church, the nadir, the point of zero. But only two of them have caught a glimpse of the positive elements, those that create the paradox; and not one of them has been really perceptive in regard to the basic movement of the final shot: that the parson, *in the middle of* the nadir, turns a pallid, restrained, "cleansed" face towards the future; towards something quite new.

THURSDAY 21 FEBRUARY 1963
The last TV interview

IB went away in conjunction with the première. He was in Switzerland for a week. So I never got his spontaneous reaction to the Stockholm press. He had the première at more than a week's distance when we did the last TV interview this morning. I asked whether he could really keep his thoughts off the première down in Switzerland.

IB: Yes, I was right away from it. Oh yes, on Monday evening I did think of it a bit, and then on Tuesday I had asked Kenne Fant to send me a telegram as to how it had gone. We had agreed that it was to be worded very briefly. That brief telegram arrived too. It said: "Two for, two against, one in between." So then I went about feeling slightly infected that day. But the next day it was gone again. And then when I got home on Sunday, I read the whole lot— everything that had been written.

INT: Well?

IB: By then I was far enough away from it to escape that usual feeling that I wanted to rush to its defense. You know, you want to write letters to the editor, you want to call people up and thank them or abuse them or something like that. It's quite a natural feeling, but you have to control yourself like hell sometimes.

INT: Well, you have a rare opportunity here to write letters to the editor.

Supposing you were to do so — — — what points would you take up?
IB: Well, there are two things chiefly that I attach importance to. One is that to mention God's name and to talk about God in certain circles in Sweden today— well, it's almost like saying a dirty word at a vicarage tea party. There's terrific indignation and terrific distress. The second thing is part of it in a way. So many people have said, why can't he busy himself with something *else* besides these religious problems. Sooner or later, after all, he must devote himself to something more interesting. And I've been given an enormous amount of well-meaning advice to stop all this silly nonsense, and then I ask myself: *can* you in fact advise an artist what he is to busy himself with? These are the two reflections that I've mostly made.
INT: Isn't one influenced if people say "Stop doing that?"
IB: No, one isn't. One isn't influenced. What you think is this: that what is such a great reality to you, a matter of such deep concern— you can't just drop it just because some people think you should. You must carry out your themes in the way you feel them and in the way you want to give shape to them.

I'm hoping for quite a lot from this last program. Usually the critics have the last word; here, for once, the creator of the film has a chance to have it. My hopes are dashed. IB can't be bothered to make any comments. The whole of the artist's resistance rises up inside him: oh, don't go into details, don't explain, simplify .... if they can't understand, never mind! I notice this when we give the final touches to the editing before transmission. During the interview I inveigled him into commenting on Thomas and Märta as characters:

IB: What astonishes me is that they (the critics) have taken the parson to be nothing but a boor, while they look on the schoolmistress as the bearer of almighty love and goodness. They can't see the woods for the trees— because the awful part about the schoolmistress is to my mind, that she's very much a mixed personality— just like the parson. They are two stray, injured, anxious people. — — — The schoolmistress is indeed both a bossy person, very dominating, and a woman with an unmistakably hysterical disposition.

Out goes *that* description of character at once. The characters must speak for themselves! Anyway, it's wisest to let the critics have the last word.

IB: You learn that from many years' experience: whatever you do, don't *answer* a critic. Never discuss anything afterwards with a critic. Don't have anything to do with critics at all. There must be in some way a sterile gap between the artist and the critic. I don't like it myself, but I know from bitter experience that it must be like that.

Short dialogue about notices in general:

INT: The nasty thing about notices after all is that somewhere they do hit home. They often hit crookedly and obliquely, but they do hit things that are sensitive.

IB: Horribly sensitive! And it's just like— I was about to say— just like erogenous zones. Either you can touch them gently and it feels lovely. Or else you can touch them the wrong way and it's terrible. A kind of awful aggressiveness awakens in one, doesn't it?

UNDATED, SPRING 1963

Secularized press reactions (cont.)

I shall quote the Stockholm newspapers most fully— their power is greatest. Moreover they turn out to be representative of a certain type of reaction to WINTER LIGHT: that of the secularized intellectuals. The Stockholm notices indicate tendencies for both approval and disapproval. I shall attempt a grouping:

Artistic appreciation under respect for the religious theme (type Ellen Lilliedahl): Hugo Wortzelius in *Upsala Nya Tidning*, 2.12.63; Åke Perlström in *Göteborgs-Posten*, 2.12.63; Marianne Zetterstrom in *Vecko-Journalen*, no. 8.63, and others.

Artistic appreciation with an attempt to translate religion into psychology (type Lasse Bergström): This approach, with all its ambivalent see-sawing between doubt and appreciation, is best studied in Jörn Donner's article in *Bonniers Litterära Magasin*, February issue 63.

Artistic criticism on account of the film's "lack of warmth" and its "fellow feeling" (type Mauritz Edström): Gösta Andrén in *Ny Tid*, 2.12.63; Margareta Edström in *Chaplin's*, February issue; Carl-Eric Nordberg in *Vi*, no. 7, 63.

Solely esthetic criticism can be studied in Carl Axel Backman's article in *Göteborgs Handels- och Sjöfartstidning*, 2.22.63; he finds the film "as lacking in scent and life as a herbarium flower." (Backman has quite a different esthetic ideal from IB. Backman thinks that it is chiefly "the small, apparently insignificant happenings in life" which give a film "spontaneity, life and atmosphere.")

239

Pure symbolic analysis, with no Christian involvement, lies behind Sven E. Olsson's article in *Scen och salong*, no. 4, 1963. The film is "obviously mediocre" but is worth examining for its theme, since Thomas, according to Olsson, symbolizes a (stern, Old-Testament) God-the-Father figure. Opposite him is Märta, who symbolizes Christ. (Many Christians conceive of Märta in the same way.)

UNDATED, SPRING 1963
Christian press reactions

The reaction pattern alters completely the minute the religiously committed are drawn into the debate. With them, the film arouses an astonishingly self-evident response.

Admittedly quite a few unpleasant feelings are apparent among certain clergy and laymen. Some are offended by both the portrait of the parson and the portrayal of the church. Some regard the end as a mockery of what they believe in.* But appreciation predominates.

The official organ of the Swedish church, *Vår Kyrka* (Our Church) reacts with an enthusiastic article by Margit Strömmerstedt in no. 9, 1963, and the pseudonym "Parson" speaks feelingly in no. 10 of "our fellow clergyman Thomas Ericsson."**Tore Zetterholm analyzes the gulf between the secularized press reactions and the Christian ones in *Vår Lösen* (Our Watchword) 1963. The strength of the Christian reaction can best be studied by reading Ulf Söderlind, student parson in Lund, in *Kvällsposten* (The Evening Post) 2.28.63; Ludvig Jönsson in *Chaplin's*, February issue; Cordelia Edvardsson in *Damernas Värld* (Women's World), no. 4, 63; Manne Eriksson in *Svensk Veckotidning* (Swedish

—

*Read some of the nine clergymen in *Norrköpings Tidningar's* questionnaire 3.5.63 or Berndt Hollsten in *Såningsmannen (The Sower)* no. 9 and no. 10, 1963. One writer of a letter to the editor of *Falu-Kuriren* 3.2.63 is indignant that Bergman was allowed to use Skattungby church for shooting the film.
** In passing, this very pseudonym takes up the cudgels with Bishop Bo Giertz who, on one of the days after the première, expressed his opinion to *Göteborgs-Posten*. Giertz thought that the film was "a mighty and upsetting document about the Swedish church in its deepest abasement." WINTER LIGHT thereby came into the firing line between the protagonists of the high church and the low church, and Ingmar Bergman, who can hardly be said to belong to the high church, found he had made a film which Church Assembly could use in its campaign.

Weekly Magazine), 3.8.63; Sylvia Edmund in *Bonniers Litterära Magasin*, March issue; Hans Nystedt in an article in *Sydsvenska Dagbladet*, 4.21.63. (Both Sylvia Edmund and Hans Nystedt take it that Märta Lundberg is a Christ symbol.)

Common to all these deeply-felt interpretations is that they *fill in* what Ingmar Bergman has left out. Not once during the course of the work— not even at the manuscript stage when he was most of all concerned to capture in the final scenes "the sprouting of a new faith" in Thomas Ericsson— would he say anything about the content of the new God image. But the religiously committed make it clear beyond all doubt what god image awaits Thomas after the silence: the "compassionate god" (Cordelia Edvardsson), he who "with his own helplessness, his doubt and his suffering fills the night of our suffering with his nearness" (Ludvid Jönsson).

The opposition in the intellectually theological camp comes, oddly enough, from those who represent the church play. Jan O. Bonnevier thinks that the Christians kotow to something that is really only a "pretentious reportage" (*Evangeliskt Drama, Meddelande från Förbundet for liturgi och dramatik, no. 1, 1963*)— Evangelical drama, message from the society for liturgy and drama. Tuve Nyström in *Vår Lösen*, no. 3, 1963, constructs a huge argumental edifice to show that Bergman's religious problems are not representatively Christian— they are too "neurotic." Birger Norman replies ironically to this in *Stockholms-Tidningen*, 3.29. 63.

These are about the most important Swedish arguments with a religious viewpoint.

UNDATED, MAY 1963

I can't find any critic who thinks of the religious mysticism in the title (in Swedish, "The Communicants") and the course of the service. But during the introductory communion service the very ones who *carry* the drama (even the messenger, the old woman from Hol) kneel down in the communion's confession about the dependence of everyone on everyone else.

UNDATED, MAY 1963
The religious line of crisis

What does he think himself of the Christian interpreters? Have they grasped what he was aiming at? I imagine that I will get a lot

241

of post-rationalizations by way of answer, if I ask. The IB who *now* talks about WINTER LIGHT is not quite the same person who wrote it. THE SILENCE comes between.

He got the idea for THE SILENCE while in the middle of shooting WINTER LIGHT. (It pushed aside THE FOLKTALE, just as WINTER LIGHT pushed aside the Sergel film.) He started writing the new script at once. *Then* he edited WINTER LIGHT; *then* he shot THE SILENCE; *then* WINTER LIGHT had its première. So the two films are dovetailed into each other.

The answer he *wanted* to give with WINTER LIGHT was never forthcoming. Instead an even greater stripping bare took place, an even more anguished silence. This is the religious line of crisis I seem to notice. (But he never explained it in our talks.)

So what he now thinks about WINTER LIGHT is colored by the state of feeling in THE SILENCE. Even the best religious analyses strike him like a boomerang.

"What did you think of Hans Nystedt's article in *Svenska Dagbladet*? That was feelingly written, wasn't it?"

"Ye-es .... "

"Have you yourself thought of Märta as a Christ symbol? If you did, you never spoke of it."

"Hah, nothing could be farther from the truth!"

"But those who think so certainly find a lot of symbolic material: Märta is thirty-three years old; she has eczema on the stigmata spots .... "

"But you know quite well that it never occurred to me that the eczema was on the stigmata spots until I was in the middle of the production!"

"But this fact that Nystedt points out: that ROUGH PROOFS is printed across the photographs of the dead wife. Have you ever thought of that as a kind of symbolic stamp on the old god image?"

"No, *that's* not why. I just wanted to give a feeling of sudden death, photographs taken in a hurry."

"But Nystedt has noticed a lot!"

"Oh yes. But he has *not* seen that Algot Frövik is an angel; he has *not* seen that Algot and Märta bear the lame Thomas; he has *not* seen that .... "

There is a curious reluctance in his appreciation of the Christian analyses.

THURSDAY 9 MAY 1963

Hurried conversation up at Hotel Siljansborg. Ingmar came here on Saturday with the technical assistants on the new film, TO SAY NOTHING OF ALL THESE WOMEN, the farce about the cellist Felix and his biographer.

He is going to venture after all to publish his film trilogy in Sweden; and when he lunched last spring with the publisher's representative, Lasse Bergström, he explained how the three films hung together. They were about a kind of reduction, on the plane of life conception.

"In THROUGH A GLASS DARKLY it was a question of certainty," he said *then*. "In WINTER LIGHT of a glimpse. In THE SILENCE of a negative print."

Supposing he were to intimate this in a short preface? He could use the same words as he did then.

Sudden hesitation. The need to change the words.

He still knows quite clearly what he feels about the latest film: THE SILENCE gives a "negative print" of God. But what words will he choose about the first two, which are now at a distance?

He tries out "anguished certainty" for THROUGH A GLASS DARKLY.

"Aren't you post-rationalizing now?" I ask.

" 'Convulsive certainty' then?"

"But is that being fair to the film? Did you really feel that way when you were making it?"

"But it *was* a convulsive certainty! I *wanted* to feel it like that. (Pause.) 'Conquered certainty' then? Is that better?"

WINTER LIGHT then?

He decides on the wording: "Seen-through certainty."

Oh, all our post-rationalizations!

It *is* difficult to sum up in one key word a whole film's dreams and ambitions.